D1590745

The Singlish Controversy

Singlish is the colloquial variety of English spoken in Singapore. It has sparked much public debate, but so far the complex question of what Singlish really is and what it means to its speakers has remained obscured. This important work explores some of the socio-political controversies surrounding Singlish, such as the political ideologies inherent in Singlish discourse, the implications of being restricted to Singlish for those speakers without access to Standard English, the complex relationship between Singlish and migration, and the question of whether Singlish is an asset or a liability to Singaporeans. These questions surrounding Singlish illustrate many current issues in language, culture and identity in an age of rapid change. The book will be of interest to scholars and advanced students of World Englishes and sociolinguistics. Its detailed analysis of the Singlish controversy will illuminate broader questions about language, identity and globalization.

LIONEL WEE is a professor in the National University of Singapore's Department of English Language and Literature. He has written extensively about New Englishes and language policy, particularly in relation to the Singapore context. He served for a number of years as a member of the committee of the Singapore government's Speak Good English Movement.

The Singlish Controversy

Language, Culture and Identity in a Globalizing World

Lionel Wee

National University of Singapore

CAMBRIDGE
UNIVERSITY PRESS

CAMBRIDGE
UNIVERSITY PRESS

University Printing House, Cambridge CB2 8BS, United Kingdom

One Liberty Plaza, 20th Floor, New York, NY 10006, USA

477 Williamstown Road, Port Melbourne, VIC 3207, Australia

314–321, 3rd Floor, Plot 3, Splendor Forum, Jasola District Centre,
New Delhi - 110025, India

79 Anson Road, #06-04/06, Singapore 079906

Cambridge University Press is part of the University of Cambridge.

It furthers the University's mission by disseminating knowledge in the pursuit of
education, learning, and research at the highest international levels of excellence.

www.cambridge.org
Information on this title: www.cambridge.org/9781107181717
DOI: 10.1017/9781316855331

© Lionel Wee 2018

First published 2018

Printed in the United Kingdom by Clays, St Ives plc

A catalogue record for this publication is available from the British Library

ISBN 978-1-107-18171-7 Hardback

Contents

Figures

Tables

Preface

Several years ago, just before I was invited to become a committee member of the Singapore government's Speak Good English Movement in the early 2000s, I was involved in a meeting with senior civil servants who were tasked with handling the Singlish 'problem' and improving standards of English in Singapore. The meeting took place in a small office in my Department of English Language & Literature at the National University of Singapore.

After the meeting, I bumped into a colleague who had happened to walk past the office while the meeting was in progress. She told me that she had heard shouting coming from within and wondered what the fuss was about. I told her that one of the civil servants had reacted angrily when I tried to explain that (i) there is no necessary correlation between the presence of Singlish and any drop in standards of English, much less any evidence that the former is the cause of the latter; (ii) it is difficult, if not impossible, to ascertain with any objective certainty that standards of English are actually dropping, since the distinction between linguistic innovations and errors is a fluid one; and (iii) the global spread of English means we have to accept that there will be changes to the language as it takes root in different societies and is both adopted and adapted by various users for multiple communicative purposes. The indignant civil servant found these points difficult to accept and, instead, accused me (and linguists in general) of being far too willing to tolerate variations in language use and therefore of irresponsibly contributing to the undesirable divergences from good/standard/proper English.

The heated discussion did not prevent the government from inviting me to join the Speak Good English Movement. A cynical interpretation (one that is perhaps not without merit) would be that the invitation was motivated by the goal of bringing into the fold and thereby co-opting potential 'troublemakers'. Nevertheless, I accepted the invitation because I thought it would provide me with a good opportunity to engage in extended discussions with government representatives about language matters and, specifically, about various assumptions concerning Singlish and Standard English.

I have to say that, in retrospect, my time as a member of the Speak Good English Movement was indeed quite rewarding. The other committee members with whom I had the privilege of working were often open-minded about the complexities of language. In turn, I came to be more appreciative of the kinds of pressures that civil servants work under and from which, as an academic, I was relatively free. For example, running an official campaign such as the Speak Good English Movement meant being answerable to politicians and members of the public about how resources were being spent and having to show that some 'progress' was being made each year (such as reducing the rampant use of Singlish, raising awareness of the importance of Standard English or simply increasing appreciation and sympathy for the Movement's goals).

Despite this, my concern about the ways in which Singlish is being understood and debated in the public sphere has continued to grow. This is because there has been no significant change in the premises and parameters of the debate. Each time Singlish is discussed in public, the same arguments tend to be thrown up and the same responses made. The result is that previously established views and attitudes (simplistically, either 'for' or 'against' Singlish because it is a 'good' or 'bad' thing) are further entrenched; there is no evidence of a closer meeting of minds, a better appreciation of different positions or a more nuanced understanding of the ideological assumptions involved.

This book is born out of my concern with the ways in which the Singlish controversy has unfolded in public debates. Though the impetus for the book is personal in nature, I have tried to provide an objective analysis of the controversy, looking at both sides of the debate. I should make clear, however, that the points I tried to convey to that senior civil servant all those years ago remain valid, and because of this, I am largely unsympathetic to those who would argue that Singlish is a problem, a linguistic menace that needs to be eliminated. This does not mean, however, that the arguments that have been proffered in favour of Singlish are unproblematic. The arguments put forward by the supporters as well as by the detractors of Singlish tend to be based on questionable assumptions.

In what follows, I show that viewing Singlish as a liability or an asset in fact sidesteps many of the important and complicated issues involved. And because the issues involving the Singlish controversy are by no means unique to Singlish but are in fact relevant to broader concerns about language and identity in the context of rapid globalization, I am hopeful that the discussion in this book will be of interest to a fairly wide audience and not just those concerned with promoting or retarding the use of Singlish.

Acknowledgements

Parts of this book are based on previously published materials. Chapter 2 is based on 'Metadiscursive convergence in the Singlish debate' (*Language & Communication* 31: 75–85, 2011). Chapter 3 is based on 'Linguistic chutzpah and the Speak Good Singlish Movement' (*World Englishes* 33/1: 85–99, 2014). Chapters 5, 6 and 7 draw on 'Evolution of Singlish in late modernity' (in S. Bushfeld, T. Hoffman, M. Huber and A. Kautzsch, eds., *The Evolution of Englishes*, 126–141. Amsterdam: John Benjamins, 2014) and my review of Leimgruber's *Singapore English: Structure, Variation and Usage* (*English World-Wide* 36/2: 259–263). Parts of Chapter 6 also draw on 'The party's over? Singapore politics and the "new normal"' (*Journal of Language and Politics* 14/3: 455–478, 2015). These materials have been revised and reorganized so as to better fit in with newer ideas and discussions. I am grateful to Elsevier, John Benjamins, and Wiley-Blackwell for permission to include these materials in the book. I also thank Gartbooks for permission to reproduce the illustration from *Essential Guide to Singlish*, and Marshall Cavendish for permission to reproduce the illustration from *The Complete Eh, Goondu!* My thanks also to Simone Khoo, Gerald Tan and Alan Tea for their comments on an earlier draft of the manuscript.

Introduction: Questions about the Singlish Controversy

Varieties of English

One of the consequences of the global spread of English has been the identification and naming of multiple varieties of English across many societies. A quick and simple internet search, for example, will throw up references to Chinglish in China (Jing and Zuo, 2006), Manglish in Malaysia (Muniandy, Nair, Shanmugam, Ahmad and Noor, 2010), Konglish in South Korea (Hagens, 2005), Japlish in Japan (Pierce, 1971) and Spanglish in Puerto Rico (Nash, 1970), to mention just a few. These varieties all manifest different levels of influence from indigenous languages, receive different amounts of public support as to their social legitimacy and desirability, and display different degrees of empirical justification for their presumed linguistic reality.

The last point in particular has led Bruthiaux (2003: 168) to criticize what he sees as the overeager tendency among scholars to contribute to the proliferation of new Englishes, suggesting that such 'me-too' calls for additional varieties to be recognized lack validity:

The question of what constitutes a variety of a language is a thorny one. The key issue is whether there exists in a particular location a core of speakers who not only know some English... but also use it to a reasonable level of proficiency for a substantial part of their daily activities, whether for international communication in a multiethnic society, for international communication with other native or non-native speakers of the language, or for academic purposes in a location where English plays a significant role as a medium of instruction despite not having a substantial presence locally. This is fundamental because for a variety to emerge, local practices must surely gain norm value through recurring, spontaneous use across a range of communicative functions as well as in emblematic domains such as the media, artistic creation, and popular culture.[1]

---

[1] I will continue using the term 'variety' for want of a better alternative. Other options such as 'dialect', 'code' or 'language' are just as problematic, if not more so. We already know that the traditional linguistic distinction between dialects and languages, where the former are supposedly mutually intelligible while the latter are not, does not always hold true. And the notion of a code suggests an already well-formed, independently existing autonomous linguistic system – which is essentially what is being questioned in current sociolinguistic theorizing (see the later discussion in this chapter on modernist conceptualizations of language).

1

Bruthiaux's criticism is well-taken since premature scholarly claims that new varieties have emerged indicate careless uses of the notion, raising the danger that it risks losing its value as an analytical concept.[2] As Park and Wee (2013: 341) point out, 'while the constitution of varieties through naming is a common phenomenon, when such names become part of our scholarly vocabulary for research, careful and critical attention must be given to the relationship between the name and the language practices that the name apparently refers to'.

The situation is different, however, when the names of varieties are being evoked in popular usage. The very fact that a specific variety's name is being bandied about in public discourse indicates that there are publicly contested ideologies regarding language at work. It is even entirely possible that such contestations can over time ultimately lead – via a kind of self-fulfilling prophecy – to a linguistic situation that does satisfy Bruthiaux's criteria for varietal status. This can happen because those speakers who view the variety favourably may calibrate their linguistic practices so as to further develop the phonological, morphosyntactic and pragmatic properties that (in their view) exemplify the variety in question. They may also try to clarify the scope of its usage in order to better distinguish this contested variety from other adjacent varieties (Pullum, 1999: 44). At the same time, other speakers who find the variety objectionable, perhaps because it runs counter to what they see as acceptable, appropriate and 'hygienic' linguistic behaviour (Cameron, 1995), may attempt to denounce and even eliminate what they consider to be deviant linguistic practices. In so doing, they may highlight examples from the stigmatized variety of linguistic practices that ought to be avoided. The consequence of this language ideological debate (Blommaert, 1999) could well be a strengthening of the ontological status of what may have at one point been little more than a name: the name now becomes associated with a (potentially growing and increasingly robust) set of linguistic practices, and to the extent that these practices are continually highlighted as exemplars that ought to be replicated or avoided depending on which side of the debate the speakers affiliate with, these then come to stereotypically exemplify and constitute the corpus of the variety.

But regardless of how well grounded in objective linguistic practice the name of a presumed variety may or may not have been initially, its use in public discourse is interesting from a socio-political perspective for a variety of reasons. One, competing assumptions about culture and identity as well as language are involved. Both supporters and detractors of the named variety are usually

---

[2] It is important to note, though, that Bruthiaux's (2003) own proposed criteria require that a lot of the actual conceptual work be done by notions such as a 'reasonable level of proficiency', 'a substantial part of their daily activities' and 'emblematic domains' – notions that are by no means uncontroversial themselves not least because there will be varying interpretations of what counts as 'reasonable', 'substantial' and 'emblematic'.

less concerned with linguistic issues per se than with how the variety in question might affect their ideas about the integrity of, among other factors, ethnic or national unity. Thus, it is no accident that the names of these varieties are often a blend of some ethnic or national identity prefix and the *–glish* suffix, such as Chinglish or Manglish (see the examples mentioned earlier). The name is itself intended to suggest the nativization of English in a society where it had hitherto been a foreign language. And while there will be some who welcome such nativization, there will also be others who see it as a threat to the sanctity of traditionally inherited indigenous identities or as a bastardization of proper/standard/good English, or both.

Two, in addition to competing assumptions, shared assumptions are also involved, for how else might the contesting parties be said to even be taking part in the same language ideological debate? These shared assumptions often tend to remain in the background of debates, however, since it is the points of difference that usually get foregrounded. Nevertheless, such shared assumptions can in fact go on to shape the debate in subtle yet significant ways. A simple example of such a shared assumption might be that ethnic or national identities are, indeed, at stake. Supporters of the variety might argue that it enriches or strengthens the ethnic or national identity, whereas detractors might assert that it compromises or undermines the same. In either case, the assumption that the debate carries significant implications for the future vitality of the wider community (be this ethnic or national in scope) is never in doubt, much less seriously interrogated.

Three, many of these ideological assumptions, whether competing or shared, are based on modernist precepts about the stability of both conceptual boundaries and the links between concepts. So, a traditional conceptual assemblage comprising essentialized links between language X, culture X and identity X is treated as being intrinsically distinct from equally essentialized links between language Y, culture Y and identity Y. More concretely, there is, for instance, assumed to be a Malay language, culture and identity that, taken together, constitute a naturalized package that must be kept separate from other similar packages, such as the Chinese language, culture and identity nexus. In this way, discourses about the need to maintain the integrity of specific languages, specific cultures or specific identities usually also involve attempts to sustain the links that keep an entire assemblage intact. Such essentialist views are, however, being increasingly challenged by phenomena such as commodification, migration and even reflexivity. Quite aside, then, from the issue of competing or shared assumptions is the question of how modernist orientations may or may not need to be re-evaluated in the context of life in late modernity.

Bearing in mind the foregoing, the case of Singlish becomes particularly interesting. Notionally, the label 'Singlish' describes the colloquial variety of English that is native to Singapore, though, as I show shortly, things are in fact much more complicated. As a well-established and deeply entrenched cultural category, Singlish is influential in calibrating the linguistic practices of Singaporeans through which identities of various sorts are indexed, including metalinguistic identities that index the speakers as being 'for' or 'against' Singlish, often on the grounds that this variety is something that Singaporeans should be either proud or ashamed of. In other words, precisely because of its cultural salience, Singlish represents a highly contested concept that has provoked very open and public disagreements amongst Singaporeans as to its legitimacy and desirability, particularly because it is seen to have very different implications for the national identity and, indeed, the national economy as well.[3]

Some Singaporeans, as well as the Singapore government, denounce Singlish as a problem on the grounds that it supposedly compromises the ability of Singaporeans to learn proper/good English (which is usually a synonym for Standard American English or Standard British English). In contrast, other Singaporeans defend Singlish as an important marker of national identity that is worth preserving, and they reject the idea that it adversely affects the learning of Standard English. Instead, these supporters of Singlish usually offer a defence loosely based on assumptions involving diglossia and situational code-switching: Singaporeans, they claim, know when to use Singlish and when not to, restricting its use to informal situations involving fellow Singaporeans and adopting the more standard variety in formal situations, including situations where non-Singaporeans are present.

The preceding paragraph, while largely accurate as an informal description of the broad contours of the Singlish controversy, nevertheless contains developments that beg further analysis. In the rest of this introductory chapter, I therefore expand on the various issues surrounding the Singlish controversy that demand further investigation.

As I elaborate on these issues, it should become evident that an examination of the arguments surrounding Singlish can provide insights into the discourses of identity and ethnicity in a globalizing world, with implications for issues such as the possible emergence of a post-national identity, the commodification of language and the impact of 'superdiversity' (Vertovec, 2006; 2007) on language policy. Such arguments pertain not only to the Singlish controversy or Singapore specifically; they have broader ramifications for our general

---

[3] The notion of Standard Singapore English has also been occasionally touted in addition to Singlish, either as a variety that can coexist with Singlish or as a nationally more acceptable alternative (Wee, 2005: 61). Standard Singapore English, however, is spoken of with far greater tentativeness than Singlish. Many Singaporeans in fact appear unsure that Standard Singapore English actually exists, even considering such a notion to be chimerical. In contrast, the idea of Singlish has struck a much bigger cultural chord and enjoys a much more robust cultural reality, so much so that supporters of Singlish celebrate its existence even as its detractors consider it a clear and present national danger.

understanding of language, culture and identity, as will become clear as the discussion in the rest of the book progresses.

Singlish is therefore interesting not necessarily because of its linguistic properties per se,[4] but because it is at the center of a socio-political controversy that is symptomatic of the anxieties and concerns that revolve around language, culture and identity in the context of rapid globalization, and an analysis of the Singlish controversy helps to bring into clear relief many of the major issues that are implicated.

Ideology Pooling and Meta-Discursive Convergence

It is clear that an analysis of the Singlish controversy cannot help attending to the conflicting representations that make it controversial in the first place. But it is also useful to focus on the shared ideological assumptions that influence the positions assumed by parties involved in the controversy. This is because such ideologies may 'become socially dominant to the extent that they become a natural part of discourse production; in such cases, speakers may (consciously or unconsciously) adopt those ideologies in their discourse even though the ideologies may not necessarily be supportive of their interests' (Park, 2009: 84).

The value of focusing on the shared ideologies is nicely illustrated by Park (2009) in his discussion of the Official English debate in South Korea, where various parties argued over whether or not to accord English the status of an official language. Park (2009: 84) points out that 'the distribution of ideologies in a debate does not necessarily align with the fault lines of social positions, but instead shows what I call ideology pooling, where both sides of a debate draw upon a common set of socially shared ideologies despite differences in their political orientations'. In particular, he emphasizes that both sides of the Official English debate subscribed to the three ideologies of necessitation (where knowledge of English is constructed as a necessity), externalization (where English is presented as a language of an Other), and self-deprecation (where Koreans view themselves as being generally incapable of mastering English). The shared nature of these ideologies makes them less vulnerable to critique. Thus, even as participants in a language ideological debate, scrutinize and contest those claims that are foregrounded as points of difference between

---

[4] This is not to deny that there has been a fair amount of interest in the linguistic properties of Singlish. Lim (2004) provides a good overview of its various grammatical properties. Gupta (1994), and Wee (2002a) propose different theoretical perspectives on how to understand the pragmatics of the Singlish particles. There are also discussions about whether Singlish ought to be considered a pidgin, creole or creoloid (Platt, 1975), and more recently, there have been theoretically sophisticated attempts at accounting for the aspectual system of Singlish in terms of substrate influences (Bao, 2005). I discuss some of these works in Chapter 7.

them, shared ideologies constitute the backdrop against which the debate itself is made possible.

Park's observations raise questions about the influence of ideology pooling in the context of the Singlish controversy. Put differently, the question we need to ask is how the shared ideologies might lead otherwise opposing parties to come to a meta-discursive convergence so that, even as the parties remain in conflict, they make very similar assertions that are not always consistent with their various interests. In the case of the Singlish controversy, there is a tendency for both supporters and detractors of Singlish to extend the use of the label so that, in public discourses, 'Singlish' is used to describe not only colloquial uses of English but also instances of ungrammatical/broken English. This raises the question of why this extension of the label should occur on both sides of the Singlish controversy. That is, in what way does this extension serve (if at all) the opposing aims of legitimizing and stigmatizing Singlish? It also raises the related question of what effect this elision of the distinction between the colloquial and ungrammatical has, if any, on the specific arguments and assumptions being made about Singlish. We therefore need to ask what are the assumptions in the ideology pool that have led to a meta-discursive convergence between the Singapore government and supporters of Singlish, so that, despite their very different views regarding the merits of Singlish, both parties end up making rather similar assertions about its nature.

The Role of Experts and the Double Hermeneutic

A reasonable question to ask in connection with ideology pooling is under what circumstances it might be possible for parties to the debate to actually start questioning their shared assumptions. One possibility is of course to rely on the intervention of language experts, who might directly highlight and draw attention to the problematic nature of the shared assumptions. For example, from a scholarly perspective, it makes no sense to conflate the ungrammatical with the colloquial, even if the distinction is not an easy one to maintain in actual practice. Yet, scholarly contributions seem to have had little impact on the tendency to use 'Singlish' interchangeably for both broken and informal uses of English. This brings up the issue of the relevance of linguistic expertise and its role in public debates, especially in trying to change entrenched ideologies about language. There are certainly 'non-public spaces' where experts are brought in as consultants by the government, and their views regarding language and education are occasionally reported in the media. But these represent highly limited interventions that are also usually given coverage only because they do not constitute an in-depth critique, much less a direct contradiction, of extant government policy. We will therefore see that the direct influence of language experts in the public domain – for reasons both specific to and beyond the Singlish controversy – tends to be rather limited.

The other possibility is for the parties themselves to gradually become more appreciative of the problems underlying some of their assumptions, usually as a result of contact with language experts via education or mass media, the avenues by which expert knowledge is more widely circulated (in the course of which it may get appropriated and modified by the general public). Here, the influence of language experts is less direct, and it speaks to the effect of what Giddens (1987) has described as the 'double hermeneutic' – that is, the notion that there is a two-way relationship between lay/everyday concepts and social-scientific ones. Unlike the natural sciences where scientists study objects and phenomena (e.g. chemical processes) that lack awareness, the objects and phenomena studied by social scientists (i.e. people, society) can come (via education, the mass media, socio-political debates, etc.) to not only appreciate social-scientific concepts such as 'citizen' and 'sovereignty' (Giddens, 1987: 20) and more recently, 'diaspora' or 'inflation', but even to use them themselves. As Giddens (1987: 18–19) puts it,

> the subjects of study in the social sciences and the humanities are concept-using beings, whose concepts of their actions enter in a constitutive manner into what those actions are. Social life cannot be accurately described by a sociological observer, let alone causally elucidated, if that observer does not master the array of concepts employed (discursively or non-discursively) by those involved . . .
>
> Unlike in the natural science, in the social sciences, there is no way of keeping the conceptual apparatus of the observer – whether in sociology, political science or economic – free from appropriation by lay actors.

I will say more about the double hermeneutic in my examination of the Speak Good Singlish Movement (SGSM). This is a movement that, as its name suggests, arose in response to the Singapore government's own Speak Good English Movement (SGEM). The SGEM was initiated by the government to help promote 'good English' while at the same time eradicate Singlish. The SGSM, in contrast, is notable not only for challenging the tendency to elide the distinction between the colloquial and the ungrammatical but also, more relevantly, for making this challenge on the basis of relatively sophisticated linguistic arguments. Thus, with the SGSM, we see at least some of the hitherto shared assumptions being foregrounded as problematic and then rebutted.

Voice and the Shaping of the Controversy

While it is of course unrealistic to expect all Singaporeans to each weigh in with their individual views on the Singlish controversy, it is worth noting that one important segment of the population remains largely unheard from. This is the group of Singaporeans who have little or no competence in what is conventionally known as Standard English and who as a consequence are portrayed by active parties to the Singlish controversy as speakers of ungrammatical/ broken English. Extending the label 'Singlish' to include ungrammatical/ broken English immediately implicates them in the controversy. Despite this, their views are not heard in the Singlish controversy.

These speakers are instead represented by proxy via the contributions of the active participants in the Singlish controversy. The latter are generally well-educated and articulate Singaporeans, both inside and outside the government. Because the arguments both for and against Singlish have tended to come mainly from well-educated individuals who are also competent in a standard variety of English, many of whom having been educated in local, British or American tertiary institutions, this raises the issue of voice. Who gets to contribute to the Singlish controversy, who gets excluded, and why?

Attention to voice therefore allows us to identify the kinds of personas that are enabled to and indeed obligated to speak, as well as the kinds of personas that are, in contrast, disallowed from or at the very least not expected to contribute to debates over Singlish. We need to examine the implications of this situation for the Singlish controversy. This is because the possibility of voice functions to mediate the indexical relationship between named varieties and personas, reflecting conventionalized understandings of this relationship while also constituting and perpetuating it.

This way of thinking about voice recalls Spivak's (1988; 1999) critique of postcolonial theory and subaltern studies, where she insists on a need to move away from treating the economically dispossessed as a homogeneous group and from relying on Western-educated academics to speak on their behalf. Spivak herself rejects as a viable project the desire to 'confer visibility and voice to the subaltern' and she suggests that it is instead necessary to understand the practices 'through which postcolonial subject-power is consolidated' (Roy, 2011: 311). The Singaporean experience with English is still very much a postcolonial one, and this includes the emergence of Singlish (Schneider, 2007: 153ff). In this regard, we need to ask about the extent to which the considerations that accompany Spivak's remarks about the subaltern might also apply to the linguistically dispossessed in the context of the Singlish controversy.

Singlish as Commodity

The overwhelming focus in the Singlish controversy has been on whether Singlish can be seen as an asset or a liability to Singaporeans. Detractors of Singlish insist that it impedes the learning of Standard English, and because of this, they assert that allowing Singlish to flourish would penalize its

speakers by limiting their social and economic mobility. This is the ghettoization argument. Relatedly, detractors also suggest that because Singlish is a low-
status variety, its use, especially on the global stage, gives a bad impression of
Singapore and Singaporeans. This is the symbolic capital argument, which is
logically independent from the suggestion that Singlish compromises the learning of Standard English.

Nevertheless, the ideological relationship between these two arguments per-
sists, because when two erstwhile distinct varieties of English come into contact, it is the stigmatized variety that is typically construed as infecting or contaminating the prestige variety. The possibility that the prestige variety might
itself be enriched as a result of such contact is never considered. This construal is of course predicated on the assumption that the labels 'Singlish' and
'Standard English' refer to objectively bounded varieties that can be reliably
distinguished and kept separate from each other.

The issue of Singlish's economic and symbolic capital (or lack thereof) leads
to another reason why the Singlish controversy bears closer examination. There
are signs that Singlish is becoming increasingly commodified as a cultural
product that is exportable. Singlish lessons are offered to non-Singaporeans,
skits prominently highlighting the use of Singlish are available on YouTube,
and Singaporean-made films that feature Singlish-speaking characters are gaining international recognition. Commodification can potentially lead to the delinking of Singlish from Singaporeans. As Budach, Roy and Heller (2003: 606–
607) point out, this is a possible scenario when language is commodified in the
new globalized economy:

In these conditions, the tight connection between language and identity is disturbed;
language skills can have value independent of the 'identity' of the speaker, and 'identity' can be sold – in the forms of dance, music, museums, art, and so on – without
the producers' having to be able to provide any of the historically related linguistic
performances. Nonetheless, uncoupling does not always happen; groups understanding
themselves historically as a community will use the notion of inheritance to legitimize
privileged access to linguistic resources and to their new markets (see Rampton, 1995
on the notion of inheritance).

Since no single individual or group holds any proprietary claim to Singlish,
even as some Singaporeans might object to Singlish becoming delinked from
Singaporeans, other Singaporeans might celebrate its spread and embrace by
non-Singaporeans. In this regard, it is worth noting that the Netflix series
Orange Is the New Black has even had one of its characters, a Black American female, speaking Singlish[5] in order to promote the series to a Singaporean
audience. Moreover, the Singapore government itself is not immune to the

---

[5] See www.youtube.com/watch?v=wO0-hvXc9kY; accessed 7 August 2016.

advantages that might accrue from the commodification of Singlish. Almost to the point of contradicting its own anti-Singlish stance, the Singapore Tourism Board (STB), a government statutory board that comes under the Ministry of Trade and Industry, actually describes Singlish as Singaporeans' 'own brand of English', one that they 'fondly refer to'; it even offers light-hearted dictionary entries that are intended to help foreigners understand various Singlishisms (Wee, 2011: 82):

> Over the years, Singaporeans have developed their own brand of English fondly referred to as 'Singlish'. With our multiracial background, it's not surprising that 'Singlish' borrows from the many different languages spoken in Singapore. Here's a collection of 'Singlish' terms which you might find handy on your visit to Singapore...
> (i) Action (verb)
> Derived from the English language meaning to show off.
> Example: That fellow always like to action, walking around with his Rolex over his shirt sleeves
> (ii) Boh-Chup (adj)
> Derived from the Hokkien dialect meaning couldn't care less.
> Example: Ah, boh-chup, I'm not going to hand in my assignment.

Likewise, in its attempt to reach out to Singaporean communities overseas, the Singapore government has started organizing Singapore Day, a somewhat annual event that is usually held in major cities such as London or Shanghai, where Singaporeans are encouraged to gather and celebrate their Singaporeanness. On Singapore Day, then, Singlish is occasionally used, and this, too, raises questions about how this practice might undermine the government's claims that Singlish is a national liability. More recently, Koh (2016) reports that, to mark the celebration of Singapore's National Day, the budget airline Jetstar would be making announcements using Singlish on 9 August:

> These include announcements on, say, duty-free sales: 'Later we'll also be coming around for duty free. If you haven't buy from the airport yet, then you can buy from us *lah*. All same price, confirm plus chop.'
> Singlish lines will be provided to the crew, but they are free to add their own flair to the announcements, a Jetstar Asia spokesman told *The Straits Times* ...
> 'Singlish is part of Singapore's identity and heritage so we hope the public will see this as a fun celebration of local culture on National Day', the airline said.
> But pre-flight safety demonstrations and announcements will still be made in standard English.

Notice that in this example, Jetstar is restricting the use of Singlish to relatively nonserious topics, such as duty-free shopping, whereas announcements regarding more serious topics such as those relating to safety issues are made using Standard English. This bears on the commodification of Singlish because commodities become indexed to different kinds of social personas (Agha, 2011: 28). As with the STB's marketing of Singlish, Jetstar, too, treats Singlish as a variety that is to be used for fun and lightheartedness. Singlish, it would seem, is manifestly inappropriate for the discussion of serious topics. There are, then, semiotic constraints on just how Singlish might be commodified.

The issue of commodification therefore lends a different dynamic to language practices (Agha, 2011; Budach, Roy and Heller, 2003). It can inform and influence the relationship between language and identity in interesting ways, so that the impetus for retaining and expanding the use of a language variety becomes less reliant on solidarity considerations. Together with the issue of migration (see the next section), the commodification of Singlish bears on the increasingly global scale at which Singlish might be seen to operate. We need to interrogate the relationship between the global commodification of Singlish and its symbolic capital.

Singlish, Migration and Mobility

Just as commodification problematizes current arguments for as well as against Singlish, so, too, does migration and mobility. The main defence coming from supporters of Singlish is that it marks the Singaporean identity and, because of this, helps to develop solidarity amongst Singaporeans. It is argued that Singlish cuts across social classes and, in this way, can lay some claim to unifying Singaporeans regardless of their socio-economic backgrounds. In making these arguments about Singlish and solidarity, supporters of Singlish have often relied on assumptions involving diglossia and code-switching: (i) that uses of Singlish correlate with situations where only Singaporeans are present and (ii) that the situations where Singlish is used can be described as informal ('Low') as opposed to the formal ('High') situations where Standard English would be expected.

The rhetorical emphasis on Singlish as a builder of solidarity across all Singaporeans seems to ignore or at least downplay those cases of Singaporeans who are either unable or unwilling to speak Singlish. The cultural reality of any named variety is such that there inevitably arises a distinction between those who speak it and those who do not. Non-Singaporeans who do not speak Singlish are less of an issue. Especially where foreigners make attempts to learn Singlish, their lack of competence may well be viewed good-humouredly as forms of crossing (Rampton, 1995). But, unsurprisingly, Singaporeans who do not speak Singlish are treated differently. This is less of an issue for those who lack competence in Standard English: since their 'broken English' is also categorized as Singlish, they end up being characterized as Singlish speakers by default. In contrast, those Singaporeans who are well-educated speakers of Standard English and who still resist using Singlish risk being seen as elitist, snobbish and pretentious. However, even those Singaporeans who happily code-switch between Standard English and Singlish, too, need to have their linguistic practices carefully examined. This is because there is evidence to suggest that educated speakers who can speak Standard English and who decide to switch into Singlish are in fact strategically performing Singlish for humorous or ironic effect. This is fundamentally different from the kind of Singlish produced by speakers who lack competence in the standard variety – a difference that gets ideologically erased when claims about Singlish's efficacy in cultivating social solidarity are made.

Related to and complicating the claim that Singlish unifies Singaporeans is the phenomenon of migration. Especially in a world where migration is on the rise, we need to ask about the implications of inward migration (of non-Singaporeans into Singapore) and outward migration (of Singaporeans overseas) for the argument that Singlish helps to foster solidarity. Migration also raises the possibility that Singlish might come to be acquired by non-Singaporeans. If this is the case, then we also have to ask just how much of a role Singlish actually plays in marking the Singaporean identity and developing solidarity among Singaporeans. In fact, the arguments advanced by both the detractors and supporters of Singlish fail to sufficiently take into consideration the issue of migration. We need to therefore inquire about the extent to wich Singlish figures in the interactional patterns of individuals who take up residence in Singapore, and how significant Singlish might be in creating bonds between these incoming migrants (some of whom are new citizens) and Singaporeans.

What Is Singlish? Conceptualizations of Language

These are just some of the questions that this book will be concerned with, and in the chapters that follow, I discuss answers to them and other related concerns. But perhaps the most important and most fundamental question of all is one that, in the context of the Singlish controversy, appears (rather ironically) to have remained unasked. This is the question, 'What exactly is Singlish?' In making this observation, I am by no means suggesting that the parties to the controversy necessarily agree on an answer to the question. Rather, what is interesting is that the question itself hardly ever takes center stage. As a result, the complexities that it masks are rarely brought to light. This entire book can be taken as an attempt to answer this question.

Modernist conceptualizations about language treat it as a stable entity with clear boundaries, one that bears a historically continuous relationship to its speakers (Blommaert and Verschueren, 1998; Gal, 1989). As generations inherit the 'same' language over time, this language then comes to be seen as helping to define the contours of this community of speakers (Anderson, 1991). The language is as a consequence also viewed as an inalienable aspect of their shared cultural identity, where it serves in the transmission of traditional knowledge and values. The emphasis in modernity, then, is on language as a homogeneous entity that bears an enduring relationship to a well-defined community of speakers.

Critics of the modernist conceptualizations point to what they see as uncritical appeals to notions such as 'language' or 'French' and, of course, 'Singlish' and 'Standard English'; they also note the concomitant tendency to assume that varieties can be unproblematically distinguished and counted; and they argue that historically inherited assumptions about the nature of language are in serious need of 'disinventing' (Makoni and Pennycook, 2007 and the contributions therein). Heller (2008: 505) drives home the point that such modernist conceptualizations need to be carefully reconsidered:

Indeed, if we are asking questions about what it means these days to try to understand what language and social process have to do with each other, it is not because the goal now seems meaningless, but rather because the tools we have inherited are encountering some of their built-in limitations in current confrontations with the way things are unfolding in the world around us, confounding our attempts to understand them.

The worry, then, is that much of social science and humanities research continues to be in the thrall of outmoded concepts. These concerns about the inadequacy of modernist conceptualizations of language and other related notions such as identity and culture are not merely abstract or theoretical in nature. The main issue is that modernist conceptualizations of language critically underestimate the complex relationship between language, culture and identity – a complexity that is in fact growing in a rapidly globalizing world.

In contrast, the conditions of late modernity have drawn the attention of scholars to the importance of taking into account fluidity, heterogeneity and change (Rampton, 2006: 12, citing Bauman, 1992: 187–204). Language itself can no longer be assumed to be stable, especially when hybrid forms emerge under conditions where speakers mix semiotic resources (linguistic and non-linguistic) to project various kinds of identities (Rampton, 2006: 16). The links between language, identity and community (otherwise presumed to be straightforward) also become problematic (Heller, 2008). Under the effects of globalization, the demographic profiles of many communities have altered drastically as a result of migration. Populations are becoming more diversified in terms of ethnicity and social class, as relatively unfamiliar languages, patterns of interaction, cuisines and religious practices all become part of the local semiotic landscape (Jaworski and Thurlow, 2010). As a consequence, what is often unproblematically assumed to be a bounded territory with stable membership and cultural values is in fact undergoing significant changes.

We will see that underlying the arguments for as well as against Singlish are modernist conceptualizations of language as an *a priori* entity whose existence as a 'whole, bounded system' (Heller, 2008: 505) and thus a socially neutral object can be presumed, coherently referred to and described. While these modernist conceptualizations also fall under the category of ideology pooling (in that they are largely shared by parties involved in the Singlish controversy), they merit being discussed separately from the shared pool of assumptions that inform the ideological debates about Singlish. This is because these conceptualizations are far more abstract and much harder to challenge, and they remain a source of controversy even among language experts. The difficulty here, even for those who acknowledge problems with such modernist conceptualizations, is how to move forward. That is, in lieu of some other estab- lished ways of thinking and talking about language (and related concepts), there is the danger of simply falling back onto historically inherited notions, despite an appreciation of the problems involved.

Organization of the Book

In the chapters that follow, I explore the issues presented earlier before conclud- ing with a detailed discussion of how we might answer the question, 'What is Singlish?' The reason for organizing the discussion in this manner is twofold. One, the focus of this book is on the public debates surrounding Singlish. And a proper appreciation of the ideological assumptions and the arguments involved will help us recognize just how severely neglected the question 'What is Singlish?' has been throughout. In this regard, my decision not to provide an answer to this question before having examined the Singlish controversy in detail is a rhetorical strategy to avoid detracting from the intensity of the disputes.

Two, the question 'What is Singlish?' is not merely about Singlish of course. It goes to the very heart of a major socio-linguistic issue concerning language ontology. As Bell (2013) observes, socio-linguists do not often enough ask the question 'What is language?' even though such a question is not merely one of abstract metaphysical interest but also has major social and political implica- tions. The answer I propose to the question 'What is Singlish?' then, will carry general implications for socio-linguistics. With that in mind, it is appropriate to defer addressing it until the end of the book because that is the point where we move beyond the specifics of the Singlish controversy and try to come to grips with more general issues about the nature of language in society. I therefore organize the chapters as follows.

Chapter 1, *Language Policy in Singapore: English, Singlish and the Mother Tongues*, sets the stage for the discussion in the rest of this book by provid- ing a brief description of Singapore, its language policy of encouraging bilin- gualism in English and an officially recognized mother tongue, as well as the background to the Singlish controversy. The rationale behind Singapore's lan- guage policy is explained, linking it to the country's history, including its brief

and fractious membership in the Federation of Malaysia. The highly instrumentalist role that English is expected to play in helping Singapore (both the
country as a whole and its individual citizens) become globally competitive
is highlighted, as is the corresponding fear that Singlish will then undermine
this competitiveness because it compromises competence in Standard English.
The government's initiation of the Speak Good English Movement, a campaign
intended – certainly in its early days at least – to help eliminate Singlish, is discussed. The chapter ends with an ironic observation. The government has been
exhorting Singaporeans to be innovative and entrepreneurial in order to maintain their competitive edge. Yet while it is explicit and enthusiastic in applying
the discourses of innovation and entrepreneurialism to the domains of science,
technology and service, it seems unable or unwilling to extend these discourses
to that of language, including English and Singlish. There is an ideological
blind spot here that smacks of linguistic conservatism. This is a blind spot
that warrants excavating, and the chapter closes by providing the necessary
extraction.

   Chapter 2, *Ideology Pooling and Meta-Discursive Convergence in the
Singlish Debate*, deals with the notion of ideology pooling mentioned earlier,
delving into the question of why the debate never seems to progress in that the
same old questions and issues are constantly being raised. The reason for this, I
argue, is that even as the two sides disagree on whether to stigmatize or valorize
Singlish, the following occurs:
 (i) They both assume that Singlish is a fully extensive social language (Gee,
     2001). That is, it is a variety that serves as the medium for conducting
     entire exchanges.
(ii) They consistently contrast Singlish with Standard English, so that the for-
     mer is characterized as nonstandard. The public understanding of 'non-
     standard' is broad enough to accommodate both 'colloquial' and 'ungram-
     matical'. As a consequence, both sides tend to use without much reflection
     the label 'Singlish' to refer to the colloquial usage by fluent speakers of
     Standard English, as well as to the kind of English produced by less edu-
     cated speakers who may not also have a good command of the standard
     variety.
(iii) They both treat Singlish as a variety that has wide scope. That is, it is a vari-
     ety that has the potential to affect the entire society. As a consequence, the
     Singlish debate becomes constructed as an issue that has national impli-
     cations, since it can either adversely affect the economy or it can forge a
     sense of national solidarity across class differences. In this way, the deci-
     sion about whether to eliminate or legitimize Singlish is presented as a
     matter that is consequential for all Singaporeans.
The cumulative force of (i–iii) is to conflate different uses of English that arise
from different kinds of competencies and to gloss over the ways in which

socio-linguistically distinct groups of speakers may employ language as a resource for style and identity work (Coupland, 2007). As a result, the points in (i–iii) actually undermine some of the claims made by the parties involved in the Singlish controversy, particularly claims concerning the role that Singlish plays in the neutralization of class differences and the expression of a national identity. But despite the problems that (i–iii) create, because both sides of the debate are committed to them, they are never seriously contested, much less critically examined. We will see how these shared assumptions that constitute the ideology pool lead the opposing parties to meta-discursively converge onto a number of similar assertions.

The possibility of progress in the debate over Singlish is further taken up in Chapter 3, *Language Experts, Linguistic Chutzpah and the Speak Good Singlish Movement*, where we see how the Singlish controversy might actually show signs of moving beyond covering the same old ground (although as Chapter 4 then shows, there is still a strong tendency to repeat the same old claims). The Speak Good Singlish Movement was started as a response to the Speak Good English Movement, the latter having been initiated by the Singapore government. The Speak Good Singlish Movement represents a good example of linguistic chutzpah, where speakers demonstrate confidence in their language choices while also having the meta-linguistic awareness and sophistication needed to articulate rationales for these choices. The chapter argues that linguistic chutzpah is especially important in relation to the global spread of English, where speakers are often confronted with the need to make decisions about language while not being able to rely on traditional sources of authority (such as the speech community or prescriptive grammars). Under such circumstances, speakers need to be able to adopt confident stances about their language choices, even while knowing that these choices may be met with criticism. Linguistic chutzpah therefore provides important counters to the anxieties over language usage that are fostered by various mechanisms of insecuritization (Lazzarato, 2009), such as technologies of surveillance (Foucault, 1977) of appropriate language practices and institutional narratives about the social and cognitive penalties/dangers of using language incorrectly. In this regard, the chapter also explores how linguistic chutzpah can be cultivated and the role that language experts can play in this cultivation.

Chapter 4, *Voice: Who Speaks about Singlish?* addresses the fact that certain segments of society appear to be more able and willing than others to contribute to the debates about Singlish. I suggest that the absence of voice from monovarietal speakers of ungrammatical English (that is, speakers who speak only Singlish and are thus unable to code-switch into Standard English) affects the controversy on two levels. On one level, it shapes the trajectory of the controversy, since claims about what Singlish *does* (whether this is about its effect on learning Standard English or its role in fostering solidarity and marking the national identity) reflect the concerns of parties that do have voice. It also does not help that the Singlish controversy is presented as a matter of national consequence. Whether rightly or wrongly, this gives the controversy a gravity that might lead those who are less educated to feel that they lack the qualifications or insights to contribute to such a 'momentous' discussion. That is, because the controversy is prominently located in the high-prestige realm of discussions about public policy or matters of national interest, less educated individuals may shy away from participating. It may be that speakers of ungrammatical English share the concerns that have been expressed so that their views are already well represented, or it may be that they have other as yet unexpressed concerns. But their lack of direct contribution to the Singlish controversy means that those who do participate can sometimes claim to be speaking on their behalf and therefore attribute specific concerns to them, regardless of whether this is in fact the case.

On another level, the absence of voice from speakers of ungrammatical English also shapes understandings about what Singlish *is*. Active participants in the controversy often provide illustrative examples of Singlish, both to bolster the points they are making and to counter the claims they hope to discredit. Many of these participants are also producers of novels, movies, plays, television series, dictionaries and other textual products whose circulations inform public understandings about what Singlish looks and sounds like. And since any social use of language is inherently indexical, these circulations also inform broader understandings about what kinds of persons speak Singlish. Especially as Singlish becomes commoditized, these characterological consequences (Agha, 2011) help to perpetuate particular understandings about the motivations that might lead speakers to 'consume' Singlish. That is, speakers might be drawn to Singlish because it is associated with particular kinds of personas, and conversely, via iconization, speakers of Singlish are constructed as being particular kinds of persons. For example, the title character in the sitcom *Phua Chu Kang* is widely seen as a representation of the kind of person who speaks Singlish. This is a sitcom character whose humour derives from him being brash and down-to-earth and whose use of Singlish is contrasted with that of his uptight and proper sister-in-law, who speaks Standard English. Singlish then becomes associated with particular kinds of social attributes: being uneducated, unpretentious, vulgar and humorous. As a result, the serious Singlish speaker – someone who is thoughtful, cultured and has gravitas – is largely perceived as a cultural oxymoron.

I suggest that the pertinent issue raised by the absence of representations from speakers of ungrammatical English is less one of remedial voicing, where the hitherto 'voiceless' are encouraged to speak up. Instead, I put forward the argument that the relevant focus ought to be more one of remedial conceptualization, where, along the lines highlighted by Spivak (1988; 1999), active contributors to the Singlish controversy should be encouraged to reexamine their own assumptions about Singlish.

Chapter 5 deals with the commodification of Singlish, an aspect of Singlish that is not widely discussed. This is despite the fact that a number of Singaporean films have been produced that have done relatively well at the local box office, and other locally produced films have also gone on to win a number of regional and international awards. In addition to films, Singlish features prominently in plays, novels and poems. And as pointed out earlier, Singlish also figures in the Singapore Tourism Board's attempts to attract tourists to Singapore.

The commodification of Singlish, then, is very much tied up with the culture industries, and the discussion in this chapter will draw on Peterson and Kern's (1996: 3) notion of cultural omnivores, which refers to a broadening of the scope of cultural consumption amongst elites such that there is a 'change from exclusionist snob to inclusionist omnivore'. Brown-Saracino (2009: 192) points out that this omnivorous orientation is tied to an 'appreciation for the underdog', resulting in 'an ethos that values a sort of cultural democracy that embraces a familiarity with low-, middle-, and highbrow cultural objects alike – that celebrates the idiosyncratic character of people and place'. I argue that Singlish holds an attraction from a consumption perspective precisely because it suits the cultural omnivore's diet. It is positioned as a celebration of low culture that simultaneously indexes an authentically Singaporean experience.

At the same time, if presented in sufficiently small doses or if accompanied by a local translator, Singlish does not become so unintelligible as to make the act of cultural consumption unnecessarily difficult. In this regard, this chapter will also examine how Singlish populates the linguistic landscape of Singapore, such that visitors can lay claim to having experienced what is linguistically idiosyncratic and exotic about Singapore in a relatively painless and enjoyable manner. This also means investigating how Singlish is deployed as part of the aesthetic and emotional labor performed by those individuals and organization that are concerned with shaping the tourism experience (Jack, 2010: 14).

Chapter 6, *Singlish, Migration and Mobility*, looks at the extent to which Singlish serves as a resource for strengthening the Singaporean identity. Supporters of Singlish claim that it fosters solidarity amongst Singaporeans in various ways. According to one line of argument, it is a class leveler that allows Singaporeans to communicate amongst themselves regardless of class background. This claim is usually made in relation to National Service, the mandatory military service where Singaporean males from widely varying linguistic and socio-economic backgrounds have to work together for a period of two years. Given these diverse backgrounds, Singlish serves as a lingua franca that apparently carries little or no class pretensions. This is in contrast to Standard English: even though English is expected by the government to serve as a lingua franca in Singapore's multiracial society, supporters of Singlish argue that Standard English's unavoidable indexical associations with class and education mean that, even where it facilitates communication, it does so without fostering solidarity and may in fact widen social gaps. Other contexts in which Singlish is claimed to perform a similar function include ordering food in local coffeeshops or hawker centers (open-air complexes housing many different food stalls), where the relatively humble nature of these establishments makes the use of Standard English socially anomalous.

A related but distinct line of argument has to do with Singaporeans relaxing amongst themselves. This bears clear similarities to the preceding argument in that social solidarity is once again emphasized. But it needs to be considered separately because interactions here often involve social peers. Social class is once again implicated, but only because the interactants here tend to share similar social and educational backgrounds. A careful comparison of both these cases, then, raises the question of whether the overly liberal use of the label 'Singlish' for both types of situations obscures more than it reveals.

The Singlish controversy, then, is inextricably intertwined with notions of class in Singaporean society. Public political discourses, we shall see, are greatly concerned with avoiding the entrenchment of privilege and class boundaries. Whereas the official rationale for positioning English as a lingua franca is to facilitate communication across different ethnic groups so as to minimize ethnic conflicts, modern Singapore also has to consider how best to position English or, as the case may be, Singlish, so as to facilitate communication across social classes. This is an important question that bears on the issue of solidarity. It is also an unavoidable question because Singapore prides itself on being an open society where talented foreigners are encouraged to take up residence and even citizenship.

The government is aware that the presence of incoming migrants is a sensitive issue, but has nevertheless insisted that this openness to foreign talent is critical to Singapore's continued economic success. If it is the case that Singlish can play a role in helping to integrate incoming migrants, then the official argument that Singlish undermines Singapore's economic competitiveness needs to be reexamined for its validity. Conversely, we also need to ask whether, as has been popularly claimed by its supporters, Singlish indeed plays an important identity function in fostering solidarity among Singaporeans located overseas. This, too, is an important question if the role that Singlish plays in the Singaporean diaspora is to be better understood.

The discussions in the preceding chapters will have consistently served to highlight the importance of giving attention to the influence of ideology in shaping the Singlish controversy. The attention to ideology is carried over into the final chapter, *What Is Singlish? Language, Culture and Identity in a Globalizing World*. Chapter 7 begins by comparing two specific attempts at theorizing

Singlish – Alsagoff's (2007; 2010) cultural orientation model and Leimgru-ber's (2013) indexical model – with more general accounts of the global spread of English, namely, Kachru's (1982; 1985) three circles model and Schneider's (2007) dynamic model. The strengths and weaknesses of all four models, along with much earlier attempts to characterize Singapore English in terms of a cre-ole continuum (Platt, 1975; Platt and Weber, 1980), and their difficulties in accounting for not just linguistic variation but also ideological variation (given that the label 'Singlish' itself is slippery) are highlighted.

The key problem, this chapter argues, is that all these models start with a par-ticular linguistic label ('Singlish', 'English') and they then attempt to account for the linguistic variation associated with that label. They do not take seriously enough the fact that meta-linguistic labeling is itself of analytical interest. Thus, all these models are trying to focus on questions such as 'What are linguistic properties of Singlish?' or 'When do speakers use Singlish?' These questions are undoubtedly important, but – and this is the critical point of the chapter – they cannot be adequately addressed without at the same time engaging with the question, 'When and why does the label "Singlish" come to be used in relation to certain linguistic properties and not others?'

In this regard, the chapter argues for treating Singlish as an assemblage of linguistic and nonlinguistic resources. This final chapter shows how the notion of an assemblage allows for a coherent analysis of Singlish as a 'mul-tiple object' (Farías, 2010: 13). The relations between different enactments of Singlish to phenomena such as commodification, migration, and class are then foregrounded as ideological stances that serve different agendas in the Singlish controversy, thus returning our discussion full circle to the issues presented in the Introduction. More fundamentally, this is not an account that is specific to Singlish, but one that has broader implications for our understanding of lan-guage and how this understanding shapes the dynamics of language ideolog-ical debates. The chapter therefore closes with some comments on the future directions for linguistic work.

1 Language Policy in Singapore: English, Singlish and the Mother Tongues

Arguments for and against Singlish are ultimately matters of language policy, and to better appreciate these arguments, it is important to understand the official language policy of Singapore. There are historical reasons why the official language policy, which emphasizes bilingual competence in English and an officially recognized ethnic mother tongue, is the way it is.

It is the goal of this chapter, therefore, to provide a description of the official language policy as well as an analysis of the ideologies that inform it. While I draw on a number of sources, the main reference for the government's language policy comes from the writings of Lee Kuan Yew (Han, Fernandez and Tan, 1998; Lee, 2012), who was not only Singapore's first prime minister but was also arguably the country's most important and influential policy maker.

I begin with Singapore's reluctantly acquired status as an independent state.

Independence, Nation-Building and Multiracialism

Singapore is a linguistically and ethnically diverse country with a population of about 5.7 million[1]. Officially, its ethnic composition is approximately 74.2% Chinese, 13.3% Malay, and 9.2% Indian, while the remaining 3.3%, classified as 'Others', comprise mainly Eurasians and Europeans. Because Singapore has no natural resources of its own, in the 1960s its leaders were convinced that economic survival was possible only if Singapore joined the Federation of Malaysia, and they worked hard to bring about that political membership in 1963. However, just over two years later, Singapore reluctantly gained its independence when it left the Federation in 1965. This departure was in no small part due to political differences over the issue of whether ethnic Malays ought to be granted special rights. The Federation of Malaysia preferred a *bumiputra* policy, which would recognize Malay as the sole official language and endow ethnic Malays with special rights. In contrast, Singapore's leaders were

---

[1] 2016 *Census of Population*, www.indexmundi.com/singapore/demographics_profile.html; accessed 27 April 2017.

uncomfortable with adopting a policy that privileged one particular ethnic group over others.

Singapore's independence meant that its leaders were faced, quite suddenly, both with the task of building a nation out of an ethnolinguistically diverse population and with the need to develop the country's economy without access to any natural resources. Under such conditions, a careful consideration of just what kind of language policy Singapore ought to be aiming for became especially critical, as Lee Kuan Yew (2012: 224–225) points out,

Language policy is a vital instrument for achieving national interest objectives and meeting the needs of governance. Rightly conceived, it can help unite a population that is racially and linguistically diverse, as well as build a platform for communication with the outside world. We did not stumble on this realization by chance. Rather, we were made acutely aware of it from the outset. From the day we assumed the reins of government, we had to give serious consideration to this matter. Unlike countries with ethnically and linguistically homogeneous populations where the language of administration follows that of the population, it was not obvious to us at the start which language we should choose as our official or working language.

Economic development took the form of a strategy aimed at attracting foreign investment and multinational corporations. This in turn meant that Singapore's language policy needed to have a correspondingly strong emphasis on learning English so that the local workforce would be able to meet the communicative expectations of these investors and corporations. In other words, despite the negative associations that English might have held for some Singaporeans given that Singapore used to be under British colonial rule, an emotional rejection of the language was not an option as far as the government was concerned. It would have meant eschewing the potential economic benefits that knowledge of the language would have brought to a country that was newly independent and struggling economically. According to Lee (1970),

The deliberate stifling of a language which gives access to superior technology can be stifling beyond repair. Sometimes this is done not to elevate the status of the indigenous language, so much as to take away a supposed advantage a minority in the society is deemed to have, because that minority has already gained a greater competence in the foreign language. This can be most damaging. It is tantamount to blinding the next generation to the knowledge of the advanced countries.

But the emphasis on English also led the government to worry that exposure to the language would lead Singaporeans to become increasingly 'Westernized', 'decadent' or 'morally corrupt' (Wee, 2002b). Thus, in the eyes of the government, knowledge of English had to be balanced by knowledge of one's mother tongue. The government's definition of mother tongue is that of an ethnic community language, to which an individual bears an official relationship by virtue of ethnic parentage. In the case of mixed parentage, this is by default taken to be the ethnicity of the father. This official understanding of what is a mother tongue, of course, ignores the complexities of an individual's sociolinguistic biography, and while the government has in recent times tried to take into account cases of hybrid identities (see the later discussion), it still insists on individuals accepting as their mother tongue an official language affiliated with their ethnic identity.

Knowledge of one's mother tongue, the government rationalized, would provide Singaporeans with a link to their traditional cultures and values and would thus serve to counter any undesirable effects of Westernization. This emphasis on the mother tongue was also motivated by the country's ethnolinguistic diversity. Recall that it was the differences over how to manage ethnolinguistic diversity that were contributing factors to Singapore's departure from the Federation of Malaysia. For Singapore's political leaders, the promotion of English had to take into account the presence of Singapore's other languages, as well as the feelings of the speakers of these languages.

The Singapore government has therefore consistently encouraged Singaporeans to be bilingual in English and in a mother tongue that is officially assigned to them on the basis of their ethnicity. There is no official mother tongue for the 'Others' category since it does not constitute a specific ethnic community. Given Singapore's ethnic diversity, official mother tongues are recognized for each of the major ethnic groups: Mandarin for the Chinese, Malay for the Malays, and Tamil for the Indians. To maintain harmony among Singapore's ethnically diverse population, there must be respect and equal treatment accorded to each ethnic group. This policy, which emphasizes the equal status of all ethnic groups, is sometimes referred to as 'multiracialism' (Benjamin, 1976).

In Singaporean public discourse, the terms 'multiculturalism' or 'multiracialism' tend to be used interchangeably, even though scholars often prefer to maintain a distinction between the two. A policy of multiculturalism, broadly speaking, aims at integrating erstwhile distinct cultural communities. The assumption here is that cultural differences are porous and malleable, and the emergence of shared practices and understandings can and ought to be encouraged. A policy of multiracialism, in contrast, aims to encourage the relatively peaceful coexistence of distinct communities traditionally built along ethnic lines or racial subdivisions, as is commonly found in many former British colonies. Such divisions are assumed to represent hard boundaries. For Lee, the differences between the various ethnic 'tribes' is a 'primordial fact' so that any policy that tries to force these 'tribes' to submerge their distinctiveness (as would have been the case with the Federation of Malaysia's policy of privileging ethnic Malays) would have most likely exacerbated ethnic tensions (Lee Kuan Yew, quoted in Han, Fernandez and Tan, 1998: 163–165). In Singapore, ethnic divisions inherited from the country's colonial past have been retained, thus leading to an official 'mother tongue' being assigned to each ethnic community in the hope that this would help mitigate any extremist tendencies that might otherwise try to impose a single language on the entire nation.

Although the language policy of Singapore recognizes English as an official language, it is not deemed appropriate by the government to be an official mother tongue. This denial of official mother tongue status to English is a core aspect of Singapore's language policy, as can be seen from Lee's (cited in Bokhorst-Heng, 1998: 252) assertion that English is not 'emotionally acceptable' as a mother tongue: 'One abiding reason why we have to persist in bilingualism is that English will not be emotionally acceptable as our mother tongue ... To have no emotionally acceptable language as our mother tongue is to be emotionally-crippled.'

There are various reasons for this insistence on the apparent emotional unacceptability of English. One, English is supposed to serve as an inter-ethnic lingua franca, facilitating communication and interaction across Singapore's ethnically diverse society. If the language officially belongs to no specific ethnic group, then it can be ideologically positioned as ethnically neutral (Wee, 2010), and it would not be seen as privileging any particular ethnicity. Thus, as Lee (2012: 226) points out, 'By choosing English as our language of administration, we managed to avoid the political fallout that would have come had we chosen either Malay over Chinese or Chinese over Malay. Language issues can stir strong emotions.' Two, and relatedly, as the major language of socio-economic mobility, maintaining an ethnically neutral status for English helps to ensure that the distribution of economic advantages is not seen as being unduly associated with a specific ethnic group, which would otherwise raise the danger of inter-ethnic tension. Three, English, as the language of Singapore's former colonial rulers, is viewed by the government as a language that is essentially Western and thus unsuitable to be a mother tongue for an Asian society such as Singapore. While the government does not take the position that 'worthy values can be transmitted only via the mother tongue' (Lee, 2012: 227; see the later discussion), it nevertheless seems to insist, somewhat contradictorily it has to be said, that the mother tongue is the only feasible way for each individual Singaporean to 'tap on the rich heritage that their respective culture has to offer':

Language is more than a tool of communication; it transmits values too. That is why we have insisted that all school-going children learn their mother tongue, whether Chinese, Malay or Tamil, as their second language. This way, they will have the means to tap on the rich heritage that their respective culture has to offer ...

I am not saying that one must know one's mother tongue in order to have a well-developed sense of identity or that worthy values can be transmitted only via the mother tongue ... What I am saying is that each ethnic culture has its own unique heritage that is worth preserving and teaching young Singaporeans about.

The result of these three considerations, then, is a language policy that posits the equal value of languages by acknowledging that both English and the official mother tongues are *equally essential* but for different reasons: the former for economic prosperity and the latter for maintaining ties to one's cultural heritage where this heritage is defined in terms of membership in an officially recognized ethnic group. In a similar vein, all three mother tongues are officially of *equal status* so that no single ethnic group can or should claim privilege over any other.[2]

To summarize, the architecture of Singapore's language policy attempts to address the twin goals of ensuring economic competitiveness and maintaining ethnic harmony by doing the following:

(i) Recognizing a total of four official languages; of the four, English is not given a status as an official mother tongue because it is not 'Asian';

(ii) Encouraging bilingualism in English and an ethnic mother tongue; and

(iii) According a specific mother tongue to each of the three major ethnic groups.

These, then, are the fundamentals of Singapore's language policy, a policy that was formulated in the context of an unexpected and reluctantly acquired independence as a result of its departure from the Federation of Malaysia.

The Positioning of English in Singapore's Language Policy

We have seen that Singapore's language policy makes a distinction between English and the official mother tongues so that, despite being officially recognized, English is considered by the government to be 'emotionally unacceptable' as a mother tongue. However, this particular positioning of English is increasingly problematic because there are already signs that, for many

---

[2] Against this backdrop of the government's emphasis on respecting and maintaining ethnic distinctiveness, the Eurasian community occupies an uneasy position. This is because, together with the Chinese, Malays and Indians, the Eurasians are considered among the 'founding races' of Singapore (Hill and Lian, 1995: 103). In the case of language, this is highly consequential, since the Eurasian community does not have its own official mother tongue alongside the other major ethnic groups. As a result, there have been anxieties about the place of Eurasians in Singapore society. As Benjamin (1976: 127) pointed out some time ago, 'The more that Singapore's national culture demands that each "race" should have a respectably ancient and distinctive exogenous culture as well as a "mother tongue" to serve as the second element of a bilingual education, the more will the Eurasians come to feel that there is no proper place for them'.

One reason given as to why the Eurasians do not have their own official mother tongue is that the community is numerically too small (Wee, 2002b). However, the lack of a specific mother tongue for the Eurasians is not just a matter of numbers. The choice of language is also problematic because the Eurasians generally feel that English should be their official mother tongue (Wee, 2002b; 2009). This is due to the fact that, since the time of British colonial rule, many Eurasians have grown up with English as the home language (Gupta, 1994: 19; Rappa, 2000: 168). However, as noted (see the main text), there are reasons why the government is reluctant to recognize English as an official mother tongue.

Table 1. *Language Most Frequently Spoken at Home (in %):*
2000 Survey

Chinese homes	English (23.9) Mandarin (45.1) Chinese dialects (30.7)
Malay homes	English (7.9) Malay (91.6)
Indian homes	English (35.6) Tamil (42.9)

Singaporeans today, the language of the home is English, rather than one of the official mother tongues (Li, Saravanan and Ng, 1997; Pakir, 2000: 262; Saravanan, 1994). Rather ironically, this broad society-wide shift towards English in the home is occurring because Singaporeans have taken seriously the government's message that English affords its speakers significant socio-economic advantages.

The data in Table 1, based on the 2000 Census of Population, show that, except for the Malays, the officially assigned mother tongue is often not necessarily the home language.

Ten years later, in 2010, English became even more widely used in Singaporean homes (Table 2). Among the Chinese, 32.6% now report speaking English compared to 23.9% a decade earlier. Among the Malays, the figure is now 17% compared to 7.9%. And among the Indians, 41.6% is the new figure versus 35.6%. This shift towards English is further underscored by the findings of the General Household Survey that was conducted by Singapore's Department of Statistics. In a recent newspaper report that discusses these findings, Lee (2016) notes that English has become the language spoken most often at home in Singapore. Whereas the 2010 census recorded that 32.3% of those aged five and older speak English at home, this figure had risen to 36.9% in 2016.

In the case of the Eurasians, many grow up speaking English at home (see note 5). But because English is the medium of instruction and cannot be counted as a mother tongue, upon entering school, Eurasian students are required to learn a second language simply to meet the government's bilingual requirement, even though this second language may bear no ethnic or heritage affiliation for them. Consequently, most of them end up choosing either Mandarin (because of its perceived economic advantage in relation to China's

Table 2. *Language Most Frequently Spoken at Home (in %):*
2010 Survey

Chinese homes	English (32.6), Mandarin (47.7), Chinese dialects (19.2)
Malay homes	English (17.0), Malay (82.7)
Indian homes	English (41.6), Tamil (36.7)

development) or Malay (because it is supposed to be relatively easy to learn; Braga-Blake, 1992: 11, 19). For many Eurasian parents, however, there still remains the anxiety that their children are being 'handicapped' in comparison with their Chinese, Malay or Indian counterparts since, for the latter, the second language also happens to be their official mother tongue (Wee, 2002b: 290).

However, this perception amongst some Eurasians that the other ethnic communities have a linguistic advantage in the education system because their official mother tongue is also the language of the home is increasingly suspect. Lee (2016) reports that English has been steadily growing as a home language:

The use of English has been rising steadily: 23 per cent in 2000, 28.1 per cent (2005), 32.3 per cent (2010) and 36.9 per cent (2015). During this period, the use of Mandarin at home has remained relatively stable, between 35 per cent and 36 per cent. Similarly, Tamil stayed stable, at around 3.3 per cent. But the use of other Chinese dialects and Malay has fallen steadily. Last year, 12.2 per cent reported using mainly Chinese dialects at home, down from 14.3 per cent in 2010 and 18.2 per cent in 2005. For Malay, just 10.7 per cent of residents used it most often at home last year, down from 12.2 per cent in 2010 and 13.2 per cent in 2005.

While the use of Mandarin and Tamil appears to have stabilized in relation to English, this has to be seen against a wider historical backdrop where English has actually been gaining ground even vis-à-vis these languages. For both these communities, the general explanation for this shift offered by community leaders has been the appreciation among Malays and Indians of the economic value of English as well as a rise in interracial marriages (Hussain, 2011).

Mandarin appears to have maintained a strong presence in its particular ethnic community, that of the Chinese. But even here, 'while the growth in the share of English-speaking households has accelerated in the last decade, the growth of Mandarin-speaking households has slowed' (Cai, 2011). More interestingly, the resilience of Mandarin is actually aided by the inflow of Mandarin-speaking permanent residents from Malaysia and China. It is not unlikely, therefore, that as these new permanent residents settle into Singapore society, subsequent generations might also demonstrate a shift towards English. One consequence of the increase in English-speaking households among Chinese Singaporeans is that a number of Chinese Singaporean students actually have great difficulty coping with Mandarin despite the fact that it supposed to be their official mother tongue. This has recently forced the government to introduce a simplified language 'B' syllabus for Mandarin (Ministry of Education press release, 9 January 2004), and also to acknowledge that only a minority, an elite estimated at about 10% of the student population, can be expected to be fully bilingual in English and the official mother tongue, with similar reviews also being initiated for the Malay and Tamil curricula (Wee, 2006: 355–357).

It is also questionable if the government can continue denying English the status of a mother tongue on the grounds that Singapore is an Asian society and English is a Western language. The reason for this is that this Asian character of Singapore society is already likely to change not least because the government has recently decided to reposition itself as 'a cosmopolitan, global city' in order to attract talented foreigners as potential new citizens, replacing those Singaporeans who may decide to emigrate permanently (see Chapter 6). Thus, Goh Chok Tong, Lee's successor as Singapore's second prime minister, pointed out in a 1997 National Day Rally speech,

Attracting global talent is essential for creating the best for Singaporeans. . . . Singapore must become a cosmopolitan, global city, an open society where people from many lands can feel at home . . .

Therefore we must incorporate into our society talent from all over the world, not just Chinese, Malay or Indians, but talented people whatever their race or country of origin.

Here, we have an implicit admission by the government that Singapore's national identity may need to be reconstructed into one less dependent on an Asian 'us' versus Western 'them' dichotomy. This possibility was acknowledged as much by Goh two years later in a 1999 National Day Rally speech:

When Singapore becomes a first-world economy, it will become more international and more cosmopolitan. This has a cost for our society. It will be less Asian. There will be many more people of different nationalities, races and lifestyles in Singapore. This place will feel and look like any other cosmopolitan city in the world.

According to a 2016 report from the government's National and Population Talent Division,

There were 20,815 new citizens last year [i.e. 2015], largely unchanged from the previous three years. About 38.9 per cent of them were aged 20 and below, 13.4 per cent aged between 21 and 30, 27.1 per cent aged between 31 and 40, and 20.5 per cent aged above 40.

The majority (58.7 per cent) of the new citizens were from other Southeast Asian countries, while 35 per cent were from other parts of Asia and 6.3 per cent from other countries outside of Asia. The Government takes a 'calibrated approach to immigration', and plans to continue taking in between 15,000 and 25,000 new citizens each year to prevent the citizen population from shrinking, the report said.[3]

It is clear that, all things being equal, the government's preference is to recruit new citizens from other Southeast Asian countries so as to maintain as far as possible the relative proportions of Chinese, Malays and Indians. But the need to prevent the population from 'shrinking' and the fact that it is not always

---

[3] See 'Singapore population rises 1.3% to 5.61 million', National and Population Talent Division, 27 September 2016, www.channelnewsasia.com/news/singapore/singapore-population-rises-1-3-to-5-61-million-7779450; accessed 28 April 2017.

possible to attract foreign talent only from Southeast Asia mean that it is also sometimes necessary to bring in new citizens from other parts of the world. Thus, trying to maintain a balance between the cosmopolitanism that the government sees as being critical to its global city ambitions, on the one hand, and the need to also continue presenting itself as a robustly Asian nation, on the other, remains an ongoing challenge for Singapore's language policy. Indeed, the results of the government's attempt to attract foreigners has been a growth in the number of permanent residents, from 287,000 in 2000 to 541,000 in 2010 and 524,000 in 2016.[4] It is therefore a distinct possibility that this will in time to come require that the government abandon or at least rethink the strict dichotomy between English and the official mother tongues (Stroud and Wee, 2010; Wee and Bokhorst-Heng, 2005).

Given all these factors, there are good reasons why the government may need to reconsider its decision to deny English the status of an official mother tongue. But until this happens, English continues to be positioned by the government as a language that is to be valued mainly on pragmatic or instrumentalist grounds and not one that Singaporeans should be viewing as part of their heritage. Such a perspective has implications for how English is taught in Singapore and, by extension, why Singlish tends to be stigmatized. I first consider the teaching of English.

Teaching English in Singapore

Not surprisingly, in the early days of Singapore's history, British English was treated as the reference model for language teaching given the country's colonial past. Chew (2005: 4; see also Foley, 1998: 246), describing early English-language teaching (ELT) in Singapore, notes,

ELT continued in much the same way that it had operated in the 1950's when it was under British colonial rule ... stated objectives were to develop pupils' ability to 'carry on a simple conversation in grammatical English and understand simple English prose; as well as write simple connected English prose' (Ministry of Education 1958). This was to be acquired by the mastery of the English sound system and the basic patterns of English sentences and phraseology.

This meant that mastery of English was understood exonormatively as the ability to approximate, if not reproduce, the speech and writing associated with the British English. Even up until the 1980s, the policy was that 'the English taught in Singapore should be British Standard English with an RP [Received

[4] Population Trends 2016, Department of Statistics, Singapore, www.singstat.gov.sg; accessed 26 April 2017.

Pronunciation] accent' (Gupta, 2010: 57). However, 'by the 1990s, school text-books knowingly incorporated local cultural terms, and there was a generally confident, tolerant, and empowering approach to Singapore English. Books and websites celebrating the local non-standard dialect, Singlish, appeared. In writing, Singlish was confidently used in informal communication and in creative writing, especially in dialogue and humour' (58).

It is not clear, however, just how widespread or institutionally accepted Singlish was in the schools, despite Gupta's comments. Chong (2011: 106) points out that the Ministry of Education was highly reluctant to fully support arts education in part because of the use of Singlish in local works, but slowly came around to the idea because of the more progressive attitudes of younger teachers and principals:

In the early 1990s, the local classroom was still a relatively new space for the arts ... the classroom was still jealously regarded by the Ministry of Education (MOE) as an exclusive space for traditional academic learning.

MOE's initial reluctance to support fully the NAC-AEP (National Arts Council- Arts Education Programme) was also due to local theatre's checkered history ... Local theatre, especially during the late 1980s and early 1990s, often explored Singlish (the local vernacular hybrid of English, Malay and Hokkien) as a key element in the search for national identity, thus making it rather inappropriate, in the eyes of local education officers who saw it as 'broken English', for the classroom.

Given MOE's resistance, it fell on NAC to ensure that artistry and creativity would not come packaged with perceived political or ideological agenda. It set up an inhouse endorsement list where a panel of arts education experts, principals and officials from MOE and NAC would assess and select the arts education modules offered by arts groups ... Furthermore, with a younger generation of teachers and principals who are more aware of the benefits of arts education, as well as the People's Action Party (PAP) state's persistent exhortation of local institutions to impart to young Singaporeans creativity and innovation for the sake of economic growth and high-value manufacturing, attitudes towards arts education have undergone a sea-change from the early 1990s. Today, the early suspicion many MOE officials and school principals had of theatre appears to have dissipated for good.

Nevertheless, this apparent acceptance/tolerance of Singlish was largely limited to 'creative' works where students were taught directing, acting and playwriting; this was far from a full endorsement of Singlish's legitimacy/acceptability. Also, to the extent that local words and accents were considered acceptable, this was predicated on the assumption that they would be part of the 'local *Standard* English' (Gupta, 2010: 57). This of course further assumes that the linguistic entity 'local Standard English' was relatively easy to define, which in turn relies on the assumption that 'Standard English', whether a local variant or not, is also a fairly unproblematic notion.

Unfortunately, there is 'no general consensus' as to what Standard English is (Bex and Watts, 1999: 1), despite Honey's (1997) assertion that Standard English is the variety spoken and written by educated speakers. Honey's assertion is problematic (see Crowley, 1999) because there are significant differences between the grammar of spoken and written English. Therefore, characterizing both the spoken and written varieties as Standard English simply evades the important question of how such differences do not undermine the claim of unity; that is, whether there is need to distinguish between Standard Written English and Standard Spoken English. This is not a trivial issue because grammatical differences are also the kinds of things that presumably distinguish Standard English from its nonstandard counterparts – and therefore between 'local/Singapore Standard English' and 'Singlish'. This issue, if left unaddressed, means that we are left with the arguably even more perplexing question of how much variation (and of what kind) is tolerated before the differences in linguistic practices that distinguish Standard Written from Standard Spoken English become characterized as nonstandard.

There is also the problem that the group of 'educated speakers' that Honey relies on to ground his definition of Standard English is not at all homogeneous, since there are different levels of education and, of course, different educational institutions that enjoy varying degrees of prestige and credibility. All these considerations bring up the question of just what kind of education is needed before a speaker is deemed to be a speaker of Standard English. This in turn raises the highly contentious question of who decides that a speaker has been sufficiently educated so as to be considered a speaker of Standard English. Simply asserting that other speakers of Standard English are the best judges, as Honey seems to be doing, will not do because of the vicious circularity involved in this line of argument. Claiming that there is an ineffable nature to Standard English that is clearly recognized even by those who may not be competent in it is equally problematic, because it shifts the grounds of argument from scholarly debate to matters of taste and faith and the contentious issue of who specifically ought to be the arbiters of such taste and faith. This shift needs to be avoided as far as possible because, as we see shortly, what counts as Standard English can have a significant impact on the social and economic fortunes of individuals. The intersection between Standard English and matters of social justice is too important to be left to the tastes and faith of a (self-)selected few.[5]

---

[5] A more reasoned and moderate position against non-Standard English is offered by Quirk (1990). While generally sympathetic to the idea that non-Standard English is just as linguistically legitimate as Standard English, Quirk is nonetheless concerned that the lack of institutional support for the former means that learners would be penalized socio-economically (as opposed to cognitively) if encouraged to learn non-Standard English (1990: 9): 'It is neither liberal, nor liberating

Needless to say, despite these problems with the notion of Standard English, the concept continues to exert a powerful influence on English language education. But rather than being understood as ideologically laden and changing, Standard English is all too often construed as an independently existing and timeless entity (Park and Wee, 2012).[6] Learners are then expected to strive towards this Standard English, and their English language competence can be objectively measured by using this supposedly timeless linguistic entity as the yardstick. The misrecognition of the actual nature of Standard English therefore fosters a sense of linguistic insecurity (see Chapter 3) that tends not to encourage variations that lack the aura of respectability, tradition and certainty bestowed by established grammars, dictionaries and teachers who are perceived to be native speakers. As a consequence, it is perhaps not too surprising that this period of relative endonormativity in Singapore's English language teaching history did not last too long. The popularity of nonstandard usages – collectively labeled as 'Singlish' – alarmed the Singapore government, who felt that it was threatening the ability of Singaporeans to learn good/proper/standard English. This was a point that was forcefully made by Goh Chok Tong during his 1999 National Day Rally Speech:

We cannot be a first-world economy or go global with Singlish...The fact that we use English gives us a big advantage over our competitors. If we carry on using Singlish, the logical final outcome is that we, too, will develop our own type of pidgin English, spoken only by 3m Singaporeans, which the rest of the world will find quaint but incomprehensible. We are already half way there. Do we want to go all the way?

Thus, in 2000, the government launched the Speak Good English Movement, whose goal was to promote Standard English and discourage the use of Singlish. As Gupta (2010: 58) points out, the SGEM

was promoting a narrow concept of Standard English, which did not allow for anything local, or informal, rejecting even words that had been unproblematically accepted since

---

to permit learners to settle for lower standards than the best, and it is a travesty of liberalism to tolerate low standards which will lock the least fortunate into the least rewarding careers.'

Quirk is correct that even in those countries where a non-Standard English might be considered indigenous, a sense of stigmatization tends to be attached to both the variety and its speakers. This is despite the fact that there is no evidence to suggest that acquisition of a non-standard variety in any way impedes the acquisition of Standard English (Siegel, 1999). However, as Kachru (1991) points out, by focusing on what is institutionally accepted, Quirk is limiting his concerns to a status quo that unjustly discriminates against non-standard varieties of English and, by extension, their speakers. Moreover, Quirk's position risks legitimizing and perpetuating the status quo rather than calling it into question. For Kachru, Quirk fails to acknowledge the vibrancy and reality of 'invisible language planning' (Kachru, 1991: 8), where informal usage amongst non-elites in unofficial contexts (including creative works) reflects an acceptance of the growing legitimacy of non-standard varieties.

[6] In the rest of this book, unless the ideological nature of Standard English bears on the argument at hand, I will simply use the term 'Standard English' without further qualification.

the 1980s ... Once again, Singaporeans are being told to look overseas for correction of their English, and are being given advice that is often based on the strictest possible concept of correctness. Even the notion that a Singaporean accent is wrong has been resurrected.

To this day, the language policy as regards the English language still remains focused on exonormative standards with traditional native speaker norms as the target (Rubdy, 2011). Even as recently as September 2011, when the Singapore government launched the English Language Institution of Singapore, the guest of honor, Lee Kuan Yew (Singapore's first prime minister and main architect of the country's language policy), suggested that English language teaching in Singapore might want to shift its normative target to American English, given the cultural and political influence of the United States, saying, 'I believe we will be exposed more and more to American English, and it might be as well that we accept and teach our students to recognize and, (if) need be, to speak American English.'[7] Lee's suggestion that American English serve as the target for English language teaching is not as radical as it might seem, given that the tendency to cling to exonormative standards remains unchanged and, more disturbingly, unexamined. But in a sense, this privileging of exonormativity is not surprising given that the government expects English in Singapore to serve an instrumentalist or practical function (C. J. W.–L. Wee, 2007: 253–254; Wee, 2003) and shows little interest in the possibility that the language might also serve an identity or heritage function (in contrast to the official mother tongues).

The overwhelming concern in Singapore regarding the teaching of English has therefore been about (i) deciding which external variety of English will best serve this instrumentalist function and (ii) ensuring that the integrity of this external reference variety is protected. The emphasis on integrity is one key reason why – despite the temporary shift towards endonormativity in the 1990s – the official tendency is towards exonormativity. In this regard, an endogenous variety like Singlish is considered doubly problematic: it is viewed both as 'contaminated' by the local linguistic ecology (as in the influence of Malay and Chinese) and as a potential contaminant that, if allowed to flourish, might go on to infect exogenous varieties (such as British/American/'standard' English).

The emergence of Singlish has in turn raised concerns in official quarters that it poses a threat to Singaporeans' ability to learn the standard variety of English, a concern exacerbated by the importance that knowledge of Standard English

---

[7] 'LKY: English gave S'pore its edge', 7 September 2011, schang@sph.com.sg, www.asiaone .com/News/AsiaOne+News/Singapore/Story/A1Story20110907-298079.html; accessed 16 January 2012.

is expected to play in Singapore's economic competiveness. This is where the Singlish controversy arises.

Problematizing Singlish

Before looking at how the Singapore government has responded to the 'Singlish problem', it is important to realize that, among ordinary Singaporeans themselves, there is no real consensus as to the merits of Singlish (Cavallaro, Ng and Seilhamer, 2014). Those rejecting Singlish claim that it is not 'proper/good' English while those favouring Singlish claim that it is a crucial part of their national identity. For example, some Singaporeans have labeled Singlish an 'enemy' of English, and have suggested that 'it is parochial to adopt a nationalist stance towards the use of Singlish' (quoted in Wee, 2005: 57). Similarly, another Singaporean noted (quoted in Chng, 2003: 2), 'It is indeed worrying that the standard of English used in Singapore has been dwindling steadily . . . I certainly hope that Singaporeans will embrace the coming years with the common, fervent endeavor to speak and write proper English, as far as possible'. In contrast, others have suggested that

Singlish is a mark of how we have evolved as a nation and should surely have a place in our culture. Embracing Singlish as part of our heritage is not self-deception . . . but the educated and wise will know when to use Singlish: use it among Singaporeans and close friends. Do not use it at job interviews or when making public announcements. (quoted in Chng, 2003: 53)

And even for those Singaporeans who view Singlish favourably, there is a tendency to see it as more appropriately restricted to communication involving family and close friends; those who feel 'it should be used with non-Singaporeans and spread beyond Singapore's borders are definitely few and far between' (Cavallaro, Ng and Seilhamer, 2014: 393).

While ordinary Singaporeans disagree about the status of Singlish, the position of the government appears unequivocal. 'Good/proper' English, which it equates with Standard English, is considered crucial for Singapore's continued economic competitiveness, particularly in a global economy (Bokhorst-Heng, 2005; Chng, 2003). And the government sees Singlish as a problem because it fears that speaking it will adversely affect the ability of Singaporeans to learn 'good' English.

Singlish is known to show a high degree of influence from other local languages, particularly Hokkien, Cantonese, Malay and Tamil (Platt and Weber, 1980: 18). The following are sample Singlish utterances,[8] showing how it is

---

[8] These are constructed utterances intended specifically to demonstrate prototypical Singlish features. But Singlish, of course, evolves, and beyond the prototypical features, there may also be

characterized by, among other features, a lack of inflectional morphology (1a), productive use of reduplication (1b) and discourse particles (1c), and lexical items borrowed from Malay and various Chinese dialects (1d). In (1c), the particle 'lor' indicates a sense of resignation, and in (1d), the word *suay* 'cursed/unfortunate' comes from Hokkien.

(1)   a. He eat already.
           [He has already eaten.]
      b. This room cold-cold one.
           [This room is very cold.]
      c. I won't go for holiday, lor.
           [I have no choice but to forego a holiday.]
      d. You always make me suay!
           [You're always bringing me bad luck!]

To better understand the social and historical circumstances under which Singlish emerged, it is helpful to know that, in 1834, the British colonialists established a Singapore Free School with the aim of providing 'instruction in Asian languages as a means of reconciling the Natives to European education and ensuring them to regular habits of subordination and study, and beyond this, the Institute should concentrate on providing an elementary education in the three Rs [reading, 'riting and 'rithmetic] in English' (Bloom, 1986: 351, quoted in Lim, 2004: 3). The British were also intent on cultivating a group of English-educated elites, mainly comprising the Peranakans or Babas and the Eurasians (Lim, 2009; Wee, 2009), and by the late 1800s and early 1900s, English had become established as the language of socio-economic mobility. After the Second World War, the language became 'even more the *lingua franca* of the more elite sections of society' (Lim, 2004: 4).

There are two things worth bearing in mind from this admittedly brief historical description. The first is that seepages between classroom instruction and social interactions outside the classroom are almost inevitable, so that it is unrealistic to assume that the taught language will somehow remain unaffected when learners interact with their peers (Stroud and Wee, 2011), even when taking the form of being used playfully or even mockingly in the playground (Rampton, 1999). The second is that even though there was a deliberate attempt to create a class of elites who would have a better command of English than the masses, some basic or elementary English was nevertheless being taught to a wider segment of the population. In this regard, Eurasians formed a significant segment of the local teacher corps up until the early 1920s; thereafter, Chinese teachers were increasingly common, being former students who had entered

disagreements on what other specific features can be properly characterized as Singlish. This is an issue that I return to in the rest of the book.

the teaching profession (Lim, 2010: 27, citing Gupta, 1994: 39–40). As Lim (2010: 28) emphasizes,

The significant point to note here is this: such a predominance in the early nineteenth century of both Eurasians and Babas as teachers and/or students in the local English-medium schools would mean that there would also have been extensive use of Malay there (Gupta, 1994: 41), since, as mentioned earlier, in addition to English, both groups had a variety of Malay as a dominant language in their repertoire. This is testified in the comments in early reports on the extensive use of Malay in English-medium schools, not just outside but also within the classroom (Gupta, 1994: 41–42). It should be noted that this would have been Bazaar or Baba Malay ... and not the Malay variety spoken by the Malay community ... In other words, Bazaar/Baba Malay would have been in significant contact with English, even within the schools. With the presence of the Straits-born Chinese, there would also have been Hokkien, and a number of other Chinese languages such as Teochew and Cantonese, in particular with the increase in Chinese teachers and students in the twentieth century.

And precisely because English was being associated with socio-economic mobility, there would be aspirations from the masses to improve their command of the language. The not surprising outcome is that the English spoken by the local elites would then serve as a model for their less privileged counterparts. As Ansaldo (2004: 143) puts it, 'in the light of Mufwene's Found Principle (Mufwene, 1996), Babas and Eurasians can be regarded as the most influential groups in transmitting a set of linguistic features bound to become the stable core of what constitutes SE' [Singapore English: LW].From a structural and typological perspective, Ansaldo (2004) therefore suggests that Singlish (or Singapore English)[9] shows significant influence due to language contact, with Bazaar Malay (also known as Baba Malay), the vernacular Englishes spoken by the Peranakans and Eurasians, and Chinese varieties such as Hokkien and Cantonese exerting the greatest influence:

The point I am trying to make here is that, though the existence of an English-based pidgin is not proven nor necessary, the existence of an early English variety pre-dating SE, probably modeled on the Peranakans' English, is plausible from a careful inter-pretation of the historical and literary documents of the early years of Singapore. This also explains why it is ultimately irrelevant to establish whether the substrate origins are to be found in Hokkien or Malay: they are more likely to be found in Bazaar Malay, *i.e. typological convergence had already taken place before the formation of SE*, which explains even better the hybrid structures observed so far ...

For all these reasons, it may be more appropriate to describe SE as a 'creolised' variety of an early colonial English, if by that we mean something like 'undergone a type of shift

---

[9] The contributions to Lim's book, *Singapore English: A Grammatical Description*, deliberately refrained from using the term 'Singlish' because of its derogatory associations (Lim, 2004: 17; note 1).

due to heavy contact mechanisms as can be typically observed in Creoles, *that brings about a typological shift'*. (Ansaldo, 2004: 143, italics in original)

It is this influence from the various local languages that detractors usually point to when they dismiss Singlish as not being a proper language. In this regard, Lee Kuan Yew's recounting of his visit to Jamaica and his encounters with Jamaican Creole is particularly telling (2012: 146–147):

I was in Jamaica in 1975. Most Jamaicans are descended from West Africans brought to the Caribbean as slaves. They learned, first Spanish, then English from their slave masters. Yet, apart from those at the top of their society, they spoke not English, but Jamaican Creole, which I could not understand. It hit me like a sledgehammer: despite learning English in school, they were back to pidgin Creole once out of school.

Here, Lee presents his inability as a foreign visitor to understand Jamaican Creole as sufficient reason to indict the language. In addition, the school environment is powerless to promote the learning of English because of the widespread use of the Creole 'once out of school'. Hence, extrapolating from the Jamaican situation, for the Singapore government, any attempt to deal with the Singlish menace cannot be just a matter of providing quality instruction in Standard English in Singapore schools; the socio-linguistic environment outside the school (family interactions, workplace activities, leisure pursuits, etc.) has to be modified accordingly to minimize the likelihood of students being tempted to use Singlish once they leave the classrooms. However, it is this very same influence from the local languages that supporters of Singlish highlight when they want to assert its role as a national identity marker; for these supporters, it is precisely this hodge-podge of linguistic influences that iconizes (Gal and Irvine, 1995) what is authentic about being Singaporean, namely its multiculturalism and multilingualism.

Around August 1999, the Singapore government became increasingly concerned about the popularity of Singlish and took serious steps to address it, though these were not the first official expressions of worry about Singlish; for example, in 1993, there was an attempt to ban the use of Singlish in the local media (Poedjosoedarmo, 1995). However, it is reasonable to take 1999 as the starting point for the current Singlish controversy (Bokhorst-Heng, 2005), since this was when momentum for the Speak Good English Movement (SGEM), which was officially initiated the following year on 29 April 2000, began building. The government was aware that the popularity of Singlish stemmed from its construction as a cultural expression of Singaporean identity, but argued that it was essential for Singaporeans to 'speak English everyone understands' and that Standard English was a 'rational trade-off' if the country was to be economically competitive globally (Chng, 2003: 48). The SGEM was thus created

with the goals of simultaneously promoting 'good English' while also elimi-
nating Singlish. And as we will see in the following chapters, it is the SGEM
that has since become a focal point for voicing both opposition to and support
for Singlish.

A major reason why the government was impelled to launch the SGEM was
the popularity of the locally produced sitcom *Phua Chu Kang* (*PCK*). The central character, PCK, is a Chinese male who runs his own business as a building
contractor. He and his wife speak Singlish unabashedly and have values that
are decidedly blue-collar in orientation. They are both unpretentious and occasionally even vulgar. The humour in the sitcom often derives from the contrasts
and clashes between PCK and his wife, on the one hand, and his highly educated sister-in-law, Margaret, on the other. Margaret speaks Standard English
and is decidedly much more snobbish in her outlook. A 1999 newspaper article
described language as a 'major appeal of the show', which set off a national
discussion:

Because Phua Chu Kang and his wife speak Singlish, they were able to strike a chord
of identity with Singaporeans (unlike another sitcom where the characters speak in an
'American accent that is totally unreal' (*The Straits Times*, 30 May 1999). The report
sparked off a spate of 'pro' and 'con' articles, letters, discussions and opinions pieces
in the press about the use of Singlish on television. There was mounting concern among
some that the use of Singlish on television legitimizes 'poor English', and may encourage Singlish to become Singapore's lingua franca. The debate expanded when the press
informed readers that some teachers in neighborhood schools use Singlish in the classrooms for pedagogical purposes, raising questions about the standards of English in
education. (Bokhorst-Heng, 2005: 189)

The country's second prime minister, Goh Chok Tong, even suggested that
PCK might improve his English by attending language classes. This suggestion was ultimately accepted by the assistant vice-president of the local TV
station responsible for creating *PCK*, who said that 'it is a great idea to have
'PCK sound like PCK without resorting to Singlish' and 'that PCK will still be
recognizable after his linguistic make-over' (Chng, 2003: 49). In her discussion of the SGEM, Rubdy (2001: 346) even suggests that '[m]aking Phua Chu
Kang the focus of attention was a masterstroke [on the part of the government],
for this immediately served to capture the attention of readers ... provoked a
number of reactions both in favor of and against Singlish, helping ... to generate public debate and sensitize Singaporeans to the government's point of
view'.

The Singlish controversy has been continuing since then in much the same
vein, although with some interesting developments. One, even though *PCK*
went off air in 2007, the series continues to be available on Toggle, an online
service run by Mediacorp, the company originally responsible for the show,

that provides free videos. This means that even younger Singaporeans who may not have grown up with a first-hand experience of *PCK*'s role in the Singlish controversy are still able to access the programs and appreciate the association between the character of PCK and his use of Singlish. Thus, even if PCK is today not as central a figure in the Singlish controversy as he used to be, the series featuring him and his language use is still publicly available. Of course, some of the most articulate supporters of Singlish in public discourse are older Singaporeans who would remember PCK well; many are successful professionals currently in their early forties and fifties (see Chapter 5). In any case, while *PCK* may have played a central role in the early days of the Singlish controversy, many of the contemporary issues involved in the Singlish controversy are independent of the TV program.

Two, it has been noted that in recent years the SGEM appears to have toned down its anti-Singlish rhetoric (Bruthiaux, 2010). Indeed, in its booklet *Grammar Rules*, published in 2017, the SGEM avoids any reference to Singlish, having instead sections on 'Grammar Gaffes' and 'Common Errors in Singapore'. Examples of such errors and their SGEM-prescribed counterparts are shown next (2017: 99–100):

> Singaporean Blunder: Please on/off it.
> Standard English: Please turn it on/off.
> Singaporean Blunder: You got eat already?
> Standard English: Have you eaten?

Some of these 'blunders' might be considered Singlish but the SGEM has decided to avoid using that label altogether, at least in Grammar Rules. Some members of the SGEM have even denied, rather disingenuously, that the SGEM was ever anti-Singlish in the first place. This denial, however, is belied by the fact that the SGEM's website 'carries an unambiguous endorsement' of the government's definition of Singlish as 'English corrupted by Singaporeans' (Chng, 2003: 51). Moreover, we only need to consider the following extracts from various ministerial speeches launching the Speak Good English Movement to see how, especially in its early days, the SGEM was clearly targeting Singlish as part of its efforts to foster good English.

Speech (1) shows that, in the lead-up to the official launch of the SGEM, the prime minister approvingly highlighted the fact that, as part of the attempt to promote good English, schools were fining pupils for speaking Singlish.

(1)   Speech by Prime Minister Goh Chok Tong, 1999 National Day Rally Speech
        (www.moe.gov.sg/media/speeches/1999/sp270899_print.htm; accessed
        15 May 2016)
        Schools already organize many programmes and activities to encourage the
        use of proper English. They have Speak English Campaigns, they fine pupils

caught speaking Singlish, and they run speech and drama programmes to promote good English. MOE has been working hard to upgrade standards of English in schools. First, it is revising the English Language syllabuses, to make them more rigorous and to strengthen the teaching of grammar.

In speech (2), the deputy prime minister expresses a concern about Singaporeans being 'stuck with Singlish' and Singlish speakers not appreciating that they are 'using the words wrongly'.

(2)   Speech by Deputy Prime Minister Lee Hsien Loong, 2001 launch of the Speak Good English Movement, 5 April 2001 (www.nas.gov.sg/ archivesonline/speeches/view-html?filename=2001040502.htm; accessed 15 May 2016)
The course of least resistance is to end up with Singlish, because that is what we get when the English language is mixed with Malay words, Chinese grammar, and local slang. But once we are stuck with Singlish, and children grow up learning Singlish as their first language, it will be very difficult to get them to learn standard English in schools. Singlish will not be cute or amusing, because those speaking Singlish will consider Singlish sentences and words quite normal, and not even know that they are using the words wrongly. And it will be even harder later on to get our whole society to switch languages a second time, from Singlish to English.
We must consciously and deliberately strive to avoid this outcome. We must make the effort to learn proper English grammar, sentence structures and pronunciation. We need not speak with a British or American accent; a Singaporean accent is fine. But Singaporeans must speak a form of English that is readily understood by people all over the world.

In speech (3), Teo Chee Hean, the minister for education and second minister for defence, highlights how the broadcast media have managed to reduce the use of Singlish (though whether they have actually done so is debatable; see Chapter 2) as part of the government's attempt to create a 'conducive social environment' for learning good English.

(3)   Speech by Minister for Education and Second Minister for Defence Teo Chee Hean, 2002 launch of the Speak Good English Movement, 18 April 2002 (www.moe.gov.sg/media/speeches/2; accessed 14 May 2016)
To speak a language properly, it is vital to have a conducive social environment. We can only excel in a language if people around us speak it well and if we use it often enough. Each of us, as parents, teachers, community leaders, students and the media, have a role to play in upholding good language skills so that we can inspire others by example. Since the launch of the Speak Good English Movement, the Ministry of Education has conducted courses for English Language teachers in primary and secondary schools to update and upgrade their skills. The broadcast media has also reduced the use of Singlish. Characters in popular TV sitcoms like *Living with Lydia* and *Mr Kiasu* speak English that is readily understood by

everyone, including foreigners. *Phua Chu Kang* has attended BEST classes, and his progress is commendable.

In addition, the SGEM produced a booklet titled *Speak Well, Be Understood* in 2001, which included statements such as the following in the preface (Chng, 2003: 51): 'This book has a simple aim: to sensitize Singaporeans to features of Singlish so that they will make the effort to speak good English. The use of Singlish can be a problem because it gives the impression that the speaker is unprofessional or poorly educated.' Finally, as one Singaporean noted in a letter to the editor (Sim, 2002, quoted in Chng, 2003: 53–54), the SGEM seemed to reinforce negative stereotypes and prejudices against Singlish. Sim (2002) specifically refers to an SGEM lesson that contrasts Simon (who speaks 'good' English) with Gary (who speaks Singlish or 'bad' English):

It soon becomes clear to the reader that Gary is made to be more than just a speaker of bad English. He is childish and irresponsible. He asks to drive Simon's car without being properly insured . . . Furthermore, there is the suggestion that the bad English speaker is less well-off than the good English speaker . . . On the other hand, Simon's English is not only grammatical, but also forceful: his speech does not merely reveal linguistic proficiency, but a personality that is steady and mature . . .
 The text is therefore a good example of the entire galaxy of prejudices people have in their estimation of those who do not speak the same type of English as them. These prejudices produce an image of deficient speakers as vulgar and stupid, lacking the refinement and culture of the speaker of good English. Texts that reflect prejudices stigmatize less able speakers as not only linguistically deficient, but also culturally and intellectually deficient. Using such a strategy to compel people to learn a language is, quite simply, hitting below the belt.

Officially, Singlish is still a *lingua non-grata*[10] and the government's attitude towards it alternates between strong anti-Singlish rhetoric and varying degrees of unenthusiastic/reluctant acceptance. In contrast, for supporters of Singlish, their enthusiasm appears to be still going strong. In 2009, the second edition of the *Coxford Singlish Dictionary* (C. Goh and Woo, 2009), a tongue-in-cheek dictionary that celebrates Singlish, was released. The following year, a Speak Good Singlish Movement (SGSM) was started precisely as a counter to the SGEM. And as we see in Chapter 6, Singlish lessons are also being offered in workshops and Singlish is celebrated, if not actively promoted, in a number of YouTube videos – all of which indicate a new dimension to the Singlish controversy: its commodification.

---

[10] This is not to say that government ministers do not themselves switch occasionally into Singlish. It is not uncommon for someone to switch between different varieties while at the same time expressing disapproval of such switches (cf. Blom and Gumperz, 1972).

The Paradox of Linguistic Conservatism and Technological Innovation

The preceding discussion makes clear that as far as the Singapore government is concerned, English is something that needs to abide by exonormative standards and Singlish represents an aberration in terms of what constitutes good acceptable English. This is a position that we may describe as *linguistic conservatism*: it views changes to language use with suspicion and accepts them only with great reluctance, because of the presumption that the proper use of a language respects its history – which involves being faithful to linguistic tradition as construed, in Singapore's case, by the language's usage by traditional native speakers such as the British.

Linguistic conservatism is by no means unique to the Singapore government, of course. As Milroy and Milroy (1999: 40) point out, it is common to lament changes to English because of the mistaken belief in a non-existent 'Golden Age' when speakers supposedly 'really' knew how to use the language properly. Nevertheless, linguistic conservatism contrasts starkly with the government's official exhortations to and support for Singaporeans to be innovative and entrepreneurial in providing services and developing new technology. For example, Prime Minister Lee Hsien Loong 'encouraged technology leaders to use Singapore as a breeding ground for new developments, which can then be scaled up and adapted to other situations' (Loh, 2015). The National Research Foundation (NRF), which was launched in 2006 and comes under the Prime Minister's Office, was set up precisely to encourage and support innovation and enterprise in technology:

The NRF sets the national direction for research and development (R&D) by developing policies, plans and strategies for research, innovation and enterprise. It also funds strategic initiatives and builds up R&D capabilities by nurturing research talent. The NRF aims to transform Singapore into a vibrant R&D hub that contributes towards a knowledge-intensive, innovative and entrepreneurial economy; and make[s] Singapore a magnet for excellence in science and innovation. (www.nrf.gov.sg/innovation-enterprise/innovation-enterprise-milestones; accessed 15 May 2016)

Singapore also has a unit under the Ministry of Trade and Industry, SPRING Singapore, that has been given the mandate to increase international recognition of Singaporean products and services:

SPRING Singapore is an agency under the Ministry of Trade and Industry responsible for helping Singapore enterprises grow and building trust in Singapore products and services. As the enterprise development agency, SPRING works with partners to help enterprises in financing, capability and management development, technology and innovation, and access to markets. As the national standards and accreditation body, SPRING develops and promotes an internationally-recognised standards and quality assurance infrastructure. SPRING also oversees the safety of general consumer goods in Singapore. (www.spring.gov.sg/About-Us/Pages/spring-singapore.aspx; accessed 15 May 2016)

SPRING Singapore's 'Strategic Outcomes' include 'Productive, Innovative and Resilient Industries and Enterprises; Good Jobs; Trusted Products and Services'.

Here, then, we have a paradox: the Singapore government is extremely keen to support and encourage innovation and entrepreneurship in technology and services, but at the same time is extremely linguistically conservative. This paradox cannot be resolved by suggesting that innovations in technology and services are marketable, whereas their linguistic analogues are not. This is because the government acknowledges that sometimes the markets for innovations in technology and services do not necessarily yet exist and may have to be created – which is where entrepreneurship comes in and where an agency such as SPRING Singapore finds its rationale: it is 'responsible for helping Singapore enterprises grow and building trust in Singapore products and services'. There is no reason why the same line of reasoning might not apply to linguistic innovations: these, too, will need to find their own markets, which might not exist at the time when those innovations are first introduced.

As mentioned earlier, the Singapore government is most certainly not alone in adopting a highly conservative view of language. Even in cases of linguistic entrepreneurship, which De Costa, Park and Wee (2016: 696) define as 'an act of aligning with the moral imperative to strategically exploit language-related resources for enhancing one's worth in the world', usually greater emphasis is placed on the mode and motivation for learning a language than on 'tampering' with the conventions of grammar or lexical innovation.[11] De Costa et al. describe a number of examples where, by articulating the rationales behind the languages they choose to learn and by showing initiative and determination in how they go about learning the chosen languages, learners are approvingly seen by their parents, teachers and even government authorities as demonstrating linguistic entrepreneurship.

De Costa and colleagues highlight a specific example from Gao (2015), who describes how a tour guide became multilingual so she could better perform her job. This tour guide, Xu XiuZhen, who is able to speak German, French,

---

[11] Researchers have used the term 'linguistic entrepreneur' on occasion to describe individuals who act as brokers between linguistically and culturally distinct groups (Holmes, 2013: 227; Miles, 1998: 232). In these cases, the use of the label 'entrepreneur' tends to be based on these individuals' initiative and risk taking (i.e., these brokers boldly move beyond the safety of their own linguistic community to seek new contexts in which the utility of linguistic resources may expand). The difference between these earlier uses of the term and the definition offered by De Costa et al. is that the latter draws specific attention to how language is appropriated by neoliberal governments as key to enhancing the value of one's human capital.

Hebrew, Danish, Italian, Korean, English and Swedish, was featured in a local documentary whose aim was to showcase 'moral values, record social change, and foster nationalism' (14). initially Xu's daughter-in-law, who had learnt some English in high school, helped her to learn these many languages, but later Xu relied more on her own memory work and interactions with foreigners. According to the documentary (15),

> when she learnt several [English] phrases, she would not go to sleep, because she feared that she would forget everything after sleeping. But even so, she still felt worrisome in the early hours of the morning, and woke up her daughter-in-law to check if she had remembered everything correctly . . . Then through her interactions with tourists, Xu also managed to pick up many other foreign languages.

Xu was presented in the Chinese media as persistent, hardworking and eager to learn different languages (Gao, 2015: 16): 'It is these qualities that enabled her to make the extraordinary achievement of speaking several foreign languages. In other words, what distinguishes Xu from other people in her village, is not her social or educational background. In fact, despite many obstacles (age, education, social status, etc.), Xu relied solely on her diligence to achieve competence in foreign languages.'

As De Costa and colleagues point out, there is a media construction of Xu as a linguistic entrepreneur – a construction that is encouraged by the Chinese government seen by the documentary's aims to 'foster nationalism' – in which ordinary Chinese from impoverished backgrounds are held up as exemplars of language learning. These individuals are presented as acquiring multilingual competence despite having to overcome a number of difficulties, such as low social status, low levels of education, and lack of access to systematic or 'proper' language instruction. It is their determination, initiative, and commitment to learning multiple languages so they can perform their jobs more effectively that the government aims to highlight as indicators of national loyalty and good citizenship.

There is no doubt that Xu's use of the various languages in her multilingual repertoire would be considered non-standard. But allowances are made for any departures from the standard varieties given the humble and challenging circumstances under which she managed to learn the languages. Crucially, in Xu's language use, there is no deliberate 'tampering' with the linguistic nuts and bolts; that is, with the linguistic rules and conventions that are presumed to constitute the existing and even sacrosanct autonomous linguistic system. This contrasts with the case of Singlish, where a key element in its successful promotion and commodification is the flouting of the 'rules' of Standard English (see Chapters 4 and 6). This key feature explains why the Singapore government clings to linguistic conservatism that is at odds with its calls and support for innovation in other arenas.

More generally, this paradox exists because, in contrast to services and technology, language is seen as a non-material body of lexical and grammatical knowledge that serves primarily as a medium for the transmission of both traditional values and cultural heritage (by Singapore's official mother tongues) and of scientific and technological developments (as in the case of how English is positioned in Singapore's language policy). To mess with the medium – that is, to recklessly disregard established lexical and grammatical 'rules' – is to risk compromising its ability to faithfully transmit values and knowledge.

Undergirding this paradox is a view of globalization as a primarily economic-technological phenomenon (Perrons, 2004: 35–54; Wade, 2001) that may or may not have political, cultural and linguistic consequences, depending on how specific communities respond. That is, political, cultural and linguistic strategies are construed as resources that may help communities take advantage of or protect communities from the globalization juggernaut, rather than as further aspects of the multidimensionality of globalization (Giddens, 2002:10; Kennedy, 2001: 8). But as Teschke and Heine (2002: 176) point out,

globalization refers to a conscious re-structuring of state-society and inter-state relations in response to the onset of the long economic downturn of the 1970s. Globalization is neither a techno-economically induced, nor a purely politically driven, phenomenon, but the result of private and public strategies of reproduction under conditions of long-term negative growth.

This re-structuring of relations is further affected by developments in transportation and communication technologies leading to 'the intensification of worldwide social relations which link localities in such a way that local happenings are shaped by events occurring many miles away and vice versa' (Giddens, 1990: 64). What this means is that a willingness to innovate and change cannot be restricted to a narrow understanding of the economic and the technological that brackets out language, culture and identity. Those latter elements are also integral parts of the globalization process, and an insistently static view of them merely serves to distort and foreclose the ways in which communities can thrive under conditions of increased diversity and change. Globalization has made it both necessary and urgent to appreciate language as a mobile resource (Blommaert, 2010), one that moves across the globe and transforms the markets into which it enters while also being transformed in the process of such movement (see Chapter 7).

Conclusion

The Singlish controversy has from its very beginning been concerned with whether or not the use of Singlish harms its speakers. This is because Singlish is presented as a variety that is not intelligible outside of Singapore. Arguments about its legitimacy and desirability have thus tended to be linked to the issue of exonormativity. Those who are against Singlish rely on the 'fact' that speakers outside Singapore, especially traditional native speakers of English, find it unintelligible and consider that a major reason why the use of Singlish should not be encouraged. Those who are for Singlish claim that Singlish is valuable in bringing Singaporeans together and that code-switching into Standard English when non-Singaporeans are present will resolve the issue of unintelligibility.

That public discussions of the Singlish controversy have remained largely mired in these same issues for nearly two decades can be seen in the recent responses to a report that the *Oxford English Dictionary* has included more than five hundred Singapore English words and phrases in its 2016 update ('Oxford English Dictionary confirms: "That ang moh is blur like sotong" is a perfect English sentence', *The Independent* 11 May 2016, http://theindependent.sg/oxford-english-dictionary-confirmsthat-ang-mo-is-blur-like-sotong-is-a-perfect-english-sentence/; accessed 12 May 2016). Words like *blur* 'slow in understanding', *ang moh* 'a light-skinned person, especially of Western origin', *sotong* 'squid or cuttlefish' and *shiok* 'cool, delicious, superb' are now official entries in the OED. This has led *The Independent* to point out that these words 'can now be officially be used in an English sentence ... [making] "That ang mo is blur like sotong" a perfect English sentence'. A number of local personalities were quickly interviewed for their reactions ('Some find new Singlish terms in Oxford dictionary "ridiculous"', http://news.asiaone.com/news/singapore/some-find-new-singlish-terms-oxford-dictionary-ridiculous; accessed 17 May 2016). An academic commented, 'The pity is that we in Singapore have often tended to deride our own and place value when others (especially the Westerners) say it's okay'. A film-maker noted, 'I am disappointed whenever Singlish is deemed improper or uncouth. Now the international experts are recognizing Singlish as proper. You should probably ask those who put down Singlish how they feel about this topic.' Yet another interviewee, a local DJ, was not impressed with these new inclusions: 'The OED sets the standard for English and I am surprised that Singlish words are included.'

In addition, a local newspaper was also spurred by the OED's recognition of Singlish words to email me to request an urgent interview (which I declined) to discuss the following questions (typos, boldface and upper case are in the original email from the news reporter, dated 12 May 2016):

I have some questions regarding this that I hope you can answer:
1. What does this acceptance of Singlish means for Singapore?
2. What are the implications?
3. Do you think the additions mean that Singlish should be accepted more westerners are more receptive to Singlish? Why or why not?

4. Will there be a time when Singlish is accepted as an official language? Why or why not?

I would really appreciate it if you could help us out with this ASAP as we are rushing this story for **TOMORROW (May 13)**.

Thus, anxieties about the acceptability of Singlish, in which one important consideration is that of exonormativity, continue to beset the Singlish controversy. This, then, leads us to the question of why there does not seem to be little change in the discussions relating to Singlish. To understand why this should be so, we need to begin with the issue of ideology pooling.

Ideology Pooling and Meta-Discursive
     Convergence in the Singlish Debate

In this chapter, I focus on the notion of ideology pooling and demonstrate why the arguments surrounding the Singlish controversy seem to continue to revolve around the same issues. I show that this occurs because both the detractors and the supporters of Singlish share several key assumptions – that Singlish can serve as the medium for conducting entire exchanges, that Singlish should always be contrasted with Standard English, and that the Singlish controversy is ultimately a matter of national consequence.

These shared assumptions constitute the ideology pool and tend to remain unchanged throughout the various interventions into the Singlish controversy. But unless they are highlighted and critically examined, the possibility of the Singlish controversy being resolved is slim, and we are destined to remain stuck in a socio-linguistic version of that Bill Murray movie, *Groundhog Day* (1993), doomed to revisit the same language ideological grounds over and over again.

Language Ideological Debates: Conflicting and Shared Assumptions

An understandably common theme in the study of language ideological debates – 'in which language is central as a topic, a motif, a target, and in which language ideologies are being articulated, formed, amended, enforced' (Blommaert, 1999: 1) – is that of struggles over conflicting assumptions and representations. Though the ideologies shared by the contesting parties are also noted, they usually form the point of departure for analyses that tend to concentrate more on the articulation of divergent viewpoints and the propagation of conflicting agendas.

For example, Jaffe's (1999a: 39) discussion of language debates in Corsica highlights the tensions that surround attempts to translate French literary works into Corsican. While Jaffe notes that the 'translators and their critics shared fundamental assumptions about language, identity and power', her focus is on the disagreements about 'the function/outcomes of translation in the project of resistance to French language domination'. Similarly, Milani (2007) observes that the prospect of Sweden joining the European Union led to a debate about the future of Swedish. And while he notes that the various parties involved in the debate shared the view that Swedish was 'undergoing some form of endangerment' (192), he points out that they differed in the specific stances adopted. For some, it was important that Swedish be used in all public domains, while for others, the emphasis on Swedish had to be balanced against the danger of encroaching on the rights of individuals – particularly immigrants – to maintain their 'home languages' (179). Milani (2007: 191) shows how these and other conflicting voices were reflected in *Mål I mun*, a policy document that attempted to 'mediate between unity and diversity at the civic and symbolic levels of a nation state' by asserting the role of Swedish as a societal lingua franca against a backdrop of internationalization and multiculturalism.

Certainly, an analysis of language ideological debates cannot help attending to the conflicting representations that make them 'debates' in the first place. However, it is also important to focus on the phenomenon of ideology pooling (Park, 2009: 84), which refers to the taken-for-granted assumptions shared by the different debating parties. Because these assumptions are taken for granted, they often remain unquestioned even as they continue to influentially frame the debates in subtle and not so subtle ways.

The key reason why an assumption goes unquestioned is because its status as 'truth' is taken to be obvious and therefore is treated as being so unremarkable as to not be worthy of even highlighting. For an assumption to go unquestioned, all the relevant parties must share the view that it is true: if one party to the debate considers assumption X to be obviously true whereas the other party does not, then the status of X as a valid or acceptable proposition could still be debated, and in that case X is not a likely candidate for ideology pooling. The likelihood of X entering the ideology pool is further raised when X is considered not only true by the different parties but also a matter of commonsense; that is, it is considered to be so obviously true as to not even be worthy of comment. When this happens, X acquires a status as part of the 'regime of truth' (Heller, 2011: 6, citing Foucault, 1984) and becomes more or less immune to critique. Individuals who try to question X might even risk being categorized as being difficult or deliberately obtuse.

Thus, consider as possible examples of X these propositions: 'There is an ontologically stable entity called Standard English and this entity has always been distinct from other varietal entities such as Japanese, Malay, Tamil or even broken English or bad English' and 'The best way to properly appreciate the Chinese culture is through the Chinese language'. Propositions such as these often lurk in the backgrounds of many language debates, *mutatis mutandis*. Such propositions, though, could still become the subjects of debate if problems are raised regarding their validity. For example, what we think of as the English language contains borrowings from many different languages. This makes problematic any assumption that varietal entities are intrinsically bounded and possess a systemic integrity that becomes compromised upon contact with other varieties. This insistence on maintaining or protecting varietal integrity can only be sustained on the basis of social fiat or convention. Likewise, both the Chinese culture and the Chinese language change. Moreover, these changes in language and the non-linguistic aspects of culture do not necessarily occur apace,[1] nor is it the case that language is a simple and transparent medium for knowledge transmission. These observations should raise doubt about any simplistic assertion that the best way to appreciate a given culture has to be through its affiliated language.[2] But such propositions are likely to be themselves debated only if there is someone present who has specialized knowledge about linguistics. Even then, the specialist who tries to foreground such propositions for critique would probably have to deal with questions about relevance or charges of not making constructive contributions, such as 'Why complicate the debate by bringing up such esoteric points?' or 'How does this even help to address the "real/substantive/practical" issue that we should be confronting (e.g. trying to ensure that our students learn good English or trying to ensure that our culture is preserved across generations)?'

Given the foregoing observations, there are two possible ways in which language experts might be able to contribute to such debates: directly or indirectly. A direct contribution is one where experts intervenes in their own individual capacity and as a consequence become identified as individuals who have specific views on the matters being debated, albeit views informed by their expertise. That is, experts emerge as a professional persona in their own right and provide critical perspectives on the debates, perhaps in the form of op-ed pieces or as a media pundit. An indirect contribution is one where the expert is brought in as a consultant by one of the parties already involved in the debate. In this latter situation, the expert's views will be filtered through the perspectives of the party for whom he or she is consulting. Both forms of involvement have their limitations because the role of the expert is the same: to bring up for critique assumptions that tend to otherwise form part of the ideology pool. In the case of a direct contribution, the expert's attempts to problematize taken-for-granted assumptions run the risk, as we noted earlier, of being treated as too esoteric and therefore as having questionable relevance. Such contributions are very likely

---

[1] That is, there is no clear or simple correspondence between linguistic and non-linguistic developments such that a change in one automatically triggers a correlational change in the other. Even if we limit ourselves to lexical innovations, it is hardly the case that each instance of a non-linguistic development (however this might be counted – and therefore note the problem involved in even enumerating non-linguistic developments) will necessarily result in a lexical change (note also the problematic assumption that non-linguistic developments unidirectionally drive linguistic effects).

[2] This affiliation is itself highly ideological and can change as a result of various socio-political developments.

to be dismissed as 'ivory tower' academic viewpoints. An indirect contribution, because it is filtered through the party that has brought in the expert as a consultant, may be met by a selective response, in which only those aspects of the contributions that are useful in supporting the party's agenda get taken up and other aspects that might prove too uncomfortable or are seen as irrelevant simply get ignored.

These problems do not mean that experts should refrain from contributing to language debates. Rather, they reflect the difficulties involved when the goal of the expert is to shift the parameters of the debate so that the apparently commonsensical premises shared by the different parties become themselves subject to critique. These problems are only likely to arise when the expert's contribution challenges the parameters that have already been established and publicly accepted. It is by no means easy to dislodge assumptions that are part of the ideology pool.[3]

I return to the issue of contributions from experts in the next chapter. For now, my goal is to show how, in the specific case of the Singlish controversy, shared and unquestioned assumptions in the ideology pool can lead opposing parties towards a convergence of meta-discursive regimes.

The Convergence of Meta-Discursive Regimes

As I pointed out in the Introduction, the Singlish controversy revolves primarily around the legitimacy and desirability of Singlish, with different parties having different views about the place that it should have in Singapore's linguistic landscape. There are two main parties to the debate: the Singapore government with its anti-Singlish stance and educated Singaporeans who are pro-Singlish.[4] The following discussion focuses on three shared assumptions in the ideology pool: (i) that Singlish is a fully developed social language, (ii) that Singlish is non-standard, and (iii) that Singlish represents the (potential) nativization of English in Singapore society as a whole.

These three shared assumptions result in three interesting meta-discursive convergences; that is, they lead the opposing parties to make rather similar assertions: (a) that there are Singaporeans who use Singlish for conducting entire social exchanges, (b) that the label 'Singlish' can be used to refer to both ungrammatical and colloquial usage, and (c) that the Singlish controversy is a matter of national interest or consequence.

---

[3] A longer-term solution involving the double hermeneutic is discussed in Chapter 3.

[4] This does not mean that there are no educated Singaporeans who are also anti-Singlish. The general population, perhaps not surprisingly, is divided in its attitude towards Singlish (Wee, 2005).

First Convergence: Speakers Use Singlish for Conducting Entire Social Exchanges

Social languages (Gee, 2001: 652) are sets of 'lexical and grammatical resources (whether in speech or writing) that a recognizable group of people uses to carry out its characteristic social practices'. A social language is firmly grounded in the kind of social interaction that it serves to mediate. It can therefore be as 'small' as a highly specialized register or as 'large' as an entire language, and anything in between. The extensiveness of any particular social language depends upon the degree of elaboration of its lexicogrammatical resources, which, in turn, depends upon the kinds of purposes or activities that involve the use of the language (Levinson, 1992). Such a view of language is useful because it avoids treating 'an abstract "language"' as the unit of analysis, and focuses instead on *'the actual and densely contextualized forms in which language occurs in society'* (Blommaert, 2005: 15, italics in original).

Both the anti- and pro-Singlish stances share the assumption that Singlish is a fully extensive social language (i.e. it can be used – rather like Standard English – as the medium for conducting entire exchanges). This assumption appears to have been influenced by the act of *linguistic baptism* (Park and Wee, 2013), where just the naming of a variety can lead to the belief that the name indeed refers to a fully fledged variety. For example, the Singapore government asserts that there are Singaporeans who interact entirely in Singlish because they are unable to speak Standard English. This assertion that Singlish is being used for the conduct of entire exchanges relies on the assumption that it is a fully extensive social language. In turn, this assertion gives credence to the character of the monolectal Singlish speaker, whose existence might otherwise be taken to be chimerical. This monolectal Singlish speaker is the Singaporean who speaks only 'broken English' and who, unlike his or her better-educated counterparts, is unable to switch into Standard English. The presence of these monolectal Singlish speakers in Singapore society is then taken to reflect a linguistic reality – one that is in sore need of redress. As a result, in August 1999, Senior Minister Lee Kuan Yew labeled Singlish 'a handicap we must not wish on Singaporeans' (*The Sunday Times*, 15 August 1999), and later that same month, Prime Minister Goh Chok Tong suggested that 'we should ensure that the next generation does not speak Singlish' (*The Straits Times*, 29 August 1999).

The assertion that speakers are using Singlish for conducting entire exchanges thus legitimizes the claim that there is indeed a Singlish 'problem'. If there are Singaporeans who conduct entire exchanges in Singlish, then the frequency and quantity of Singlish in Singaporean social life must be of a magnitude that cannot be ignored. In other words, the occurrences of Singlish are not merely occasional or happenstance, nor are they the result of deliberate and strategic choices made to optimize communicative effects. Rather, such occurrences are widespread and are the result of the lack of competence in the standard. Thus, this assumption posits that the presence of this 'poor English' significantly characterizes the social fabric of Singapore and, as a consequence, presents an unattractive and undesirable portrait of Singaporeans both to fellow Singaporeans and perhaps more importantly (according to the government at least) to non-Singaporeans.

If, on the other hand, however, Singlish were only a play language – perhaps one that speakers occasionally and deliberately crossed into (Rampton, 1995) so that it was limited to the 'liminal margins of everyday interactional practice' (Rampton, 1998: 229), such as greetings or farewells – then it would be more of an occasional annoyance and less of an issue that Singapore society would need to be concerned about, because it would not be in wholesale use for more 'substantive' interactions. The government is aware that some Singaporeans can easily code-switch between Standard English and Singlish, since it is precisely this particular group of Singaporeans who have been the strongest supporters of Singlish. However, the government considers that these Singaporeans who deliberately choose to speak Singlish when they can in fact speak Standard English are doing the nation a 'disservice' (Goh Chok Tong, 2000 SGEM speech), since they are not making it easy for their monolectal Singlish-speaking fellow Singaporeans to learn the standard. By contributing to the creation and maintenance of an environment where Singlish is heard, spoken, used and accepted, these educated Singaporeans are supposedly dis-incentivizing their monolectal Singlish-speaking counterparts from making serious efforts to learn Standard English. And because the government sees Singlish as lacking any economic value, these educated Singaporeans are therefore, albeit unintentionally, jeopardizing the social and economic mobility of their monolectal Singlish-speaking compatriots. Their desire to champion the use of Singlish despite the severe harms such usage would have for their less educated and less affluent Singaporeans opens them to charges of selfishness: they are more interested in indulging their own desire to enjoy speaking Singlish than in discouraging its use by others who are less fortunate and who will end up paying the price for this indulgence.

Supporters of Singlish obviously have a very different stance from that of the Singapore government, but they, too, share the assumption that it is a fully extensive social language. For example, C. Goh and Woo (2009: x) provide the following characterization of the government's anti-Singlish stance (italics in original), followed by their own rebuttal:

(1)   *Those who are able to speak both Singlish and English are somehow trying to prevent those who can only speak Singlish from being able to improve their English.*

> Our view is that this proposition is not only confusing, it's rubbish. Ask
> yourself: who's keeping whom down? The people who're trying to tell you
> there's only one way to express yourself, or the ones who're saying, go
> ahead, just speak up?

Their rebuttal contests the government's position that educated Singaporeans who are conversant in both Standard English and Singlish should refrain
from expressing support for Singlish. Observe, however, that it does not dispute
the assumption that there exist Singaporeans 'who can only speak Singlish'.
Rather, C. Goh and Woo argue that such monolectal Singlish speakers should
'just speak up' despite their lack of competence in the standard. These monolectal Singlish speakers are therefore being encouraged to take pride in their use of
Singlish. Note, however, that there is a slippage from the government's concern
with socio-economic mobility to C. Goh and Woo's interest in linguistic pride,
which does not actually address the government's claim that Singlish penalizes
those who are unable to switch into Standard English.

And in a separate statement, C. Goh (Save Our Singlish, 27 April 2002)
suggests that educated Singaporeans know when to use which variety (2), indicating that his and Woo's concern is for those who are in fact capable of code-
switching rather than for those who are not.

(2)   And I am confident that we know when to speak Singlish, and when we
         should use proper English. We are intelligent enough to know we don't write
         formal letters in Singlish. When was the last time you typed out, "Eh, give
         me a job, leh!" And we try not to speak Singlish to our foreign friends
         because we instinctively know that they might not understand.

Statement (2) is essentially an appeal to situational code-switching, since it
argues that there are particular situations where 'we speak Singlish' and other
situations (those that are more formal or that involve foreigners) where 'we try
not to speak Singlish' and use Standard or 'proper' English instead. This line
of argument once again asserts that there are speakers who use Singlish for
entire exchanges, particularly those exchanges that are informal and where the
interlocutors present are all Singaporeans. Such an assertion, as in the case of
the Singapore government, also relies upon the assumption that Singlish is a
fully extensive social language.

However, this shared assumption is problematic since Singlish is in fact not
a fully extensive social language. We can see this by comparing Singlish with
other varieties that are indeed fully extensive social languages – varieties that
we know can be used as the medium for entire exchanges. In work elsewhere
(Wee, 2010a), I point out that the Chinese dialects such as Cantonese, Hokkien
or Teochew can all totally constitute the medium for various interactions. These
Chinese dialects have also been the target of a language campaign, the Speak
Mandarin Campaign, which was designed to encourage Singaporeans to use

Mandarin in place of those dialects (Bokhorst-Heng, 1999). To discourage the use of both those Chinese dialects and Singlish, the Media Development Authority (MDA) issued the following advisories – MDA Free-to-Air Television Programme Code (4–5):

(3)   News, current affairs, and info-educational programmes where dialect interviews are given by older people who are unable to speak Mandarin. Voice-overs should be provided for these interviews.

(4)   Singlish, which is ungrammatical local English, and includes dialect terms and sentence structures based on dialect, should not be encouraged and can only be permitted in interviews, where the interviewee speaks only Singlish. The interviewer himself, however, should not use Singlish.

However, it has been much easier to implement (3) than (4), for the simple reason that as fully extensive social languages, there are conversations or programs that are entirely in Hokkien or Cantonese. These can then be banned or dubbed. But because Singlish is a less extensively developed social language[5], most Singlish usage involves switching between Singlish and Standard English; there are few, if any, movies or television serials that are *totally* in Singlish. This creates difficulties for the Media Development Authority as it tries to grapple with the use of Singlish because it 'is usually interspersed with other lexicogrammatical constructions that are, to varying degrees, more or less standard' (Wee, 2010a: 107).

Alsagoff (2007: 26) makes a similar point when she observes that 'fluidity and movement between Standard English and Singlish is not the exception but the rule in modern Singapore'. Moreover, it is not the case that the 'movement' between Standard English and Singlish involves an equal distribution of resources from the two varieties. Rather, it is usually Standard English that forms the matrix language and Singlish the embedded language, to use the terms suggested by Meyers-Scotton (1993; 2002). Indeed, Alsagoff (2007: 40) implicitly recognizes this fact in her discussion of how Singaporeans use Singlish and Standard English when she refers to the inclusion of Singlish features 'in what would otherwise be recognized as Standard English', rather than the other way round. Thus the MDA advisories (3–4) are difficult to apply to Singlish because, rather than serving as the medium for entire exchanges, Singlish is instead usually interspersed with other lexicogrammatical constructions that are more or less standard.

---

[5] By treating the dialects as more extensive social languages than Singlish, I do not mean to imply that the grammars of the dialects are complete or hermetically sealed. Nor do I mean to suggest that the grammar of Singlish cannot further develop so that it might at some point be able to be used in sustained social interactions. Extensiveness is a relative matter, contingent on the activities of language users, which is precisely what Gee's (2001) notion of social languages is trying to remind us of.

Second Convergence: The Label 'Singlish' Refers to the Colloquial as Well as the Ungrammatical

Recall that the sitcom *Phua Chu Kang* (*PCK*) described in Chapter 1 played a prominent role in the Singlish debate, since its main character PCK was well known for his regular use of Singlish. Here is an exchange between PCK and his nephew, Aloysius, in which PCK uses the analogy of picking one's nose to explain why lovemaking is a private act.[6] Clearly, the choice of analogy itself – where nose picking serves as the source domain (Lakoff, 1993) – is intended as an index of PCK's unpretentiousness and/or crudeness. PCK's contribution is also peppered with non-standard pronunciations and the Singlish particle *lah*.

(5)   ALOYSIUS: Why is making love carried out in private?
       PCK: Ah boyyyyy, use your blain, use your blainnnnn . . . . you
                        go and dig your nose in flont of your whole class izit?? Stupid
                        lah!!
                        [My boy, use your brains . . . Would you pick your nose in front
                        of your whole class? That would be stupid!]

As mentioned in Chapter 1, PCK's perceived influence in popularizing and legitimizing Singlish was so great that Prime Minister Goh Chok Tong felt compelled to ask the local television station that aired the sitcom to change the script so show PCK enrolling in a Basic English class in order to improve his English. The vice-president of the station acceded to the prime minister's request, promising viewers that PCK 'will still be recognizable after his linguistic make-over' (Chng, 2003: 49). It is unclear whether PCK's 'linguistic make-over' subsequently affected the ratings of the sitcom.

Prime Minister Goh Chok Tong, in his 1999 National Day Rally speech, described the harmful effect of the sitcom on students:

(6)   Teachers complain that their students are picking up catchphrases like:
       "Don't pray, pray." and using them even in the classroom. The students may
       think that it is acceptable and even fashionable to speak like Phua Chu Kang.
       He is on national TV and a likeable, ordinary person. The only character who
       tries to speak proper English is Phua Chu Kang's sister-in-law Margaret, and
       she is a snob. Nobody wants to be a snob. So in trying to imitate life, Phua
       Chu Kang has made the teaching of proper English more difficult.

The prime minister expressed the government's concern that the usage of Singlish interferes with the ability of Singaporeans to learn Standard English, based on the assumption that learners are confused about the boundary between

[6] Transcribed exchange from SGClub.com, forum section, posted by *missyjo* on 14 October 2007; accessed on 15 November 2009.

the two. This inability to distinguish the two, it is argued, leads students to mix features of Singlish with those of Standard English, thus contaminating their knowledge of the latter. This is an all-too-common argument stemming from a prejudice against stigmatized varieties (Siegel, 1999); it is often used to justify the conclusion that the stigmatized variety ought to be eliminated from the classroom because of the confusion and contamination it supposedly causes, even though the available evidence suggests that stigmatized varieties either have no effect on the learning of the standard or can actually have a positive effect (Siegel, 1999). More to the point of the present discussion, however, is that as far as the 'interference' argument is concerned, it does not matter whether Singlish is a colloquial variety that might be rule-governed or whether it is an ad hoc collection of ungrammatical errors. In either case, it is still nonstandard and thus 'incorrect' by virtue of its divergence from the standard variety (Milroy, 2001).

In contrast to the government, supporters of Singlish reject the claim that it is responsible for problems in learning Standard English. However, they, too, conflate the ungrammatical with the colloquial when referring to Singlish. For example, C. Goh (Save Our Singlish, 27 April 2002) describes Singlish as 'broken English'. And in their introduction to the second edition of the *Coxford Singlish Dictionary*, C. Goh and Woo (2009: ix–xi) assert the following:

(7)   Yet, every year, many employers and teachers of English express concern
        about our young people's ability to write and speak in what they deem as
        'appropriate' English.
        Don't be mistaken: the cause of this is NOT Singlish. Having a younger
        generation that writes and speaks differently is a universal 'problem',
        experienced by many different countries, including English-speaking
        countries such as England the USA . . .
        But don't misunderstand us: we love English as much as Singlish, and
        believe that mastering the rules of grammar is both empowering and
        enjoyable. It's just that we don't believe that we have to stifle one language
        to boost another.

In (7), there is a clear rejection of the government's claim that Singlish has a deleterious effect on the learning of the standard. Moreover, Singlish is contrasted with (appropriate) English, with the latter described as having 'rules of grammar' that need to be 'mastered'. The implication – that Singlish lacks such rules – was stated explicitly in the introduction to the first edition of the *Coxford Singlish Dictionary* (xiii), with its references to 'mish-mash' and 'badly spoken English', as shown in (8). At the same time, (8) also describes Singlish as involving 'conscious art' and 'ingenious and humorous wordplay'.

(8)   Singlish is unique to Singapore, and listening to its mish-mash of various
           languages and dialects, often involving bad transliterations, is also very, very
           funny.
           Contrary to popular belief, it is not merely badly spoken English, akin to
           pidgin. There is a conscious art in Singlish – a level of ingenious and
           humorous wordplay.

To summarize, because both sides of the debate consistently contrast Singlish
with Standard English, the former ends up being largely defined by its divergence from the standard. Singlish, then, is portrayed broadly as non-Standard
English, and at this relatively gross level of characterization, the distinction
between that which is colloquial and that which is ungrammatical is lost. There
is a perfectly understandable reason, of course, why Singlish (qua colloquial
variety) should share a number of features that might otherwise be associated
with the 'uneducated variety'. As Alsagoff (2007: 41–42) points out,

Singlish has many features in common with the uneducated variety of English for a good
reason – its need to mediate across different social groups means that it has to accommodate a wide range of grammaticality, even if it is to create a space for the normally
unacknowledged group of the poorly educated in meritocratic Singapore. Thus, what
should be held up as a purposeful accommodating style-shift is heaped into the same
boat as the learner of [the] uneducated variety of English.

Alsagoff is correct that the 'accommodating style-shift' is a major reason why
the Singlish that educated Singaporeans switch into shares a number of features with the Singlish spoken by less educated Singaporeans. However, it also
important to note that this accommodation occurs not only at the level of specific linguistic features but also meta-discursively. That is, when educated Singaporeans who are pro-Singlish deliberately characterize their own Singlish
as 'badly spoken English', this is intended to signal socio-linguistic solidarity
with their less educated counterparts. This explicit denigration of Singlish on
the part of those who take pride in it clearly supports the argument that Singlish
is for everyone regardless of socio-economic background.

The distinction between what counts as colloquial and what counts as
ungrammatical is admittedly a fluid one, insofar as it depends ultimately
on the conventions of particular linguistic markets (Bourdieu, 1991). Nevertheless, the classificatory practice itself has real socio-cultural force in that
both laypeople and institutions are consistently engaged in 'evaluative discourses' that aim to clarify whether certain uses of language are indeed right or
wrong, correct or incorrect (Cameron, 1995: x). And as we have seen, both the
Singapore government and supporters of Singlish are keen, for their own reasons, to exploit this fluidity so that the distinction between the colloquial and
the ungrammatical becomes even more obscured.

Third Convergence: Singlish as a National Issue

As noted in the Introduction, the names of the new varieties of English often combine an ethnic or national identity prefix with the *–glish* suffix, resulting in nomenclature such as Chinglish, Konglish and, of course, Singlish. These coinages convey the impression that English has taken root and become nativized, to varying degrees, in the local society. The morphological structure of these names further suggests that the ultimate scope of such nativization is that of the relevant society as a whole. That is, if allowed or encouraged to continue unchecked, these new varieties will come to be used at a societal level. And depending upon what one feels about the emergence, entrenchment and institutionalization of these new varieties, such developments can be a welcome or worrying trend.[7]

Reactions to such presumed nativizations can thus be highly emotive. And in the case of Singapore, because the variety that Singlish supposedly undermines or compromises (i.e. Standard English) is considered an extremely valuable and critical resource for Singapore's economic competitiveness, the government feels that there must be zero tolerance for Singlish. The Singlish 'problem' is thus elevated to the level of a potential national crisis. This adoption of a crisis discourse maximizes the scope of the Singlish debate: it becomes a matter that concerns all Singaporeans rather than, say, a specific sub-community.[8] Bokhorst-Heng (2005: 198) makes the following observation about the government's framing of the debate in crisis terms: 'And it is a discourse of crisis management: if the government's solution to the perceived problem is not adopted, the viability of the nation is threatened. The overarching objective of these discursive strategies is to reconfirm the position of Standard English in the ideological polarization of language as the language of pragmatic rationality and synonymous with the nation's continued economic viability.'

This framing of the debate is, in fact, a familiar move by the Singapore government, which has been described by various scholars as having a 'crisis mentality' (Chua, 1995: 69): 'from time to time, the mass media are mobilized to engender personal identity crises in the citizenry so that the leaders can then present themselves as possessing the means to solve people's crises and provide them with a certain "identity"' (Hill and Lian, 1995: 34). The following statement from a government minister (ibid., citing Betts, 1975: 141) succinctly explains why the government feels it is necessary to adopt a crisis discourse:

---

[7] In this regard, observe that even experts themselves may have strong disagreements about the legitimacy of these new varieties of English. See, for example, the exchange between Kachru (1986) and Quirk (1988).

[8] This is unlike the Speak Mandarin Campaign, for example, that is targeted specifically at the Chinese community in Singapore (Bokhorst-Heng, 1999).

'And one of the things we can do to get a little further down the road a little faster is to raise the specter of' total disaster as the alternative . . . Within this context, sooner or later they [the citizens] will change.'

In contrast to the government, however, supporters of Singlish obviously do not see Singlish as something intolerable. Instead they believe it should be cherished and valued as an expression of the Singaporean identity, as stated by Hwee Hwee Tan, a Singaporean novelist, in a contribution to *Time* (29 July 2002):

(9)   Singlish is crude precisely because it's rooted in Singapore's unglamorous past. This is a nation built from the sweat of uncultured immigrants who arrived 100 years ago to bust their asses in the boisterous port. Our language grew out of the hardships of these ancestors.

Similarly, consider this comment by C. Goh (Save Our Singlish, 27 April 2002):

(10)   Why we're fighting for Singlish, is because it's simply a part of our culture. In fact, it may be the ONLY thing that makes us uniquely Singaporean. It mixes all the various languages, which to me, seems to spread multi-cultural understanding. I thought this was something to be proud of.

This comment clearly appeals to iconization (Gal and Irvine, 1995), presenting Singlish as the language that embodies both Singapore's immigrant past and its multicultural present. It motivates the assertion that Singlish is a language that allows for the authentic expression of a national identity. The comment also represents a version of the pastoralist view of language (Gal, 1989), which treats language as an entity that is inherited across generations of speakers who belong to the same community, where this community is itself understood as (always) having occupied a specific territory. In the case of Singapore, this community is one of immigrants who have made the island their home. Singlish then comes to be seen as an inalienable carrier of the Singaporean community's values. Loss of the language becomes tantamount to the destruction of that culture, which is why it is something worth 'fighting for'. Thus, supporters of Singlish see it as a national 'treasure', while the government sees it as a national 'threat'.

Despite these opposing viewpoints, both sides see the continued use of Singlish – and thus the Singlish controversy – as a matter that can have national consequences that could ultimately either make or break the nation. From the perspective of the government, the continued use of Singlish jeopardizes Singaporeans' competence in Standard English, which is viewed as having significant economic value, especially in a globally competitive economy; in turn, Singlish is dismissed as having no economic value whatsoever. In contrast, the perspective of Singlish supporters is that this variety can help bind Singaporeans together by serving as the medium for the expression of a truly Singaporean identity. This is a function that Standard English cannot fulfil because it lacks any authentic connection with Singapore's multicultural 'unglamorous' history. Neither can the official mother tongues fulfil this function because they can only serve as emblems of specific ethnic communities rather than represent the nation as a whole.

The foregoing shared assumptions and their meta-discursive convergences tend not to be highlighted for discussion by either side of the debate. This is despite the fact that these assumptions and convergences are not always consistent with some of the claims made by the parties to the debate, and therefore could have been brought up by one side to undermine the claims of the other side. Furthermore, those individuals (mainly academics) who have attempted to critically examine the assumptions and convergences have largely found their contributions sidelined in the debate. In the next two sections, I discuss these points, beginning with how some of the claims being made are in fact belied by the shared assumptions and meta-discursive convergences.

Singlish Has No Value

In his 1999 National Day Rally speech, Prime Minister Goh Chok Tong asserted that Singlish has no economic value because it is something that 'the rest of the world will find quaint but incomprehensible'. This claim of Singlish's apparent lack of value and incomprehensibility motivated the creation of English-language lessons on the SGEM website, as seen in the following example (shown in 11–13), reproduced from one such lesson (Kwan, 2003: 117–118). In this example, Jane is a British expatriate who has just arrived in Singapore to work for a local company. She is met by Jaya, and on their way from the airport, Jaya uses Singlish to communicate with the taxi driver.

(11)   DRIVER: This way can?
         JAYA: No, lah! – this way cannot! Miss turn already! Mus u-turn back!
         DRIVER: Traffic heavy already – cannot change lane!

Later on, it transpires that Jane has mistaken Singlish for Chinese or Malay:

(12)   JANE: Thanks for meeting me, Jaya. I hope I'm going to manage all right in
                 Singapore. I didn't realize I'd have to learn Chinese to work here.
         JAYA: (Puzzled) Chinese?
         JANE: Or was it Malay?

This leads the narrator of the lesson to make the following commentary:

(13)   NARRATOR: First impressions are very important; in her first few hours in
                       Singapore, Jane has heard mostly 'Singlish' – and she's
                       clearly not impressed...

> [Singlish] doesn't have the features of good English that
> people outside Singapore are used to hearing. This creates a
> very poor first impression for visitors, customers from
> overseas and well-spoken Singaporeans.

The scenario in this lesson is clearly intended to evoke the concerns usually expressed by the government about Singlish. It involves an expatriate from Britain, who is therefore a supposedly 'real' native speaker of English. This expatriate is confused and unimpressed by the use of Singlish, and this can have serious repercussions for Singapore's economy, especially if foreigners find communication with locals to be a major obstacle. This scenario reinforces the pedagogical goal of the lesson: to get Singaporeans to stop using Singlish because they will not be understood by 'visitors, customers from overseas and well-spoken Singaporeans' (though presumably it is the first two categories of interactants who are more important). The lesson is executed in a heavy-handed and even clumsy fashion since it relies on a caricature of actual English usage amongst Singaporeans. It ignores the fact that it was Jaya who was using Singlish to communicate with the taxi driver rather than Jane. It also treats a foreigner like Jane as being inept or at least incredibly naïve to even think that 'Miss turn already' (uttered by the taxi driver while in traffic) might be either Chinese or Malay.

More seriously, because the SGEM insists on equating the promotion of 'good English' with the elimination of Singlish, the movement is dooming itself to failure. By declaring total war on Singlish, the SGEM will be considered by senior government officials and members of the public (or linguistic mavens) who might also be keen to see the end of Singlish as falling short of its goal as long as Singlish continues to be spoken in Singapore society. But it is difficult to see how Singlish will ever be completely eliminated since, as a colloquial variety, it constitutes a stylistic resource (Coupland, 2007) that educated speakers draw upon to perform their 'Singaporean-ness' (Alsagoff, 2007; see the later discussion). Indeed, by attempting to discourage the use of Singlish, the SGEM has set itself up for what seems an impossible task. Thus, Bruthiaux (2010: 99–100) observes,

Under the heading, 'Over the Years' the [SGEM] website does review the first six years of the project's existence in some detail. It reports that, a year into the project, a survey found that '9 in 10 Singaporeans agreed that it was important to speak good English', with perhaps a hint of a causal relationship between the project itself and this happy outcome. In 2002, a survey by *The Straits Times*, a habitual government mouthpiece, found that '66% of Singaporeans who were aware of the Movement were motivated to speak good English', a finding for which the line of causality – if indeed there was one – could have gone either way. Nothing further is reported regarding the effectiveness of the project for the rest of the period covered (2000–2005). Given that... the project can hardly have unfolded over this period without careful evaluation, this lack of publicly available information is puzzling, and it is left to an anonymous Wikipedia contributor to suggest, in the absence of hard evidence, that the project 'may have failed to substantially alter the diglossic character of language use in Singapore' (Speak Good English 2007). If this view is in error, the SGEM promoters are silent on this issue. Admittedly, it would be unfair to expect a project of this type to report on its own ineffectiveness on what is in effect a promotional website. But if demonstrable evidence that the project is succeeding is available, it is reasonable to suppose that it would be given pride of place on the website. After seven years of SGEM fanfare, the jury cannot still be out. In the absence of a public statement of outcomes, there will remain a suspicion that the news is not all good.

In other words, Singlish is proving more difficult to eliminate than originally anticipated, and if the removal of Singlish from Singapore's linguistic land-scape is one of the SGEM's 'key performance indicators', then the movement has to be considered a failure. The SGEM therefore seems to have come to the realization that it might be wiser to simply concentrate on promoting 'good' English and not equating this with the elimination of Singlish. This decision to tone down on its anti-Singlish rhetoric, however, is far from an acceptance of the merits of Singlish. And precisely because the SGEM is still a government-led initiative motivated by the comments of ministers about the deleterious effects of Singlish, any official recognition that Singlish does have merits would have to come from ministerial statements to that effect. Otherwise, as soon as a key government figure voices concerns about the dangers that Singlish poses to Sin-gaporeans' attempts to learn Standard English, the SGEM will then be obligated to go back to its earlier, explicitly anti-Singlish stance.

Ironically, the government itself is more than willing to treat Singlish as a manifestation of Singaporean-ess, particularly when it commodifies Singlish as a part of the tourist experience (Budach, Roy and Heller, 2003). Thus, in (14), the Singapore Tourism Board (STB) actually describes Singlish as Singaporeans' 'own brand of English', one that they 'fondly refer to'.[9] Pre-sumably, those ones who refer to Singlish 'fondly' do not include the very same government ministers who have denounced it as a 'handicap' and as something that 'we should ensure that the next generation does not speak'. The assertions in (14) therefore undermine the government's own claims that Singlish has no value. They present Singlish as a variety of English that tourists might indeed find 'quaint'. The STB even adds that the mixed nature of Singlish is 'not surprising' given Singapore's multiracial back-ground. This statement treats Singlish as a socio-linguistically natural phe-nomenon arising from the ethno-linguistically heterogeneous character of Singapore society – which is of course the very same argument that supporters

---

[9] See www.visitsingapore.com/publish/stbportal/en/home/about_singapore/fun_stuff/singlish_ dictionary.html; accessed 18 August 2009.

of Singlish have been making when they assert Singlish's value as an expression of the Singapore identity!

(14)   Over the years, Singaporeans have developed their own brand of English fondly referred to as 'Singlish'. With our multi-racial background, it's not surprising that 'Singlish' borrows from the many different languages spoken in Singapore. Here's a collection of 'Singlish' terms which you might find handy on your visit to Singapore.

Moreover, as the last sentence in (14) indicates, the STB has also included on its website explanations of some Singlish terms, some of which are shown in (15). These are aimed at tourists, on the grounds that they may otherwise find it difficult to understand what (some) Singaporeans might be saying. More significantly, the explanations in (15) encourage these foreign visitors to learn bits of Singlish so as to better understand the locals. This is a very different strategy from the SGEM's goal of persuading Singaporeans to avoid Singlish on the grounds that it creates a 'bad impression' and so ought not to be used at all with foreigners.

(15)   (i)   Action (verb)
              Derived from the English language meaning to show off.
              Example: That fellow always like to action, walking around with his Rolex over his shirt sleeves
        (ii) Boh-Chup (adj)
              Derived from the Hokkien dialect meaning couldn't care less.
              Example: Ah, boh-chup, I'm not going to hand in my assignment.

Thus, the 'incomprehensibility' of Singlish that left the fictional expatriate Jane unimpressed is now apparently a relatively tractable problem – thanks to the glosses provided by the STB – which suggests that Jane might herself have been less daunted by life in Singapore had she perused the STB website prior to leaving Britain.

Singlish Is Non-Elitist

Supporters of Singlish have also attempted to provide their own explanations of Singlish words and phrases to those who might be seeking to improve their knowledge of this erstwhile stigmatized variety. Possibly the most well-known attempt in this regard is the light-hearted *Coxford Singlish Dictionary* (C. Goh and Woo, 2009). The tongue-in-cheek introduction to the first edition (xiii), with its allusion to PCK ('swearing like a contractor'), indicates that the dictionary is intended for foreigners ('chao ang mor') who are trying to pick up ('chee hong') SPGs ('Sarong Party Girls' – a derogatory term for local girls who only date Caucasians); Westernized Singaporeans ('keng chio kia', lit. 'banana child'); and highly educated Singaporeans (with 'air-level' [i.e. 'A'

Level] education or about to study law at the National University of Singapore [NUS]) who wish to appear less elitist (16):

(16)   You too can talk like a Hokkien peng!
         *Accused of being 'air-level' when you joined National Service?
         *Ever been called a 'keng chio kia' or banana?
         *Are you a 'chao ang mor' who's trying to 'chee hong' an SPG?
         *Accepted into NUS Law?
         Worry no more! The Coxford Singlish Dictionary can help you fit in with everyday Singaporeans. Study it, and you'll soon impress your friends by swearing like a contractor!

The dictionary is unabashedly celebratory of Singlish, and its editors (xv) 'hope that fellow lovers of uniquely Singaporean culture will find the Coxford Singlish Dictionary a useful and fun resource'.

Consider now the actual dictionary entries themselves, with some examples presented in (17). We can note several qualities of the entries, as compared to the ones from the STB in (16). First, while the explanations are generally presented as in ordinary dictionaries, the attitude towards Singlish is less restrained and a lot more irreverent, as in (17b), where the combination of the Malay 'kena' and the Hokkien 'sai' is described as a 'happy marriage' of the two languages. This is clearly intended as a challenge to the government's stance of linguistic purism, which claims that Singlish is illegitimate because it mixes elements from different languages. For supporters of Singlish (and apparently the STB, though not the SGEM), such mixing is part of its charm and value as a marker of the Singaporean identity. Second, the examples provided do more than illustrate the particular word or phrase in question; they are liberally sprinkled with yet other Singlish expressions. Thus, in (17a), the second example sentence, in addition to showing the use of 'cheem', also includes the exclamative 'aiyoh', the particle 'hor', and the intensifier 'si beh'. Again, this liberal use of Singlish is consistent with the overall objective of the dictionary, which is not only to explain Singlish but to also promote it unabashedly.

(17)   (a) cheem: Hokkien term meaning something is profound or deep or intellectual.
              (i)   *'You study philosophy? Wah lau, damn cheem, man!' (You're studying philosophy? Whoa, that's deep stuff, man!)*
              (ii) *'Aiyoh, that Jacques Derrida, hor, is si beh cheem. I read until gong-gong.' (Man, that Jacques Derrida is really deep. Reading his stuff makes me giddy.)*
         (b) kena sai: A happy marriage of Malay and Hokkien, meaning to get into trouble. Literally, 'got hit by shit'. Not to be confused with 'kana sai'.
              (i)   *'He didn't pass up his homework, so kena sai from the teacher.' ('He didn't hand in his homework, so he got shit from the teacher.)*

However, given the consciously playful nature of the *Coxford Singlish Dictionary* and the fact that its editors are both educated Singaporeans competent in Standard English, it is worth asking to what extent the kind of Singlish represented in the dictionary can actually be said to be non-elitist (see the discussion of the Speak Good Singlish Movement in Chapter 1). This is because the playful nature of Singlish leads to the coining of forms that count as Singlish only in the sense that they are the stylized (Coupland, 2007) results of deliberate and highly creative manipulations of the language by well-educated speakers, rather than the consequence of the language being used by uneducated speakers.

Consider the following example (cited in R. Goh, 2009), taken from the TalkingCock.com website, which is managed by C. Goh, one of the authors of the *Coxford Singlish Dictionary*. The website states that it is 'committed to preserving and advancing the authentic voice of Singaporeans' (C. Goh and Woo, 2009: 9), and given this mission, we can safely assume that contributors also tend to share a pro-Singlish stance. Postings to the website tend to be both highly satirical and anti-establishment. The following posting comes from someone calling him- or herself Ter Koh (which is Hokkien for 'lecherous'). Here, Ter Koh is expressing the opinion that the level of Chinese proficiency among Chinese Singaporeans is not as high as the level of proficiency in English.

(18)   It's si beh condemn that as Chinese peepur, our standard of Chinese am not
        as powderful as our Engrand.

Ter Koh's use of *si beh*, a Hokkien intensifier meaning 'very/extremely', to pre-modify *condemn* is clearly intended to be humorous, since *condemn* is not even an adjective but a verb. Even in Hokkien, *si beh* would typically be used to pre-modify adjectives (e.g. *si beh juak* 'very hot', *sib eh sien* 'very tiresome'). Collocating *si beh* with an English verb is therefore simply Ter Koh's attempt to index this posting as intentionally and playfully non-Standard English. The phonetic representations of *powerful* as *powderful* and *English* as *Engrand* are likewise intended to achieve the same effect, especially since very few Singaporeans actually use terms such as *powderful* or *Engrand* outside a non-humorous context. These are creatively constructed terms that invoke the stereotype of Singlish speakers as speakers of non-Standard English. The closest that (18) comes to approximating naturalistic speech is with *peepur* 'people', since it has been observed that Singaporeans do tend to delete the final consonant (Bao, 1998).

In (18), then, Singlish is not being used as the medium for an entire exchange. Rather, it is interspersed with larger stretches of language that are closer to the standard. Also, when some form of Singlish is used, it is often intended as humorous or sarcastic, the effect deriving in part from the fact that the forms are exaggerations of non-standard speech rather than representations of actual use. Therefore, the assertions that Singlish derives organically from Singapore's 'unglamorous past' with its 'uncultured immigrants' and that educated elites play little or no role in its development are belied by the playful and exaggerated nature of Singlish as produced by these elites. This point emerges with particular force when we consider the fact that most of the strongest advocates of Singlish are 'linguistically and culturally elite in the context of Singapore' (R. Goh, 2009). For example, C. Goh has a law degree from University College London as well as a master's in law from Columbia University, Woo holds a doctorate in education from Columbia University, and Hwee Hwee Tan has a master's in English studies from Oxford University.

This erasure of the influence of educated elites is significant. It is a necessary move that allows Singlish to be characterized as non-elitist. The point to bear in mind is not that the playful and creative uses of language that educated Singaporeans call 'Singlish' bears absolutely no relation to the 'uneducated variety of English' (Alsagoff, 2007: 41–42; see the earlier discussion). Shared features across these varieties are to be expected given that one of the espoused advantages of speaking Singlish is that it can serve as a linguistic resource that elites can acquire as a way of bridging the class divide. But a proper appreciation of Singlish would have to give equal recognition to the existence of shared features and to fundamental differences in the linguistic competences of the groups involved.

Expert Contributions to the Debate

It is useful to ask what role played in the Singlish debate by those individuals who possess the expert knowledge needed to highlight the problematic nature of its meta-discursive assumptions. This is relevant to understanding why these assumptions were allowed to remain unexamined and thus to continue shaping the debate. Some academic contributions (including those of linguists) that tried to suggest that, as a colloquial variety, Singlish is rule-governed (Alsagoff and Ho, 1998) or to clarify the different meanings that are conflated under the label 'Singlish' (Fong, Lim and Wee, 2002) did occasionally make their way into the public domain, often via media reports (Bokhorst-Heng, 2005: 190). However, these contributions had relatively little impact on the Singlish debate.

To understand their limited impact, it is useful to consider that ideologies are necessarily sited (Philips, 2000; Silverstein, 1998). That is, to understand how ideologies achieve their effects (or not), we need to concern ourselves with their sitedness. Such sites refer to culture-specific scenes where participants enact roles that are recognizable as being embedded in normatively valued modes or patterns of interaction (Kroskrity, 2000: 19; Park, 2009: 22; Philips,

2000: 238; Wee, 2006: 347). However, it is important to distinguish between sites that are the objects of ideologies and sites in which meta-pragmatic commentary about ideologies occur. Philips (2000: 245) refers to the first as 'primary sites' and the second as 'secondary sites'. For example, in Philips's work on the Tongan concept of *lea kovi* 'bad language', which governs inter-actions between a sister and a brother by requiring that they adhere to par-ticular proscriptions on verbal behaviour, he found that a distinction is made between how *lea kovi* directly guides in real time an actual interaction between individuals and how the courts adjudicate on whether such past interactions in fact involved violations of *lea kovi*. In the former case, actually occurring interactions are, with varying degrees of faithfulness, sites of 'primary ideo-logical reproduction' (Kroskrity, 2000: 19). In contrast, in the legal setting, as magistrates ruminate on the applicability of *lea kovi* to specific situations, they necessarily engage in meta-pragmatic commentary, which is what makes this a secondary site. In the course of these ruminations, the magistrates' understand-ing of *lea kovi* may itself become more elaborated and differ from that of the participants in the primary site. Once this happens, the magistrates' ability to impose their own secondary-site interpretations of *lea kovi* onto the primary site participants relies on their judicial powers.

Since the Singlish debate is a language ideological debate, it already qualifies as a secondary site, the primary sites being those instances of Singlish usage that are either celebrated or condemned, depending upon whether the commen-tator happens to be pro- or anti-Singlish. Expert opinions that attempt to inter-vene in the debate by clarifying assumptions about the nature of Singlish can therefore be considered tertiary sites. The terminology itself is not consequen-tial, since the labelling of such sites as primary, secondary, tertiary is mainly intended to reflect the relative level of meta-pragmatic commentary that one site bears to another. But unlike the Tongan courts, whose judgements carry judicial authority, the contributions of academics impose no obligations what-soever on the various parties to the Singlish debate, who may choose to selec-tively appropriate, cite or ignore said contributions. Precisely because of this, experts may intervene by making critical observations about the assumptions, problematic or otherwise, behind the Singlish debate – but whether their obser-vations get taken up by stakeholders in the debate is ultimately up to the stake-holders themselves. There is no institutional compulsion, legal or otherwise, to do so.[10]

---

[10] An anecdote from an academic may help to illustrate this point. This academic, a linguist, was recently on a public panel and was asked to comment on whether the standard of English in Singapore was deteriorating. She pointed out that the question was not so simple since it relied on various problematic assumptions, including how deterioration might be measured given that language practices change. This was met with an angry and emotional response from the audi-ence, including from an elderly individual who identified himself as a member of one of the

Experts have, of course, been invited by the government to serve as members of advisory committees, including the SGEM committee. But even here, the committee's brief is more on how to realize the goals of the SGEM than to critique basic assumptions about Singlish. And experts will tend to interact more with those civil servants who work on these committees, rather than with the key political figures, such as the prime minister, who set the basic tasks and agendas of the committees.

The following example from the United Nations is instructive in this regard (Wee, 2011). Duchêne (2008) provides valuable insights into the processes by which the United Nations engages in policy formulation, specifically, in its handling of linguistic minorities. The kinds of documentation produced in the course of policy debates and formulation are a function of the available 'discursive spaces', namely, spaces that assign particular relations of power and expertise. The relationship between these different discursive spaces is critical for appreciating how the priorities and concerns expressed at one level may (or may not) be retained as the discussion moves on to some other level. For example, the space allocated to expert consultants – the Sub-Commission on Human Rights – is institutionally subordinate to the political space occupied by the Commission on Human Rights. Consequently, the Sub-Commission is 'a space of expertise, consisting of experts, at the service of a political space ... [and functions] primarily as an organ that proposes, while the superior echelons dispose' (Duchêne, 2008: 73–74). As Duchêne further explains, 'We can therefore see that the structure of the institution is determined by a form of top-down hierarchy ... the advocate for the Sub-Commission is always the Commission, the latter having the power to either convey concerns to the level above or to refuse to become involved' (77). This means that the work of the Sub-Commission may be ignored since there is no institutional obligation for the Commission to convey any of the Sub-Commission's findings or proposals to a higher level where political power is actually being exercised. In other words, the expert advice provided by the Sub-Commission constitutes a tertiary site, where the members have little or no binding authority that they can exert over the Commission on Human Rights, which in this case constitutes the secondary site. (The activities of the various linguistic minorities themselves would be the primary site).

In the case of the Singlish controversy, the government ministers (particularly the prime minister) are the most dominant voices (Bokhorst-Heng, 2005:

local university's board of trustees ('When I speak, even the university's president has to listen to me!'). This elderly gentleman stated in no uncertain terms that English in Singapore was indeed deteriorating and essentially chastised the academic for failing to take that position. The identities of these individuals involved in this anecdote are kept anonymous, particularly to protect the academic, who has yet to be tenured.

188). It remains unclear if the government is willing to have its own assumptions about Singlish subject to expert scrutiny.

Conclusion

The shared assumptions in the ideology pool and their associated meta-discursive convergences discussed in this chapter constrain the specific contributions that might be made in the course of a language ideological debate. In this case, because particular representations concerning Singlish are shared by both the anti- and pro-Singlish parties, they tend to remain unexamined and unchallenged. As a consequence, they come to constitute forms of 'social action, social facts and can function as agents in the exercise of social and political power' (Jaffe 1999b: 15; quoted in Makoni and Pennycook, 2007: 2). And while expert advice still has a place, its efficacy in challenging the assumptions in the ideology pool remains open to question. This, of course, raises the issue as to whether there are any conditions under which the assumptions in the ideology pool might come to be scrutinized and whether the experts might have a role in creating such conditions.

The role of expertise is the focus of the next chapter, which explores in greater detail the Singapore government's attitude towards language experts. Although the government is occasionally willing to admit that it has made mistakes, such admissions are hard to come by, especially regarding language policy. More often than not, expert advice and suggestions are dismissed without serious consideration. Given these conditions, the willingness to confront the government's assumptions regarding Singlish takes a fair amount of courage, and this is where it becomes pertinent to focus on the Speak Good Singlish Movement, which was created specifically as a direct challenge to the Speak Good English Movement.

3   Language Experts, Linguistic Chutzpah and the Speak Good Singlish Movement

Language Experts: Missed or Dismissed?

Consider the following three extracts, where Lee Kuan Yew narrates his various encounters with academic experts. The first shows that he did not always dismiss academic contributions as irrelevant. When Lee was concerned about gross differences in economic development across the various ethnic groups, he decided to look at anthropological and sociological studies:

One of the problems which has worried me is the uneven rate of development within the community, because the Chinese, Indians, Ceylonese and Eurasians progress at a faster rate than our Malays. If we do not correct this imbalance, then, in another 10 to 20 years, we will have a Harlem, something not to be proud of. So from politics I have had to go to anthropology and sociology to seek the reason for this. (speech to Southeast Asia Business Committee, May 12 1968; cited in Han, Fernandez and Tan, 1998: 181)

After consulting the works of sociologist Judith Djamour and cultural anthropologist Bryan Parkinson, both of whom emphasized differences in cultural values between the Malays and the Chinese, Lee came to the conclusion that the most feasible policy was one that eliminated ethnic enclaves and encouraged the different ethnicities encouraged to interact. It was this desire to encourage inter-ethnic interaction that, in part, led to the government's decision to recognize English as an official language that would serve as the inter-ethnic lingua franca.

The next two extracts, however, show Lee brusquely dismissing academic contributions without giving any specific reason. In the second extract, Lee describes how the suggestion by Eddie Kuo – a sociologist by training and also the appointed chair of a government advisory committee – to relax the ban on Chinese dialects (as part of the government's attempt to encourage Chinese Singaporeans to speak Mandarin instead) was simply dismissed on the grounds that 'it was not time':

In February 2003, Eddie Kuo, the dean of the Nanyang Technological University's School of Communication and Information, said that since the Speak Mandarin Campaign had gone on successfully for more than 20 years, perhaps it was time to relax the ban on free-to-air dialect TV programmes. Professor Kuo was then the chairman of a government-appointed advisory committee on television programmes. He said, 'Dialects are an important part of Singapore's multicultural environment. A considerable number of senior citizens who cannot understand Mandarin yearn to watch dialect programmes. The language is close to their hearts. Without interfering with the Speak Mandarin Campaign, we could gradually increase dialect programming, for example showing some good movies in dialect, which would also make our television programmes richer and more varied.' *His suggestion did not amuse the Ministry of Information, Communications and the Arts, which replied that it was not time to relax the ban on dialect TV programmes on national TV.* (2012: 164–165, italics added)

In the third extract, Lee describes a call by another academic, a linguist, to rethink the ban on dialects as 'daft' and 'stupid' (Lee, 2012: 166–167):

In 2009, when Dr Ng Bee Chin of the Nanyang Technological University's (NTU) Division of Linguistics and Multilingual Studies made a veiled call for dialects to return while speaking at a linguistics forum: 'Although Singaporeans are still multilingual, 40 years ago, we were even more multilingual. Young children are not speaking some of these languages at all any more. All it takes is one generation for a language to die. While many languages are in danger of dying, there is still hope that efforts can be made to preserve existent languages, and to create new ones', I thought it was a daft call. My then-principal private secretary Chee Hong Tat issued a reply on my behalf: 'Using one language more frequently means less time for other languages. Hence, the more languages a person learns, the greater the difficulties of retaining them at a high level of fluency ... It would be stupid for any Singapore agency or NTU to advocate the learning of dialects, which must be at the expense of English and Mandarin.[1]

Thus, at least as exemplified by Lee's own reactions (whose considerable influence on Singapore's language policy cannot be underestimated), the government appears willing to accept academic advice only when it already coheres with its own views or beliefs. Contrarian perspectives tend to be dismissed or rejected outright as inappropriate, irrelevant or lacking in credibility.[1]

This is not to say that the government never changes its approach to language policy. As I have pointed out elsewhere (Wee, 2011: 207), when the government first attempted to garner support for the use of Mandarin rather than Chinese dialects in the 1970s, it made the argument that the human brain could only

---

[1] This was in fact my own experience when serving as a member of the SGEM committee. I agreed to join the committee precisely because I saw it as an opportunity to engage in sustained dialogue with the civil servants responsible for running the SGEM: I would try to get them to better understand why a 'Singlish is bad' position vastly oversimplifies matters while I myself would become more appreciative of the exigencies and constraints faced by those charged with formulating and implementing language policy. Nevertheless, I came to quickly realize that even as the civil servants whom I interacted with were becoming more aware of some of the socio-linguistic complexities surrounding Singlish, they were not in a position to translate this awareness into policy. This was ultimately the prerogative of the government ministers, who were neither privy to my socio-linguistic conversations with the SGEM members nor, given their busy schedules, were likely to make the time to be educated on the fundamentals of socio-linguistics.

learn two languages. Anything more would overload the brain's capacity. This argument enabled Lee to present the government's demand of bilingualism as not only reasonable but also natural because it conformed to the capacities of the human brain (speech given at the Tanjong Pagar Community Centre Scholarships Presentation, 4 March 1978):

But let me reassure all parents: your child has a brain bigger than the biggest computer man has ever built. Whilst the world's biggest computer cannot handle two languages, most human beings can, especially if they are taught when young ... the fact is that your child has a brain which can use two languages, whilst the computer as yet cannot.

Thus, parents were faced with the dilemma of letting their children learn just two languages (English as the medium of instruction in schools and Mandarin as the official mother tongue that would be taught in schools) or, if they continued to speak Chinese dialects at home, to risk overloading their children's brain capacities.

However, given the great difficulties that many Chinese Singaporean students had in learning Mandarin in school, despite the fact that their brains 'can use two languages', the government in 2004 decided that the majority of them were not in fact capable of being highly proficient in both Mandarin and English. It held that only a minority, an elite estimated at about 10% of the student population (*The Straits Times*, 26 November 2004), could be expected to be fully bilingual in English and the mother tongue. Thus, compare Lee Kuan Yew's statement just quoted (made about forty years ago), with the following, more recent statements issued in 2004. In these two extracts, Lee describes his earlier view as a mistake, now believing that the average person cannot be expected to master two languages:

But now I believe it's only possible for the exceptionally able and the very determined ... If you spend half-and-half of your capacity on two languages, it's likely you won't master either. (Lee Kuan Yew, *The Straits Times*, 24 June 2004)

I used to believe that you can learn two languages at the same time, whatever your IQ. I was wrong. You have to master one language enough to read and to absorb knowledge for all the other subjects. (Lee Kuan Yew, *The Straits Times*, 26 November 2004)

The second admission occurred about five years after the first. Both concerned what might be considered a realistic level of bilingual proficiency, though in 2009, the focus shifted to the specific kinds of language teaching methods being employed. Towards the end of 2009, Lee acknowledged that generations have 'paid a heavy price because of my ignorance' and admitted that the policy is 'not completely right':

Reflecting on some 40 years of bilingual education in an off-the-cuff speech at the official opening of a Chinese language center, he [Lee Kuan Yew] said Singapore's policy on the learning of Chinese started on the wrong footing because he believed in the past that it was possible to master two languages equally well.

As a result, Chinese lessons in the old days were pitched at too difficult a level and 'successive generations of students paid a heavy price because of my ignorance', he said...

The policy, he acknowledged with a laugh, is still 'not completely right but I will get it right if I live long enough'...

Earlier this month ... he cited bilingualism as the most difficult policy he had to implement, and one which should have been done differently from the start. ('MM Lee wants learning of Chinese to be fun', *Straits Times*, 18 November 2009)

Of particular interest to the present chapter is his explanation that he had initially based the language policy on the assumption that general intelligence and language ability were strongly correlated. It was only recently that he had come to appreciate that the two reflected different kinds of capacities. This was a difference that the earlier policy expectations did not take into consideration. As seen in the following extract, Lee attributed this newfound appreciation for this difference to input from his daughter, a neurologist. The relevant statements are shown next (Hoe, 2009).

Mr Lee added: 'At first I thought, you can master two languages. Maybe different intelligence, you master it at different levels.'

But his conclusions now, after over 40 years of learning Mandarin, cannot be more different.

MM Lee said: 'Nobody can master two languages at the same level. If (you think) you can, you're deceiving yourself. My daughter is a neurologist, and late in my life she told me language ability and intelligence are two different things.

'Girls are better at languages because their left side of the brain to learn languages, as a general rule, is better than the boys. Boys have great difficulty, and I had great difficulty.'

As in 2004, the admission of a policy error was quickly followed by initiatives aimed at redressing the issue. In this case, if language ability is distinct from general intelligence, then cultivating the former requires a different pedagogical approach from, say, the teaching of mathematics or geography. The government's emphasis on the need to rethink Chinese-language teaching was driven home in Lee's recollection of how it used to be taught, as shown next. There had been, in his view, too much of a focus on rote learning and a lack of sufficient interactivity; there had also been little or no regard at all for the fact that an increasing number of students were coming from English-speaking homes. The result was that a significant number of Chinese students who were supposed to embrace Mandarin as their official mother tongue came to dislike the language intensely:

During a speech made at the official opening of the Singapore Centre for Chinese Learning, MM Lee said: '*We started the wrong way. We insisted on ting xie (listening), mo xie (dictation) – madness! We had teachers who were teaching in completely-Chinese schools. And they did not want to use any English to teach English-speaking children Chinese and that turned them off completely.'* (MM Lee admits 'mistake' made in his education policy. (*Temasek Review*, 18 November 2009, italics in original)

Singapore's overall language policy is built on a number of more specific policies. Its overarching focus is the division between English, on the one hand, as a non-Asian language and hence a culturally inappropriate mother tongue, and the ethnic mother tongues, on the other hand, as officially sanctioned heritage identity markers. At more specific levels, there are policies pertaining to how particular languages (such as English and the mother tongues) are to be taught in the schools, as well as what levels of proficiency might be expected of students. In the preceding discussion, the mistakes that Lee refers to were made at these more specific policy levels. In contrast, the government appears determined to stick to its general policy on the appropriate allocation of roles between English and the mother tongues (Wee and Bokhorst-Heng, 2005).

Guiding the government's overall efforts regarding language are those policies that are assumed to be so commonsensical as to not be even worth articulating explicitly (see Chapter 2). In such cases, when no explicit language policy is being formulated, ideology then 'operates as "default" policy' (Lo Bianco, 2004: 750). Arguably, this is where the assumption that Singlish is 'clearly' bad English or English that has been compromised and contaminated by contact with local languages resides. Thus, recall Lee Kuan Yew's comments regarding Jamaican Creole, which he considered to be problematic because, unlike proper English, he found it difficult to understand. His observation makes no allowance for the fact that Jamaican Creole, like any other language, has both a communicative and a communal value, that it is both a means of communication and an expression of a community's identity and values (Widdowson, 1994: 381). There is a clear lack of appreciation that language serves more than just the function of transmitting information, of the naturalness of code-switching and style-shifting, and that speakers juggle multiple linguistic resources as part of their repertoire.

This same lack of appreciation is evidenced in comments by Lee's successor, Goh Chok Tong, when he recounted his experience with an African caddy:

Let me give you an example of how a person can speak proper English when exposed to others who do. Some years ago, I played golf in Zimbabwe when I had some spare time before my meetings. I was impressed by the excellent English spoken by my African caddy. *For example, when he found me putting badly ever so often, he asked politely, "Would you permit me to test your putter?" He tried it and advised me that it was too heavy. In Singlish, we would have said, "Can try your putter or not?"* After the game, he asked me, "Would you have some used balls to spare me?" I was so impressed by his elegant English that I gave him all my used golf balls and some new ones too. In Singlish, it would be "Got old balls give me can or not?" My Zimbabwean caddy did not complete his secondary school education. He picked up his English from the white Zimbabwean golfers. (speech delivered at the launch of the 2000 Speak Good English Movement, http://goodenglish.org.sg/*f*/media/sgem/document/press%20room/2000/sgem%20launch%202000%20goh%20speech.pdf; accessed 15 May 2016, italics added)

These observations by Singapore's former prime ministers highlight the importance, in any discussion of language policy, of recognizing varying degrees of ideological entrenchment, since different policy levels are often informed by different ideologies. The more deeply entrenched the ideologies (and by implication, the policies that they inform), the less open both the ideologies and policies are to critical scrutiny. Thus, in this case, the most general policy level is informed by essentialist assumptions concerning the character of Singapore as a fundamentally Asian society and English as a fundamentally Western language. That is, the government takes it as a natural and unassailable fact that official mother tongues have to be Asian (see Chapter 1). Consequently, it is extremely reluctant to countenance the possibility of recognizing English as an official mother tongue, even as it acknowledges that it is a home language for many Singaporeans. This is despite the fact that Lee (2012: 231) has himself acknowledged that language policy should never be treated as having been set in stone; instead, it needs to be understood as a tool that has to be adapted as social circumstances change: 'Language policy must evolve as society progresses in order to remain relevant [as a] vital instrument for achieving national interest objectives and meeting the needs of governance.'

It is clear, however, that the revision of language policy occurs more at the lower levels of policy detail and implementation than at the higher levels of fundamental assumptions. It is the ideologies informing the more specific levels of the language policy, then, that are more amenable to possible change. This may be because those more specific policy levels deal with how to realize or implement the government's expectations of bilingual proficiency. In short, they concern how to teach and assess students' language proficiencies and do not impinge upon or undermine the more general rationale for the adoption of an English-mother tongue policy in the first place. But even with those specific policies, it took the government close to three decades (from the late 1970s to the new millennium) to determine that it held unrealistic expectations about language proficiency levels and was using unsuitable language teaching methods.

Importantly, the factors that led the government to reconsider its more specific policies were the accumulating data from examination results that showed students facing considerable learning difficulties and Lee's conversations with his own daughter. Absent such interventions, it is quite likely that the government would have continued to assume that equal mastery of two languages is the norm and that language ability is correlated with general intelligence. This counterfactual scenario gains plausibility from two comments made by Lee:

he insisted that 'my experience should guide the policy' and then asserted that 'I wasn't helped by Ministry of Education (MOE) officials. They were basically two groups of people, one English-speaking, the other Chinese-teaching' ('MM Lee wants learning of Chinese to be fun', *Straits Times*, 18 November 2009).

As regards the first comment, basing a policy that affects the general population on the particularities on his personal experience indicates Lee's general skepticism about the relevance of the experiences of others as input to policy formulation. It suggests that, unless the information being provided concurs with his personal experience, it will carry relatively little weight in the process of policy formulation. In the second comment, Lee, rather ironically, places blame on MOE officials for the policy mistakes, because they were unable to rise above their own language experiences. In a column written days after these comments, he expressed a similar concern both about the ability of advocates of specific language-teaching policies to rise above their narrow interests and about language issues being used as 'political football' among various interest groups. In that case, he was commenting on the concerns expressed by Mandarin-speaking Chinese that non-traditional teaching methods might lead to a decline in language standards while their English-speaking counterparts were worried that more needed to be done to help students learn a language that had 'been forced on them' ('Was Chinese wrongly taught for 30 years?' *Straits Times*, 27 November 2009). Taken together, these comments do not augur well for the role that language experts might possibly play in policy formulation, since any such involvement is likely to be limited to providing advice on policy implementation, rather than providing critical feedback on fundamental ideological assumptions.

But the ability to provide feedback on ideological assumptions is important, especially since the government's understanding of what 'bilingualism' entails is already problematic. For one, the government's construal of bilingualism is grounded on the assumption that languages are fully developed delimitable systems. Delimitable linguistic systems are assumed to each have their own internal integrity, and the maintenance of this integrity is therefore dependent on each system being kept separate from the others. This creates the belief that 'properly' bilingual individuals are those in complete control of compartmentalized sets of monolingual proficiencies, such as English and Mandarin. However, the fact is that individuals are seldom equally fluent in two or more varieties (Baetens, 1986). This is because societies are organized in such a way that different varieties are typically used in different contexts and for different purposes (Romaine, 2001). Consequently, knowledge of language is always 'partial' since it is a function of the kinds of social interactions that the individual participates in, and no individual ever fully participates in all existing social practices. There will always be social practices that some individuals are excluded from by virtue of their age, gender, education level or some other social factor. The idea of a fully developed delimitable linguistic system is therefore a myth (Hopper, 1998).

An individual's social experience of language, then, plays a significant role in the kind of competence that she or he acquires (Gee, 2001; Norton, 2000). But if Lee's remarks are indicative of the government's overall understanding, there is a tendency both to underplay the significance of the social dimension of language learning and to treat language proficiency primarily in neurological or cognitive terms. Thus, Lee's original assumption about language learning was stated in terms of brain capacity, and even his revised assumption remains couched in neurological terms.

In making these comments about the contributions of experts, I want to emphasize that I am not treating expert knowledge as being flawless and that it should be automatically privileged as objective 'truth' as opposed to the 'misconceptions' that non-experts have. There is no doubt that experts themselves can be guilty of relying on taken-for-granted assumptions without critically questioning them. The expert position is therefore also an interested position, one that is socially constructed and open to influence from vested considerations, such as the desire for fame or to be influential (Bourdieu, 1988).[2]

It is also clear that the complex nature of language policy means that language experts themselves should not adopt the stance that they are the 'final arbiters' of what should be considered appropriate policy initiatives (Wee, 2010a). The fact that language policy is inevitably influenced by existing language ideologies, as well as being intertwined with non-linguistic considerations (Spolsky, 2004), should give language experts pause before they attempt to present themselves as having a monopoly on what counts as 'good' policy. There is another reason why language experts should not assume some privileged perspective on the issues involved in developing a particular policy. Language experts are also social actors who are necessarily members of specific speech communities and consequently may have some vested interest in which language resources are to be valued or mobilized (as are policymakers themselves). Language experts therefore need to acknowledge that 'we can no longer sustain the position of neutral and objective expert which has usually been ours, and that rather the kind of knowledge we generate in this alternative way can be understood as a distinctive contribution to a conversation among stakeholders' (Heller, 2008: 519). Accordingly, experts need to adopt the perspective of 'joint problematization' (Roberts and Sarangi, 1999: 474), where the practical imperatives of policy formulation are informed but not overridden by scholarly understandings.[3]

---

[2] My thanks to Joseph Park for raising this point.

[3] Shannon (2014) proposes some interesting ways in which such joint problematization might be facilitated, including diplomat-in-residence and scholar-in-residence programs. Andreas (2014) suggests that closed-door dialogues between scholars and policymakers might allow difficult questions to be productively addressed.

Unfortunately, to the extent that the issues being disputed involve fundamental assumptions about language, then the possibility of joint problematization becomes more unlkely. In the case of the Singlish controversy, the debate concerns the basic issue of whether Singlish can be considered desirable or a legitimate variety of English. As far as the Singapore government is concerned, the official stance is a clear 'no'. Let us now see how a group of Singaporeans attempt to defend Singlish with a clear 'yes'.

Linguistic Chutzpah

The Yiddish word 'chutzpah' suggests attributes variously described as supreme self-confidence, nerve, gall, audacity or even insolence. An individual with 'linguistic chutzpah', then, is one who has confidence in his or her language choices and usage. However, linguistic chutzpah is not about making choices and usage that blatantly disregard conventions of grammar or situational appropriateness, as if they were irrelevant. Rather, it is confidence that is backed up by meta-linguistic awareness and linguistic sophistication, giving the speaker the ability to articulate, where necessary, rationales for his or her language decisions.

It is important to clarify that linguistic chutzpah is not necessarily about championing either endonormativity or exonormativity. The Speak Good Singlish Movement (SGSM) of Singapore that I discuss in this chapter clearly supports the use of a nativized variety of English, that is, Singlish. In this sense, the SGSM can be considered endornomative in orientation. But it does not promote Singlish to the exclusion of other, arguably more exonormative varieties (www.facebook.com/MySGSM/info, Speak Good Singlish Movement's notes; accessed 27 February 2013). Instead, what makes the SGSM a good case study of linguistic chutzpah is that it is a relatively linguistically sophisticated response to the Singapore government's Speak Good English Movement (SGEM). This linguistic sophistication is in clear contrast to the sociolinguistically naïve attitudes displayed by Lee Kuan Yew and Goh Chok Tong in their respective remarks about Jamaican Creole and the Zimbabwean caddy, which showed no appreciation for code-switching or style-shifting.

As regards the championing of exonormativity, consider the fact that it is common in Singapore for some local DJs to use Americanized English, though this practice has been subject to harsh criticism by some radio listeners. Nevertheless, many of the DJs still continue speaking in American-accented English, which arguably requires confidence on their part (www.digplanet.com/wiki/987FM; accessed 24 February 2013). Hypothetically, were the DJs to articulate linguistically informed rationales for why American English might be desirable for Singaporean DJs, then this, too, would constitute a case of linguistic chutzpah.

Finally, there are sometimes disagreements and uncertainties over what actually constitutes 'American English' or 'Singlish'. Another important point to appreciate about linguistic chutzpah is that it does not operate only at the level of different varieties of English; it is also relevant when variety-internal decisions have to be made about what might be considered appropriate lexico-grammatical features, orthographic conventions or pronunciation. In short, there are two key criteria for linguistic chutzpah: (i) confidence in one's linguistic choices in the face of criticism (actual or anticipated) and (ii) drawing upon linguistic knowledge to justify these choices.

A focus on linguistic chutzpah is especially relevant for the study of world Englishes, given the vagaries of English-language use in late modernity.[4] Particularly in relation to the global spread of English, speakers are often confronted with the need to make decisions about language without being able to rely on traditional sources of authority (such as the speech community or prescriptive grammars). Under such circumstances, speakers with linguistic chutzpah are able to adopt confident stances about their language choices, even while knowing that these choices may be met with significant criticism. I develop this point in the last part of the chapter.

As mentioned, the SGSM is a response to the government-initiated SGEM, which is generally concerned with promoting good English while discouraging the use of Singlish (see Chapter 1). It is therefore useful to begin with a discussion of the SGEM.

The Singapore government's strong reservations about Singlish (Chng, 2003; Bokhorst-Heng, 2005) are expressed in this statement by Lee Kuan Yew: 'Those Singaporeans who can speak good English should to help create a good environment for speaking English, rather than advocate, as some do, the use of Singlish . . . Singlish is a handicap we must not wish on Singaporeans' (*Sunday Times*, 15 August 1999). This concern about the deleterious effects of Singlish on Singaporeans' ability to speak Standard English led the government to initiate the Speak Good English Movement in 2000 (Bruthiaux, 2010; Rubdy, 2001). As is common with government campaigns in Singapore, the SGEM is re-launched annually, with the chairperson reminding the general public of the rationale behind the campaign and introducing new initiatives to maintain momentum and enthusiasm.

On 7 September 2010, the SGEM was officially re-launched with the tagline 'Get It Right' and the use of some 'creative methods' to get Singaporeans to speak good English. One such method involved

---

[4] The focus on English does not deny that similar issues might also arise with other languages. But the global spread of English has led, more so than with any other language, to the emergence of multiple varieties, in turn raising concerns about the legitimacy of these varieties and anxieties about what might be considered proper usage. Hence, the issue of linguistic chutzpah arises with particular force in connection with English.

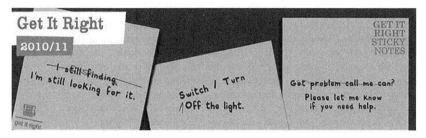

Figure 1. Stickers from the Speak Good English Movement. Reproduced by permission of the Speak Good English Movement.

pasting stickers – with handwritten notes that correct bad English – in public places. SGEM ambassador Ahmad Faizal was one of the ambassadors who recently carried out this 'guerilla-styled' activity at a food court. 'One of the initial reactions of the members of public, when I started pasting the "speak good English" stickers at the food court, was curiosity. That's when I'd pick up a conversation with them and spread the message', he said. SGEM chairman Goh Eck Kheng said: 'We put sticky notes in high-density areas and whether people like it or they don't like it, they've attracted a lot of attention to the message that we are putting out and there's a very heightened awareness.' (Loh, 2010)

The stickers were part of 'an activist toolkit' handed out by the SGEM. Singaporeans were encouraged to use the stickers to correct any English errors that they might encounter; they were to cover over signs that used 'bad' English with a sticky note with the correct version of English written on it. Vivian Balakrishnan, then minister for community development, youth and sports, kicked off the 2010 SGEM by being the first to correct a sign at a food court, replacing a sign saying 'No outside food allowed' with one that said, 'No food from elsewhere, please' (http://en.wikipedia.org/wiki/Speak_Good_English_ Movement; accessed 29 October 2012). Figure 1 shows some examples of how the stickers are intended to be used.

The Speak Good Singlish Movement (SGSM)

Just four days after the re-launch of the 2010 SGEM campaign, on 11 September 2010, the Speak Good Singlish Movement was initiated, with this rationale[5]:

---

[5] While both the SGEM and the SGSM present themselves as 'movements', arguably only the latter is a proper movement. The SGEM is a top-down government-initiated campaign whereas the SGSM appears a bottom-up initiative of ordinary Singaporeans (though it is admittedly hard to be completely certain about this since the founders insist on anonymity). I thank an anonymous reviewer for raising this point.

We not against Speak Good English Movement in Singapore hor. But we feel people should get it right with speaking Singlish and not just English. We are damn tired of people confusing Singlish with broken English. We are damn tired of people kay-kay speak Singlish but really speak bad English. We are damn tired of people picturing Singlish speakers as obiang chow Ah Bengs and Ah Lians. You dun wanna learn the subtle rules of this natural evolving language, then dun anyhow say it is simple, shallow, and useless please! Singlish is full of culture, of nuances and wordplay. It pulls together the swee-ness in the grammar, syntax, and vocabulary of so many languages. Best OK! (www.facebook.com/MySGSM/ info; accessed 27 February 2013)

Postings to the SGSM's Facebook page tend to celebrate the use of Singlish and are usually presented with lots of humour. This is not surprising since the use of Singlish, especially among educated Singaporeans, tends to be marked by a high degree of self-conscious playfulness (Wee, 2010b: 110; 2011: 84). Nevertheless, despite the generally humorous tone, some of the comments made can be substantive. Thus, light-hearted contributions – which include tips on how to complain like a Singaporean (from the SGSM) and the defence of cheap local food (from others) – sit alongside more pointed posts (from the SGSM as well as others) that critique the English used by the Singapore president and various members of Parliament to drive home the point that even such luminaries occasionally speak 'broken English' (SGSM Facebook, accessed 4 March 2013). Moreover, after the SGSM's interview with *The Online Citizen* (discussed later), a number of fairly heated exchanges took place between the SGSM and various contributors, some of whom were critical of the SGSM's pro-Singlish stance and others who were more supportive of it. The SGSM has been successful in garnering support (with 37,384 'likes' on its Facebook page as of 5 December 2016) and in maintaining active participation (with Google counting sixty-seven posts 'talking about' the SGSM on 24 March 2013).

Exactly who the founders of the SGSM are is not clear. They remain anonymous, despite having given two lengthy interviews, one with *The Online Citizen* and another with *Ms Demeanour Singapore*. This anonymity may have been maintained to ensure that focus has remained on the SGSM as a whole rather than on specific individuals. And while the identities of the SGSM founders remain unknown, it is reasonable to posit that they are well-educated Singaporeans with a strong interest and competence in language matters. The likelihood that some of them might even be linguists, novelists or poets increases when we consider that the SGSM has criticized the government for lacking any such individuals: 'You must remember that there is no linguist among them [the government]. You can't even make one between two of them. No linguist, no writer, definitely no novelist, no poet – you get the idea.'

Whether members of the SGSM are in fact linguists, novelists or poets is less relevant than the fact that their educational background probably includes some exposure to language studies or literature. The timing of the SGSM's launch and its name's syntactic parallelism both suggest that the SGSM is a direct response to the SGEM. This is further confirmed by the SGSM's own use of a sticker as part of its banner, in which 'It's not proper English' (a sentiment presumably attributed to the SGEM) has been crossed out and replaced with the defiant 'Go and die lah!' (SGSM Facebook page, http://archive.is/1U3I; accessed 30 October 2012). The latter is a Singlish phrase that is pragmatically equivalent to 'Go to Hell!' It is commonly used to aggressively reject an assertion or request put forward by someone else. Examples of this phrase at work are shown next (1–2).

(1)   A: Can lend me some money?
            'Can you lend me some money?'

(2)   B: Go and die lah!
            'No way!'
         A: You are late.
         B: Go and die lah!
            'None of your business!'

This display of defiance by the SGSM should not be dismissed as trivial for two reasons. First, the style of government in Singapore, until recently, has been highly authoritarian. Indeed, to some, it still remains too authoritarian. This authoritarianism is such that the state has had no compunctions about intervening in 'personal matters', including that of language use, as Lee Kuan Yew himself acknowledges (quoted in Mauzy and Milne, 2002: 35):

We wouldn't be here, would not have made the economic progress, if we had not intervened on very personal matters – who your neighbour is, how you live, the noise you make, how you spit or where you spit, or what language you use . . . It was fundamental social and cultural changes that brought us here.

The second reason is the government's deep concern that Singlish might jeopardize Singaporeans' competence in Standard English, which is seen as critical to Singapore's economic success by enabling Singaporeans to be globally competitive. Given the importance that the government attaches to economic development (Chua, 1995: 68; Mauzy and Milne, 2002: 54) and the instrumental role that Standard English plays in this development (Wee, 2007: 253), any attempt to champion the use of Singlish – especially when the political leaders have already spoken out against it – risks being portrayed as irresponsible. Indeed, Singapore's second prime minister, Goh Chok Tong, asserted that those Singaporeans who deliberately choose to speak Singlish when they can in fact speak Standard English are doing the nation a 'disservice' (Goh Chok Tong, 2000 SGEM speech), since they are (apparently) creating an environment where it becomes more difficult for fellow Singaporeans to learn the standard. This assertion assumes that the presence of stigmatized varieties interferes with the learning of standard varieties (see the later discussion). In combination, this assertion and the government's authoritarian nature mean that the SGSM runs the risk of being accused by the government of irresponsibility or doing the nation a 'disservice'. The reality of such a risk is brought home by the government's tendency to dismiss as 'daft' or 'stupid' proposals that are at odds with its own language policy.

Recall, however, that linguistic chutzpah is not just about being defiant, audacious or even insolent. It also includes the ability to provide support for the stance taken. To appreciate this other component of linguistic chutzpah, we need to first understand that, in trying to discourage the use of Singlish, the government has made a number of questionable claims, claims that the SGSM has felt the need to directly rebut.

Claims about Singlish Made by the Government

The government's concern that Singaporeans' ability to speak good English is affected by the popularity of Singlish arises from its view that the two cannot co-exist. In the course of trying to make this argument, it has made at least three questionable claims.

The Interference Claim

In language education, one common justification given for banning stigmatized or denigrated varieties is the 'interference' claim (Siegel, 1999). It posits that the learner experiences confusion between the grammar of the desired variety and that of the stigmatized variety. This inability to distinguish the two leads the learner to mix features of the stigmatized variety with those of the desired variety, thus contaminating the grammar of the desired variety (Wee, 2010a: 101).

Government officials have repeatedly claimed that the characters on the popular television sitcom, *Phua Chu Kang*, were responsible for popularizing the use of Singlish. Phua Chu Kang's use of Singlish contrasts with the language used by his uptight and snobbish sister-in-law, Margaret, who speaks Standard English. If Singaporeans, especially younger Singaporeans, persist in using Singlish (regardless of whether this persistence is motivated by a desire to emulate Phua Chu Kang), the government argues that this practice will only contribute to difficulties in the teaching and learning of 'proper English'.

However, he available evidence suggests that stigmatized varieties either have no effect on the learning of the standard, or they can actually have a positive effect (Siegel, 1999).

The Label 'Singlish' Can Be Applied to Ungrammatical as well as Colloquial English

The second claim concerns the use of the label 'Singlish' for both colloquial (i.e. non-standard) and ungrammatical English. We see this when Goh Chok Tong expressed the hope that, in time to come, Singaporeans will no longer speak Singlish (*Straits Times*, 29 August 1999): 'Singlish is broken, ungrammatical English sprinkled with words and phrases from local dialects and Malay which English speakers outside Singapore have difficulties in understanding ... Let me emphasise that my message that we must speak Standard English is targeted primarily at the younger generation.'

The claim here is that Singlish can be equated with ungrammatical English, even though this elides the distinction between the colloquial and the ungrammatical. The categorization of particular linguistic constructions as 'colloquial' or 'ungrammatical' is admittedly fairly fluid and open to contestation and negotiation (Wee, 2011: 80). However, the conflation of the two is problematic. For example, Singlish (qua colloquial English) does appear quite widely in various internet forums and Singapore Anglophone literature, whose contributors tend to have been educated at elite English-medium schools and universities (Goh, 2009). Nevertheless, it is important not to lose sight of the fact that speakers who confidently manipulate linguistic resources to perform (Bauman and Briggs, 1990) Singlish are socio-linguistically distinct from those who speak what might be categorized as ungrammatical English because they lack the ability to do otherwise.

Singlish Ghettoizes Its Users

The third claim exploits the fear of ghettoization by suggesting that the use of Singlish limits the socio-economic mobility of its speakers. Thus, Goh Chok Tong asserted the following in his 1999 National Day Rally speech:

We cannot be a first-world economy or go global with Singlish ... The fact that we use English gives us a big advantage over our competitors. If we carry on using Singlish, the logical final outcome is that we, too, will develop our own type of pidgin English, spoken only by 3m Singaporeans, which the rest of the world will find quaint but incomprehensible. We are already half way there. Do we want to go all the way?

As I have pointed out elsewhere (Wee, 2013), this claim is problematic if we consider the culture industries, such as the Singapore film industry (see Chapter 6 for further discussion). The domestic and international success of Singaporean films is no small part due to their significant use of officially stigmatized languages, such as Singlish and Chinese dialects other than Mandarin. This allows the films to more authentically reflect the speech patterns of their characters. A good example is *Singapore Dreaming* (2006), by Colin Goh and

Woo Yen Yen, which focuses on a Singaporean working-class family as its members aspire towards a better life. It was the first Singaporean film to win the Montblanc New Screenwriters Award at the 54th San Sebastian International Film Festival; it also won the Best Asian/Middle-Eastern Film Award at the 20th Tokyo International Film Festival. Somewhat ironically, the promotional trailer for *Singapore Dreaming* was banned from local free-to-air television by the government due to what was deemed its excessive use of Singlish and Chinese dialects. What this suggests is that the decisions of international audiences and film festival organizers to recognize Singaporean films (and possibly other cultural goods) are beyond government regulation. Consequently, a persistently anti-Singlish stance from the government would only look foolish should more such international recognition be forthcoming.

Rebuttals from the SGSM

These three claims from the government have been countered by the SGSM at length in an interview with *The Online Citizen* (2010). Relevant extracts from the interview are reproduced in the following sections.

Rebutting the Interference Argument

The SGSM takes issue with the interference claim, pointing out that it is contradicted by the government's own policy of 'institutional bilingualism':

What underlies this state hysteria over Singlish is a strange belief that most Singaporeans can speak just one language. So, if they stay with Singlish, they won't get better in English, and our investors will shun us, the economy will suffer, and we will become a fishing village again . . . to hold to the 'one language only' idea seems pretty bizarre, especially when it is coming from the same guys who brought us institutional bilingualism in Singapore.

As discussed in Chapter 1, under Singapore's bilingual policy, all Singaporeans are expected to learn both English and an officially assigned ethnic mother tongue: Chinese Singaporeans are expected to know English and Mandarin, Malay Singaporeans to know English and Malay, and Indian Singaporeans to know English and Tamil. This bilingual policy is not without problems of its own (Pakir, 1992; 2000; Siddique, 1997; Stroud and Wee, 2007), but the key point, as far as the SGSM is concerned, is its lack of internal consistency. If the government is encouraging Singaporeans to be bilingual in English and an official mother tongue[6], then it must either not be too concerned about

---

[6] Even given the government's recently revised belief that equal proficiency in both English and the mother tongue is something that can be expected of only a small elite segment of the population, the SGSM's point about non-interference still holds. This is because the government still expects that there will not be any mixing between English and the mother tongue, regardless of the proficiency level of the speaker.

interference between these two languages or it must be confident that any inter-ference effects can be handled. In either case, there is no clear rationale for why this willingness to accommodate English and the mother tongue cannot also be extended to Standard English and Singlish.

Rebutting the Extended Use of the 'Singlish' Label to Include Ungrammatical English

The SGSM also points out that there is a problem with the government's incautious use of the label 'Singlish': 'We kept hearing all these non-Singlish phrases thrown about by powerful people as examples of both bad English and Singlish. The gahmen[7] doesn't seem to have a clue to what the difference is, and it really doesn't care. It seems more than happy to throw the baby out with the bathwater.'

According to the SGSM, the failure to distinguish between colloquial and ungrammatical English stems from ignorance about and lack of sensitivity to the nuances of language use. The SGSM attributes this ignorance to the fact that there are no individuals with language expertise (such as linguists, writers, novelists or poets) in the 'gahmen'. This leads to a situation where the merits of Singlish (such as providing a 'sense of community'; see the later discussion) are being discarded in the course of the government's overenthusiastic but ill-informed attempts to improve the standard of English in Singapore. Thus, the SGSM argues that there is a groundswell of support for Singlish, making any attempt to eradicate it unlikely to be successful: 'Anyone who knows enough Singlish has been learning on our page that he or she isn't alone in sensing its importance. If we have lost much of our sense of community through missing historical landmarks and an ever-changing skyline, we have preserved a bit of this in Singlish. Bulldozing Singlish will be this gahmen's greatest challenge yet.'

Rebutting the Ghettoization Claim

The SGSM also targets the ghettoization claim by accusing the government of playing up 'popular stereotypes' in its attempt to demonize the use of Singlish:

We are also fed up with the depiction of Singlish speakers as crass, poorly educated, and unintelligent. This issue is a bit more complex as it is aided by popular stereotypes in every major ethnic group in Singapore. So the Ah Bengs, Ah Lians, Mats, Minahs, Muthus,[8] etc. are supposed to be experts in Singlish. But the gahmen turns this into a cautionary tale as well. If you don't speak proper English and persist with Singlish, you

---

[7] 'Gahmen' is Singlish for 'government'.

[8] These are colloquial and politically incorrect terms for, respectively, Chinese males, Chinese females, Malay males, Malay females and Indians. The stereotypes evoked by these terms not only carry ethnic and gender markers but are also usually understood to be uneducated and uncouth.

will have no future and everyone will laugh at you, everyone from your neighbour to Barack Obama.

Instead, the SGSM points that Singlish is spoken by professionals and other successful individuals, who are capable of switching between Singlish and standard English, as and when the situation demands it, or to frame particular interactions as humorous:

The reality itself is very different since Singlish is spoken by many Singaporean professionals too. These people are not stupid, unsuccessful, or tragic figures; they know well how, when, and where to use standard English, and when and where using Singlish is more appropriate. Singlish is often used at home and at play, with family – especially aged parents – and with friends, and to inject humour into stuffy or pointless discourses.

The Importance of Linguistic Chutzpah

Gupta (2010: 76, 86) suggests that the SGEM's efforts appear to have had a harmful effect: it has fostered a culture of insecurity about English-language competence 'rather than empowering people to extend and develop their English', with its focus on 'correctness . . . damaging to insecure users of English'. Gupta's point is certainly supported by SGEM's attempt to encourage Singaporeans to go around correcting instances of 'bad English'. More recently, in its 2017 booklet on *Grammar Rules*, the SGEM included a section on grammar gaffes, introduced with the following remarks and examples (2017: 93–95):

A gaffe is an embarrassing mistake people make in public.
This compilation of corrections to common grammar gaffes may
save you from unintended awkward moments.

> Gaffe: I am staying in Jurong.
> Correct: I live in Jurong.
> Gaffe: Divide the chocolates among the two of you.
> Correct: Divide the chocolates between the two of you.

Some of these 'gaffes' are commonly associated with Singlish, as in the use of 'stay' for 'live'. Others, such as the use of 'Divide . . . among' rather 'Divide . . . between', seem unnecessarily pedantic, especially when ordinary Singaporeans vacillate between the two, as well as the reasons for deciding when to use what. This means that (i) we might well be looking at a language change in progress, and (ii) it is not at all clear that using 'among' will indeed result in an 'awkward moment' (https://forum.wordreference. com/threads/divide-between-or-among.1496173; accessed 1 May 2017; http:// blog.oxforddictionaries.com/2015/06/grammar-myths-among-or-between;

accessed 1 May 2017; www.quickanddirtytips.com/education/grammar/ between-versus-among; accessed 1 May 2017).

However, the way in which the SGEM presents these examples – that they are 'embarrassing' and that avoiding theses 'gaffes' will 'save you from unintended awkward moments' – merely serves to strengthen Gupta's point about linguistic insecurity. Given these circumstances, the SGSM's display of linguistic chutz-pah represents a strong rejection of any fostering of anxieties about language use, especially where these emanate from the SGEM.

But are there situations where at least some such chutzpah might stand or might have stood the relevant social actors in good stead? In this section, I consider two examples in which the absence of linguistic chutzpah leads to anxiety about language use. Such anxieties stem from insecurities about how to deal with language choices, which are exacerbated by the assumption that there must always be a single correct answer to questions about language use (cf. Gupta, 2010: 82, 84).

Woodleigh: [Wudleɪ] or [Wudliː]?

Around the middle of 2011, just before the official opening of the new Woodleigh train station in Singapore's mass rapid transit system, I received a phone call from someone working for the Land Transport Authority (LTA). The caller was worried because it had just occurred to the government agency that, at the official opening, the guest of honor (usually a government official) was going to have to pronounce the name of the station, and there was some uncertainty about how it should actually be pronounced.

The LTA was aware that Singaporeans might variously pronounce 'Woodleigh' as [wudleɪ] or [wudliː], in fact, Deterding (2011) indicates that a former student of his wrote to him asking for advice about this very same issue. The presence of variant pronunciations meant that the LTA was unable to rely on the speech community (which, in this case, it construed as Singaporean society at large) as the proper authority. Clearly, in the course of its internal discussions about what to name the station, there must have been actual con-versations in which the name was pronounced, perhaps even with variations. But the pronunciation was apparently not an issue then. Or at least it was not an issue that created anxiety until the official opening was imminent, probably because of the very public nature of the event.

The name had apparently been chosen for its historical connection to a British colonial figure. But history does not provide a good guide to 'correct' pronunciation: the LTA was aware that, however the name might have been pronounced by the British, it was now no longer referring to a historical figure (although he provided the inspiration), but to a modern train station in Singa-pore. The LTA was therefore sensitive to the fact that the traditional British pronunciation for Woodleigh might not be suited to contemporary Singapore. The LTA's uncertainty over how to pronounce the name may have been heightened by the fact that Singapore has an arts and entertainment centre called the Esplanade, whose name has been varyingly pronounced as [espl∂neɪd] and [espl∂nad]. This awareness of variation in the pronunciation of 'Esplanade' may have contributed to the uncertainty about how to pronounce 'Woodleigh'. However, as the agency officially in charge of station names, the LTA may have felt obligated to provide a definitive pronunciation, rather than allow for variation. Because neither the Singaporean speech community nor British tradition was helpful, the LTA was in a quandary.

The caller from the LTA therefore was hoping that a linguist would be able to provide the needed authoritative backing as to which version was correct. And while I was sympathetic, I refused to categorically prescribe a correct pronunciation on the grounds that this was something that should be decided by the most frequent users of the train station, including those residing around the area (see the later discussion). Deterding (2011), too, makes a similar suggestion when he says that 'Singaporeans should decide. Or maybe there could be two different pronunciations, both of which are equally correct'.

'Double Confirm'

Another example of anxiety about language use comes from the MediaCorp game show *We Are Singaporeans* that aired in 2011. In this game show, contestants have to answer questions about Singaporean culture, trivia and history. In its first season, the show had a catchphrase 'double confirm'. The host of the show, Hossan Leong, used the phrase to get contestants to lock in or commit to their answers to the various questions posed. That is, when contestants first offered an answer, Leong would ask them, 'Confirm?' If the contestants were confident that their answer was indeed correct, Leong would then ask, 'Double confirm?' as a means of getting them to commit to the answer.

In January 2012, I received this email from a MediaCorp research writer working on the show:

I'm writing on behalf of my team from MediaCorp Channel 5's gameshow 'We Are Singaporeans'. As we're moving to our 2nd season, we're refining elements in our 1st season and need some help with something which we're debating about internally. In the 1st season, our host used the phrase 'Double Confirm' for our contestants to lock in their answers. However, we've been getting comments that that's not grammatically correct. Thus I was wondering if you could help verify whether 'Double Confirm' is indeed ungrammatical and whether there is any issue with our host using the phrase.

Thank you.

Apparently, there had been complaints that the phrase 'double confirm' was 'bad English'. In my response to MediaCorp, I pointed out that 'double confirm' could be considered grammatical if we were talking about the grammar of Singlish, and in a show about Singaporean culture, there was absolutely no reason why a Singlish catchphrase should not be considered appropriate. Nevertheless, MediaCorp's unease with the Singlish nature of 'double confirm' led it to change the catchphrase in the second season to 'confirm confirm'. However, this other phrase, too, has been subjected to complaints from viewers on the grounds that it, too, is ungrammatical and possibly even more Singlish in nature than its predecessor (Kok, 2012).

In the 'Woodleigh' and 'double confirm' cases, we see that speakers were faced with a uncertainty about correct pronunciation or the grammaticality of a particular phrase, respectively. In neither case were speakers able to rely on traditional sources of authority, because these sources provided either no clear guidance or conflicting information. For example, in the 'Woodleigh' case, community norms were not useful because of variation within the speech community of Singaporeans. In the 'double confirm' case, prescriptive/pedagogical grammars were not decisive since what was operative here was a desire to come up with a creative catchphrase. Although there was an attempt to extrapolate from traditional rules of grammar, there was no objective litmus test that distinguished linguistic creativity from error. And as subsequent responses from Singaporeans have demonstrated, neither 'double confirm' nor 'confirm confirm' is without controversy ('"Double confirm" more catchy than "confirm confirm"', posted by gdy2shoez, 21 August 2012, Everything also complain.com, https://everythingalsocomplain.com/2012/08/21/double-confirm-more-catchy-than-confirm-confirm/; accessed 18 December 2016).

The anxiety about language choices in both these cases arises because the actors are involved in high-performance events. Coupland (2007) suggests that performances can be located on a performance continuum from mundane to high. High-performance events tend to have the following characteristics (Coupland, 2007: 148, citing Bauman, 1992: 46ff):

They are scheduled events, typically pre-announced and planned, and therefore programmed. They are temporarily and spatially bounded events, marked off from the routine flow of communicative practice. They are co-ordinated, in the sense that they rely on specific sorts of collaborative activity, not least in that performers and audience members will establish themselves in these participant roles for the enactment of the performance. High performances are typically also public events, in that membership of the audience will not be especially exclusive. Even if it is exclusive, audience members are positioned as parts of a more general social collectivity.

The closer communicative events are to the high end of the performance continuum, the more they are open to judgement and evaluation from the audience, not least because speakers' competence is on display and they are expected to have had the opportunity to prepare for the events by carefully considering their language choices. Thus, the 'Woodleigh' case became of particular concern when the public opening of the station was imminent. The same can be said of the 'double confirm' case when members of the public complained and the producers of the game show had to start thinking about whether to retain the catchphrase for the second season.

The anxiety associated with these three factors – uncertainty, an inability to rely on traditional sources of authority, and high performance – is perhaps even more understandable when we recall that in Singapore, there is strong public awareness of arguments about the legitimacy of Singlish, heightened by the government's Speak Good English Movement – which attempts to contrast 'proper/good/standard' English with 'broken/bad' English, often using Singlish as a bogeyman.

Under such circumstances, possession of linguistic chutzpah would have served well the speakers representing both the LTA and MediaCorp. For example, the LTA personnel could have conducted a simple survey of how the residents living around the train station – a more localized speech community – tended to pronounce 'Woodleigh'. It could then have adopted the most commonly used version as its 'official' pronunciation on the grounds that it reflected the linguistic norms of the local community. Regardless of whether the writers at Medicorp stuck with 'double confirm' or switched to 'confirm confirm', they could have publicly explained the rationale behind the decision to use a Singlish catchphrase, given that the game show is about Singaporean culture. In what might be considered a truly ironic development, Singaporeans who use the Singapore Personal Access (SingPass), an electronic gateway for government e-services, are now asked by the system to 'double confirm' their personal information. In both these cases, then, the important point to keep in mind is that the actual language choices are ultimately less important than having the confidence and ability to defend the choice, especially given that there is likely to be criticism no matter what choice is made.

Conclusion

In her discussion of verbal hygiene, Cameron (1995: ix–x, italics in original) notes,

There exists a whole popular culture of language, in which many people participate to some degree. Some are occasional and fairly passive consumers, a few are fanatical crusaders, and there is a continuum of interest and commitment between these two extremes. What is clear, however, is that a great many people care deeply about linguistic matters; they do not merely speak their language, they also speak copiously and passionately about it ... The linguistic questions laypeople care most about are questions of right and wrong, good and bad, 'the use and abuse of language'. In fact, it would not be overstating the case to say that most everyday discourse on language is above all evaluative discourse.

The issue of verbal hygiene becomes even more problematic in the case of English because the global spread of the language has led, perhaps more so than with any other language, to the emergence of multiple varieties. The existence of these varieties, in turn, has raised questions about their legitimacy and anxieties about what might be considered proper usage.

This is especially the case with an outer circle country like Singapore – that is, a former British or American colony where the past use of English in government institutions continues to exert in various ways its influence on contemporary normative assumptions about what constitutes proper or good English – which is caught between the pulls of exonormativity and endonormativity (Kachru, 1985). Many Singaporeans are ambivalent about their competence in English, since claims about English-language competence have to consistently weighed against the desires to develop local norms, on the one hand, and to adhere to more dominant, global 'standard' varieties, on the other (Park and Wee, 2012: 74; Schneider, 2007: 160). But this dichotomy between exonormativity and endonormativity oversimplifies the complexity of language choices that users have to negotiate. For example, we saw that speakers in Singapore have to be cognizant that their use of English might be variously judged as ungrammatical, as being too Singlish or even as being not Singlish enough. It is not an exaggeration, then, to suggest, following Cameron, that Singapore society is characterized by 'evaluative discourses' about the 'use and abuse of [the English] language', and such evaluations do not always neatly follow the exonormative-endonormative distinction. Dealing with such evaluative discourses becomes particularly challenging when community norms change rapidly, traditional grammars provide little guidance, and both the general public and the government are quick to interject with their own views on what is right and wrong, good and bad about English/Singlish.

English-language use is particularly challenged in late modernity, when rather than simply responding to or accepting associations between language and socio-cultural values, speakers are also trying to forge or actively shape such indexical associations for localized interactional purposes. Such reflexive awareness of 'the cultural images of people and activities conjured by particular forms of speech' leads to a greater emphasis on the 'artful use of speech in expressive performance' (Rampton, 2006: 16). And, as I have argued, if speakers are not to surrender to anxieties about how such performances might be received, it will be helpful if they have linguistic chutzpah.

4   Voice: Who Speaks about Singlish?

The issue of voice is a complex one since being able to speak does not necessarily mean also being heard. Both the ability to speak and the ability to be heard are highly dependent on the roles of the speakers and the listeners. Some roles have the force of institutional backing, so that the speaker, such as a magistrate, has the judicial ability to enforce views that others cannot easily ignore (see Chapter 2). Other speakers may be considered as not having anything that is worth listening to, perhaps on the basis of their gender (see the later discussion).

In all these cases, language comes into play because it is not simply the medium for communicating. It can also serve to adjudicate on whether or not someone should even be considered a speaker in the *contextually relevant sense of the term* (given that what counts as the relevant role can involve factors such as ethnicity, gender, educational or professional qualifications, and social status). Blommaert (2005: 71, italics in original) makes this point when he observes that '*differences* in the use of language are quickly, and quite systematically, translated into *inequalities* between speakers'.

There are then categories of speakers that are indexed to differences in language use and other factors. In some categories speakers may be dismissed *en masse* simply by virtue of their category membership as not having the capacity to speak at all or as not worth listening to, which is effectively the same thing. Consider, for example, Ong's (2006) observation that in Malaysia, feminists like the Sisters of Islam, who oppose the monopoly that ulamas (traditionally male Islamic scholars and officials) have over Islamic ethics,

must first legitimize their claims as rational and therefore equal moral partners (sisters) in the interpretation of Islamic texts. The first of feminists' struggles with ulamas is over women's intellectual and moral capacity to interpret Islam for themselves, instead of relying solely on ulamas' interpretations. This assertion of women's intellectual role in Islam is part of Muslim feminists' worldwide strategy to increase higher education for girls...

By arguing that ulamas' claims are not divine revelations but man-made interpretations (however authoritative), feminists have opened a space for women's voices in debates about religious truths. (Ong, 2006: 42–43)

What is at stake in this case is the discursive right to legitimately propose alternative interpretations of religious texts (Wee, 2011). The exclusion of women on the basis of their gender and the concomitant status of men as the sole legitimate interpreters of Islam stem from the belief that men are by nature inherently more rational than women, who are characterized as being more passionate and out of control. As Ong (2004: 39) points out, 'tapping into these beliefs, ulamas use masculine speech, representing rationality, to typecast female thinking and practice as unruly, unreliable, and irrational, thus unsuitable for both understanding Islamic texts and for claiming gender rights'. Yet other categories are deemed 'speak-worthy' or at the very least, not dismissible outright. Therefore it is within such categories that certain individuals, depending perhaps on the force of their personalities or the specific nature of their contributions, might then stand out as being particularly worth listening to. The role of academics in influencing policy, arguably, belongs in this category. As we saw in the preceding chapter, some academics are considered more relevant than others depending on whether their views and inputs cohere with or at least are not seen as challenging those of the Singapore government.

The general importance of voice cannot be overstated: in some cases, the desire for voice and the sense that the speaker's concerns are not being heard may even result in the use of extreme communicative acts such as chopping off one's own finger, self-immolation and hunger strikes (Wee, 2004; 2007). Extreme communicative acts are typically employed – in conjunction with verbal expressions – as forms of political protest against institutional authority. The verbal expressions carry the propositional content of the protests (that is, what the self-immolators and hunger strikers are protesting), while the acts of self-immolation and hunger strikes are part of the illocutionary force: non-linguistic forms of communication that serve to boost the force of the protests (cf. Holmes, 1984; Sbisà, 2001). Of course, no one has yet embarked on a hunger strike to protest against or to support the use of Singlish. Nevertheless, as a very public and highly contested language ideological debate, the various participating parties have expressed, with differing degrees of certainty and vociferousness, their particular views regarding the legitimacy and desirability of Singlish.

This is why the issue of voice occupies a position of particular importance in the Singlish controversy. By taking stock of the participating parties, we are able to highlight an omission that is, if not curious, at the very least certainly significant: the absence of the group of individuals characterized as uneducated monolingual speakers of Singlish; that is, individuals who are assumed to be unable to code-switch between Singlish and Standard English and who are instead restricted to only the former. These individuals are often presented as being in greatest need of help with their English. But because their voices are absent from the Singlish controversy, it is others – the Singapore government, better educated Singaporeans who are competent in Standard English – who speak on their behalf. Exactly why is this so and what are its effects on the contours and substance of the Singlish controversy occupy us in the latter part of the chapter.

What we need first is a framework for discussing voice that allows us to capture the different ways in which different groups have voice (with complete exclusion as a limiting case), as well as the kinds of resources that they might utilize (linguistic as well as non-linguistic). This is what I propose to do in the next section.

I organize this chapter into four major sections. The next section outlines a framework for talking about voice. The two sections following that provide an inventory of the various participants in the Singlish controversy, using the framework already outlined to analyze the roles of those participating as well as those who are absent. The final section then details the effects that the voices present as well as those absent have on the trajectory of the Singlish controversy.

Voice: Indexical Orders, Pretextual Gaps and the Subaltern

Blommaert (2005) offers a comprehensive conceptual treatment of voice, anchored by these two key points:

(i) Orders of indexicality: Differences in language use may index differences in speaker identity, and some of these differences may lead to inequalities in voice. But the differences in language use are not randomly distributed; they tend to cluster with various other social and cultural features. This is why voice is not just a linguistic issue. Other non-linguistic attributes are also at play, and it is the cluster of attributes that forms ordered indexicalites 'in which some kinds of indexicalities are ranked higher than others: they suggest prestige versus stigma; rationality versus emotion; membership of a particular group versus non-membership, and so forth' and these rankings of indexicalities 'enable judgements, inclusion and exclusion, positive or negative sanctioning, and so forth' (74).

(ii) Pretextual gaps: Because these ordered indexicalities are ranked and allow for judgements of various sorts, as noted earlier, individuals are always marked by the indexicalities that they carry with them. As also noted, not all the features are linguistic; some may be ethnic or gendered. Consequently, 'people enter communication events with pretextually marked resources and capabilities: resources and capabilities that have a particular "load", a value in terms of the orders of indexicality in which they move into. Such pretextualities will condition what they can accomplish. Whenever the resources people possess do not match the functions they are supposed to accomplish, they risk being attributed *other* functions than the ones pro-jected, intended, or necessary. Their resources fail to fulfill the required functions; speakers lose voice' (77; emphasis in original).

Taken together, (i) and (ii) suggest that, to understand the possibilities for voice, it is necessary to look both at the orders of indexicalities that prevail vis-à-vis a given communication event and the kinds of pretextual resources that actors bring with them to the event. For example, in the case of the Sisters of Islam discussed earlier, attributes such as being female and emotional are, individ-ually as well as collectively, ranked lower than other attributes such as being male and rational. These rankings are well established and indeed entrenched in this particular religious context so that the social and cultural obstacles that the Sisters have to overcome to be given a seat at the discursive table, so to speak, are formidable. In contrast to the situation faced by the Sisters of Islam, the relationship between, say, academics and government policymakers does not involve any clearly established rankings regarding prestige, rationality, and the like. Government policymakers occasionally consult academics given the lat-ter's domain expertise. Nevertheless, policymakers usually face different con-straints than academics, and consequently, while academic input may be useful, it is far from being the main determinant in policy formulation.[1] Under such cir-cumstances, the issue of voice can be described as being more equivocal in that academics may sometimes be dismissed as an entire category of ivory tower thinkers while at other times, they may be considered to provide valuable and useful insights.

The case of the Sisters of Islam, where there are clear indexical rankings that disqualify a particular group from having voice, comes close to exemplifying what Spivak (1988; 1999) has described as the subaltern. Spivak first developed her ideas regarding the subaltern in relation to the ways in which knowledge is constructed. The effects of colonialism, Spivak observes, are such that West-ern ways of knowing and reasoning – including, therefore, the use of colonial languages – become constructed as legitimized knowledge, whereas the lan-guages and knowledge of the oppressed subaltern are recast as lore or myth. Under these conditions, the subaltern represents the limiting case of voiceless-ness. The subaltern can never directly speak because he or she is considered to have nothing worthy to contribute by way of knowledge construction. Others – better educated and Westernized – assume the privilege and responsibility to speak on the subaltern's behalf. Possibly the only way in which the subaltern can ever hope to speak is by trying to adopt or conform to the forms of language and ways of knowing established by the West. He or she must therefore resort to mimesis to be heard. But this begs the question of whether the subaltern has

---

[1] See, for example, the discussion in Chapter 3 on joint problematization.

voice in any meaningful sense if the only way in which he or she can bridge the pretextual gap is to abandon indigenous ways of speaking and thinking and instead assume the communicative conventions of the West.

It is important, however, to be careful not to overuse the term 'subaltern' as a shorthand for anyone who feels aggrieved or who claims to be oppressed simply because he or she feels unheard or that his or her views are not respected. As Spivak (quoted in de Kock, 1992, italics added) emphasizes,

Everybody thinks the subaltern is just a classy word for oppressed, for Other, for some-body who's not getting a piece of the pie. The subalternist historians take it from Gramsci and change it. They define it as the people, the foreign elite, the indigenous elite, the upwardly mobile indigenes, in various kinds of situations: everything that has limited or no access to the cultural imperialism is subaltern – a space of difference. Now, who would say that's just the oppressed? The working class is oppressed. It's not subaltern... When you say cannot speak, it means that if speaking involves speaking and listening, this possibility of response, responsibility, does not exist in the subaltern's sphere.

Some academics and other experts may indeed feel aggrieved that their views are given short shrift by policymakers. But they are, as Spivak puts it, 'within the hegemonic discourse' and should not be considered subaltern. The subaltern that Spivak has in mind, in contrast, is not so much denied the opportunity to speak as considered not capable of speaking in the first place, the strategy of mimesis notwithstanding.

While differences in orders of indexicality account for the pretextual gaps that some speakers might encounter, we need to be cognizant of the various strategies that they may use to close (as far as possible) the gap. Of course, this desire to close the pre-textual gap need not always be present: some speakers may not be aware of such a gap, or they may feel that it is a legitimate one. But where speakers are concerned that the pretextual gap unfairly deprives them of the opportunity to be heard, they may use a number of strategies.

If the linguistic or other resources that speakers possess are considered inadequate to enable them to be heard, then one option is to try to acquire more valued and voice-relevant resources. For example, if a variety such as Standard English or a genre such as academic discourse is the established and preferred mode of communication, then speakers might try to become competent in that more valued variety or genre. Such a strategy, especially in the case of the Singapore's government's exonormative preference for British (and possibly American) Standard English, is open to the charge of encouraging a form of mimesis, in which mimics – speakers from what Kachru calls the outer and expanding circles of World Englishes – automatically place themselves in the disadvantaged position of non-native speakers by forever trying to emulate their native-speaking counterparts. This strategy of mimesis inherently puts native speakers in an inferior position because, as mimics, their competence can at best only ever be seen as an approximation of the native speaker's competence, given the powerful influence of native speakerism (Holliday, 2005). The strategy of mimesis condemns non-native speakers to the role of playing linguistic catch-up in a world where the language and therefore notions of competence are rapidly changing (see Chapter 3). In a sense, the Sisters of Islam are also engaged in a strategy of mimesis, in this case, mimesis of affect rather than that of language. Precisely because their ability to be considered rational (given their gender) is in question, an important part of their strategy for claiming the right to offer their own textual interpretations involves cultivating 'an ascetic self-representation... to appear cool, reasonable, and morally above reproach in order to be effective in issuing rebuttals and in negotiating for (morally acceptable) gender rights... women's desires must be channeled away from pleasures that men can brand and damn as passionate and disruptive' (Ong, 2006: 46–47). The Sisters' public performances of rationality and reasonableness are measured against established masculine benchmarks.

Other strategies for being heard might take the form of protest movements, such as the Occupy Movement, which started in New York City in 2011 and was motivated by the belief that politics was being corrupted by the rich and was resulting in the exploitation of the poor (Castells, 2012: 161). The Occupy Movement, itself inspired by the Arab Spring Movement (Milkman, Luce and Lewis, 2013: 2), quickly spread to other cities such as Chicago, Boston, and even Hong Kong (Juris, 2012). Extreme communicative acts are also attempts to bridge the pretextual gap, drawing attention simultaneously not just to the speakers' political message but also to their powerlessness and frustration in effecting change. Protest movements and extreme communicative acts constitute extra-institutional strategies for being heard. They are a final resort of those who feel that intra-institutional avenues for conveying grievances have either been closed or are simply not sufficiently effective.

Notice that as we move from mimesis to protest movements and extreme communicative acts, we are moving from strategies that are less tied to the specific social and cultural factors that are being contested to ones that are more universal. That is, whereas mimetic attempts to acquire Standard English or display rationality are motivated by the fact that the pretextual gap concerns a specific linguistic variety or a particular emotional outlook, embarking on a protest or engaging in acts of self-immolation is no longer necessarily directly connected with any specific pretextual gap. Instead, those actions have a more universal application that not only draws attention to a particular grievance but also highlights the increasing frustration of the actors.

In the context of the Singlish controversy, the monolectal Singlish speaker – the speaker whose English repertoire is publicly characterized as being limited only to Singlish (in the sense of 'broken English') and who therefore lacks the facility to switch between Singlish and Standard English – has the status of a subaltern. Despite being implicated in the controversy, this is the figure that need not and is not expected to directly speak to the issues that have been raised by the presence, spread and popularity of Singlish. There is no expectation that such an individual might have the capacity to contribute in any meaningful way to the Singlish controversy. The plight of the subaltern monolectal Singlish speaker, as we now see, is represented only indirectly via anecdotes and stories about his or her presumed linguistic difficulties and travails.

An Inventory of Voices in the Singlish Controversy

Over the course of the preceding chapters, we examined assessments of Singlish made by various government ministers, as well as by various members of the public. Public opinion has been mixed: some Singaporeans are supportive of Singlish, whereas others share the government's concerns. Although ordinary Singaporeans who are concerned about Singlish have made their views known (see Chapter 1), they tend to be less engaged in the Singlish controversy than those who are pro-Singlish. This is because the government already speaks, loudly and clearly, on their behalf.

The usual suspects involved in actively contributing to shaping public discussions about Singlish are the following:

• Government officials, especially ministers
• Media and creative personalities such as DJs, film-makers, authors and bloggers
• Academics

An important characteristic that most of these usual suspects share is that they are highly educated, as shown in the following examples. Soh (2005) conducted an in-depth interview with Koh Tai Ann, a professor of English literature at the Nanyang Technological University and, at the time of the interview, chairman of the Speak Good English Movement. Among the observations offered by Koh in a newspaper article reporting on the interview are the following:

(i) Singaporeans are perhaps too comfortable in their Singlish clothes. Even though T-shirts or housecoats might be improper attire for formal occasions, they still wear the linguistic equivalent when they meet visitors and at such occasions.

(ii) We need to speak an English that is closer to international Standard English. That form could be Singapore Standard English, which at least follows the basic laws of international Standard English in terms of principles, structure and grammar. There may be some acceptable, distinctly local lexical items, like 'five-foot way' just as the British say 'pavement' and the Americans say 'sidewalk' that could be incorporated into everyday speech.

Using the metaphor of different varieties of English as different kinds of cloth-ing, Koh expresses concern that Singaporeans may not know when to use Singlish and when not to, and she calls for a more standard variety of Singapore English. But some years later, in 2011, in yet another interview featured in a newspaper (Lee, 2011), Koh offers a more sympathetic view of Singlish where she disputes the view that it is 'broken' or 'deviant' and argues that there is no shame in using it:

 (i) Linguists and native users will know, for instance, that the usage of *lah, leh, hor, meh* in Singlish is not random.
 (ii) Singlish should not be regarded as deviant and not 'proper' English, but as a spoken variety that has developed alongside the standard 'proper' English learnt in schools. Otherwise, we do ourselves a disservice by giv-ing Singlish an odour of inferiority and shame.

The website of Lee Kin Mun, better known as Mr Brown, a self-described 'blogfather of Singapore, satirist, writer, lyricist, traveler, photographer and singer of silly songs', has also offered commentary on Singlish. In a post dated 12 November 2013, Mr Brown tells us that his 'old school chum, Colin Goh, was in town for Singapore Writers Festival':

Then Colin messaged me and asked me 'Eh! Want to come to my spur-of-the-moment Singlish salon at Jing Hua Restaurant at Qun Zhong Eating House on Monday at 7pm?
    Wah, Singlish Literary Salon leh! In a noisy dumpling restaurant leh! With many cool and fun artistic peoples leh! And can talk cock sing song in Singlish! (www.mrbrown .com/blog/2013/11/inaugural-and-random-singlish-literary-salon-2013.html; accessed 23 May 2016)

Mr Brown's blog post references his school friend Colin Goh (a film-maker and co-author of the *Coxford Singlish Dictionary*) and a gathering of 'artistic peoples' at a Singlish salon. This highlights the interdiscursivity of Singlish amongst what might be described as the 'Singlitterati', a relatively closed circle of well-educated creative and artistic individuals who enjoy playing around with Singlish words and phrases and are keen to promote Singlish.

More recently, as a follow-up to the *Oxford English Dictionary*'s (OED) deci-sion to officially recognize a number of Singlish terms (see Chapter 1), a local newspaper *The Sunday Times* ran an article (Chan, 2016) suggesting that this 'recent development is seen as an acknowledgement that Singlish is a deeply ingrained part of local culture'. The article included comments from the fol-lowing individuals:

 • Gwee Li Sui, a poet and literary critic who also used to be a professor in the Department of English Language and Literature at the National University of Singapore
 • Sylvia Toh, author of humorous books that use Singlish and a former news-paper columnist
 • A schoolteacher (who declined to be named)

- Tan May Yik, an account manager
- Goh Eck Kheng, Koh Tai Ann's successor as chairman of the Speak Good English Movement
- Addul Alim Iskandar Dzulkhari Kajai, a student
- Desiree Orien Tay, a student
- Colin Goh and Woo Yen Yen, film-makers and authors of the *Coxford Singlish Dictionary* (see Chapter 6 for further discussion)

Perhaps unsurprisingly, the overall tone of the article is fairly light-hearted. Some of those interviewed were asked what other entries they would like to suggest for inclusion in the OED, for example. Nevertheless, more substantive points were also made as indicated by the following comments. Except for the last comment, which is from Goh Eck Kheng (Koh Tai Ann's successor as chairman of the SGEM) and essentially reiterates the government's position, the other three comments make clear that, while the acknowledgement of Singlish from Singapore's former colonial rulers is appreciated, it is nevertheless a development that should not be given undue significance.

SYLVIA TOH: Speaking as a Singaporean, you've got to be happy and take a sense of pride as it counts as acknowledgement that Singlish is important to, and part of, our national identity. Ironically, a former colonial master is recognizing this, while our own government campaigns fought to rid it.

COLIN GOH: Its mish-mash of various languages and dialects, often involving bad transliterations, is very, very funny. Contrary to popular belief, Singlish is not merely badly spoken English, akin to pidgin. There is a conscious art in Singlish – a level of ingenious and humorous wordplay that is equalled only perhaps by Cockney rhyming slang...

We don't need its [OED] validation, though it's quite nice, lah. Thank you, hor.

GWEE LI SUI: It's like saying French words in the OED validate French or an international report on Afrikaans validates it. Enough of the colonial mindset. The fact that Singlish continues to thrive against all odds is its own validation.

GOH ECK KHENG: Not everyone who speaks Singlish can also speak English. There are those who think Singlish is English. Others habitually use ungrammatical, fractured English.

In addition, the article also featured Dr Danica Salazar, the World English editor at the OED, who explained the reasoning behind the decision to include Singlish terms. Salazar pointed out that a word 'gets into the OED because people use it' and she cited the *Coxford Singlish Dictionary* and a local play, Michael Chiang's *Army Daze* (1985), as sources that helped validate specific lexical entries. Interestingly, Salazar also worked with a law professor, Jack Lee, from the Singapore Management University, who created www.singlishdictionary.com.

Salazar's references to those cultural influences are particularly significant as regards the issue of voice. The *Coxford Singlish Dictionary* is a tongue-in-cheek compilation of Singlish terms and *Army Daze* is a humorous play about life in National Service, the mandatory military service for Singaporean males. What we have then is a re-semioticization of Singlish terms whose trajectories include a move from their originally light-hearted and creative origins uses to the more institutionalized and established site of the OED. There is absolutely nothing wrong with this path, of course. Nevertheless, the reason why it is worth noting is that it demonstrates quite clearly that what ultimately comes to be culturally accepted and understood as 'Singlish' – both by Singaporeans and non-Singaporeans – is very much shaped by a specific segment of Singaporean society, one that is highly educated, eloquent and comfortable with Standard English.

Consider the contributions of Gwee Li Sui, one of the interviewees for the article quoted earlier. Gwee has a weekly column that appears on the website *The Middle Ground* (www.middleground.sg). Gwee's column, titled 'SinGweesh on Wednesday', discusses in detail various Singlish words and phrases, including speculations on their etymologies. This column is written with liberal sprinklings of Singlish and therefore can be assumed to be aimed primarily at fellow Singaporeans. His 4 May 2016 column (www.themiddlegr ound.sg/2016/05/04/singweesh-wednesday-head; accessed 23 May 2016) contrasts the Singlish phrase 'Your head' with its pragmatic British equivalent 'My foot'. And one of his earliest columns, dated 17 June 2015, deals with the Singlish particle 'lah' (www.themiddleground/sg/2015/06/17/singweesh-about-time-lah; accessed 23 May 2016):

So let's get the rules right for the sake of our sanity. 'Lah' is firstly used at the end of a sentence or a main clause – nowhere else. No 'Lah you is so funny' or 'I take lah the bus home'. This isn't French. But you can say 'Dun care him lah, let's go!' . . . Secondly, there's no need to use 'lah' to end every sentence. Once is enough to set the tone.

In addition to his columns directed to fellow Singaporeans, Gwee (2016) recently contributed an op-ed piece on Singlish to the *New York Times*, where the readership is clearly a much more international one. In this op-ed piece, he points out that 'the government's war on Singlish was doomed from the start: Even state institutions and officials have nourished it [Singlish], if inadvertently. The compulsory national service, which brings together male Singaporeans from all walks of life, has only underlined that Singlish is the natural lingua franca of the grunts.'

And just in case there was any doubt that the Singapore government is still strongly against the use and promotion of Singlish, Gwee's op-ed piece provoked a quick response from the government in the form of a rebuttal that was signed by Li Lin Chang, the press secretary to the prime minister. It was also published in the *New York Times*:

Gwee Li Sui's 'Politics and the Singlish Language' (Opinion, May 13) makes light of the government's efforts to promote the mastery of standard English by Singaporeans. But the government has a serious reason for this policy.

Standard English is vital for Singaporeans to earn a living and be understood not just by other Singaporeans but also English speakers everywhere. But English is not the mother tongue of most Singaporeans. For them, mastering the language requires extra effort. Using Singlish will make it harder for Singaporeans to learn and use standard English. Not everyone has a PhD in English Literature like Mr Gwee, who can code-switch effortlessly between Singlish and standard English, and extol the virtues of Singlish in an op-ed written in polished standard English. (www.nytimes.com/2016/05/23/opinion/the-reality-behind-singlish.html?_r=0; accessed 26 May 2016)

As we can see, the government's response in no uncertain terms not only re-asserts its anti-Singlish stance sixteen years after the launch of the Speak Good English Movement but also gives reasons for this stance that has remained essentially unchanged. The distinction between Standard English and Singlish is assumed to be clear and unproblematic; the relationship between the two is constructed as a zero-sum game, where competence in Singlish is claimed to undermine competence in Standard English; Standard English is treated as being valuable for earning a living, whereas Singlish is apparently useless; and educated Singaporeans who champion Singlish are (yet again) presented as being unhelpful to their less fortunate counterparts.

From the perspective of voice, the issue here is not about a pretextual gap; hence, it is not about the government contesting Gwee's right to participate in the debates about Singlish because of any paucity of linguistic resources on his part. In fact, the opposite happens to be the case. The government is claiming that Gwee (and others of his ilk; that is, other educated and pro-Singlish Singaporeans) are overly resourced in being able to 'code-switch effortlessly between Singlish and standard English'. According to the government, their relative abundance in terms of linguistic resources makes it irresponsible of them to adopt a pro-Singlish stance because doing so makes it 'harder for [other] Singaporeans to learn and use standard English'. The government is of course referring to the monolectal Singlish speaker.

The Singlish Subaltern: Already Spoken For

We saw earlier in the chapter that the inventory of voices contributing to the Singlish controversy does not include the monolectal Singlish speaker; indeed, the preceding section ended with the government's reference to those Singaporeans who need Standard English to earn a living but for whom 'mastering the language requires extra effort'. Here are further examples to drive home the point that these Singaporeans are represented only indirectly by either government officials or members of the Singlitterati who profess to speak on their behalf. They may be spoken about and spoken for, but they do not them-selves directly speak. It is for this reason that I refer to them collectively as the 'Singlish subaltern'.

Consider the following references to the Singlish subaltern from the govern-ment. Lee Hsien Loong (then deputy prime minister), in rebutting a supporter of Singlish, Imran Johri, makes reference to the 'many other Singaporeans' who will suffer from such a development (1). Clearly, this line of argument, delivered in 2001, is much the same as the one more recently delivered in 2016 as a response to Gwee (see the preceding section).

(1)   DPM Lee Hsien Loong, speech at the launch of the Speak Good English
        Movement, 5 April 2001 (www.nas.gov.sg/archivesonline/speeches/view-
        html?filename=2001040502.htm; accessed 25 May 2016):
        People like Imran Johri who argue that we should keep Singlish as a badge
        of identity can usually speak and write good English. For them, Singlish is
        something extra. But many other Singaporeans have not learnt standard
        English. Suppose they follow this advice, and learn Singlish instead of
        standard English. Will we then write our own school and university
        textbooks in Singlish? How many technical manuals and international news
        reports are written in Singlish? Will Singlish help you to write a business
        proposal? Will MNCs, banks, or even local companies prefer to hire you, if
        you speak Singlish instead of standard English?

In (2), the Singlish subaltern is represented in the figures of a hawker and a sales person. Lee Boon Yang (then minister for information, communications and the arts) suggests that those Singaporeans who can speak Standard English but who choose to 'lapse into broken, ungrammatical English' when speaking to a hawker or sales person are doing them a disservice. His analogy, that such a practice of accommodation is akin to encouraging 'bad speaking habits' in a child, merely serves to reinforce their subaltern status.

(2)   Minister Lee Boon Yang, speech at the launch of the Speak Good English
        Movement, 2 July 2003 (www.mci.gov.sg/web/corp/press-room/categories/
        speeches/content/speech-by-minister-lee-boon-yang-at-the-launch-of-
        speak-good-english-movement-2003; accessed 25 May 2016):
        It is not uncommon to hear some Singaporeans speak impeccable English
        when they are at work, or with their friends. But when they are speaking to a
        hawker at the hawker center or to a sales person in a shopping mall, they
        lapse into broken, ungrammatical English.
        It would appear that they do this so that people will not think that they are
        arrogant or that they are 'westernized'. This in itself is not a bad attitude. It
        reflects consideration for the other person's feelings.
        However, this practice, despite having a well-meant face saving reason, may
        inadvertently be perpetuating bad English. We should make an effort to
        arrest this trend. We must make speaking good English acceptable at all
        levels. Those who already speak good English should not be shy about doing

so. In the same way you would not speak broken English to a child learning to speak, you would not want to pass on bad speaking habits to those whose command of the English language is not so good. If you can speak good English, please speak out at all times. This way those who do not speak English well can learn from those who do – not the other way around. In fact, I believe that the fastest way to speak good English is to have lots of opportunities to hear good English spoken around us.

The following extract from Lui Tuck Yew's (then minister of state for education) speech (3) describes his encounters with 'residents in the constituency' who 'lamented the standard of their English and expressed sorrowfully a desire to speak better English'. Though the term is not used in this context, there is an implicit reliance on the government's reference to Singlish-speaking 'heartlanders', those humble and less-educated Singaporeans who are not as globally mobile or affluent as their 'cosmopolitan' counterparts who speak Standard English (see Chapter 6),

(3)   Minister of State for Education Lui Tuck Ye, speech at the launch of the Speak Good English Movement, 31 July 2007 (www.nas.gov.sg/archivesonline/speeches/view-html?filename = 20070731972.htm; accessed 25 May 2016):
And I must say that SGEM has been successful. More people than ever before recognize the importance of good English and are making an effort to speak good English; in schools, taxis, buses, supermarkets and other public places. There have been daily enquiries on the rules of the English language on Stomp!, Singapore Press Holdings' online platform. 'English as It is Broken', a column in the Gen Y page of the Sunday Times is so well received that it has been compiled into a book to be launched this evening. But despite making some headway in our efforts, we cannot afford to be complacent. This was brought home to me when on several occasions in my conversations with residents in the constituency this past year, they lamented the standard of their English and expressed sorrowfully a desire to speak better English. I therefore applaud the Workforce Development Agency' s efforts in putting together the Retailer's Guide to Good English as it will help a segment of our workforce improve on their use of the language in their daily transactions.

Extract (4) is from a news report (Lim, 2014), in which Goh Eck Kheng (chairman of the Speak Good English Movement) explains that we need to only 'eavesdrop at coffeeshops or on buses and trains' to 'see that English is not strong'.

(4)   'Speak Good English campaign to focus on common mistakes', 28 May 2014, Mediacorp (www.todayonline.com/singapore/speak-good-english-movement-launches; accessed 25 May 2016):
'If you just eavesdrop at coffeeshops or on buses and trains, you will see that the English is not strong. I have seen many signs with bad grammar too,'

said Mr Goh Eck Kheng, Chairman of the Speak Good English Movement. 'This is because people are not consciously speaking standard English.' Mr Goh said: 'It is not a matter of abolishing Singlish. Some of us tend to code-switch but others do not have the ability to do so. Those who speak well have a responsibility to raise the standard of English, and the way to do that is to create a stronger environment of English.'

These references to particular kinds of jobs (hawker, sales person), people (residents in the constituency) or locations (coffeeshops, buses and trains) evoke stereotypes about humble, working-class and less-educated Singaporeans that are familiar to the general public. The indexical associations between these kinds of personas and 'their' level of English – that is, they are limited in only being able to speak Singlish and not to switch to Standard English– come across as commonsense knowledge that no 'reasonable' person would be seriously expected to question.

Lest I give the impression that it is only the Singapore government that speaks for the Singlish subaltern as part of its attempts to discourage the use of Singlish, I now present a different set of examples. These show that even those who are supportive of, or at least are not against, Singlish also rely on similar stereotypes that help them to evoke and thus speak on behalf of the subaltern. Consider (5), from KF Seetoh, a Singaporean food critic and champion of hawker fare in particular. Seetoh's reference to a 'Singlish-spewing, Chinese-educated, local Ah Pek' is admittedly meant to be tongue in cheek. Nevertheless, the humour plays on existing cultural stereotypes that link Singlish to the working class, in this case, a hawker whose Chinese-educated background implicates a lack of competence in Standard English.

(5)   KF Seetoh in *Huffpost Travel*, 5 July 2014 (www.huffingtonpost.com/kf-
        seetoh/not-so-shiok_b_3204933.html; 26 May 2016):
        Perhaps more, shiok is the thrill of learning How-to-Use-A-Hawker-Centre-
        at-Peak-Hour in Singapore from a Singlish-spewing, Chinese-educated,
        local Ah Pek (old uncle) trying his level best in his brand of English to
        ensure you get your food and seat fast and comfortably.
        'You must wait one. Don't anyhow anyhow buy food then look for seat hor.
        Sure don't have one la. Anden, food cold liao. You see who wan to finis
        already, then bluff bluff lidat wait next to table, smile smile pretend a bit,
        then, chiong in when they leave. Then one fella go chope the table and the
        other buy food la. If you alone only, then put tissue paper pack on chair, like
        the fella there, and people know this one chope already, so you can go buy
        food ... line up long long also no problem one.'

Extract (6) is from the website of the Marina Bay Sands, a high-end casino, live theatre and shopping complex that attracts both local and foreign visitors. The website has a 'Singlish Guide', which is clearly aimed at helping foreign visitors better understand the various kinds of Singlish utterances that they might encounter. As with the previous example, a working-class persona, in this case, a taxi driver rather than a hawker, is presented as the likely source of Singlish utterances.

(6)   'Singlish Guide' by Marina Bay Sands (www.marinabaysands.com/singapore-visitors-guide/culture/singlish-guide.html; accessed 26 May 2016):
The ubiquitous Singaporean 'lah' is something you'll hear everywhere, and it's used at the end of sentences as an interjection. 'Cannot lah,' 'Can lah,' 'Okay lah,' or 'Let's sit here for a while lah,' are some usages of the word. When a taxi driver asks you which way you prefer to get to your destination, answering, 'Fastest way okay lah,' could be a good way to practise your Singlish!

Finally, in (7), we have a foreigner's perspective on Singlish. The blogger, who goes by the name 'Limpeh', once again makes reference to the by now fairly ubiquitous Singlish-speaking hawker.

(7)   Limpeh's quirky look at life in Singapore from the POV of a foreigner in 'Why don't Singaporeans try to speak proper English?', 29 November 2015 (http://limpehft.blogspot.sg/2015/11/why-dont-singaporeans-try-to-speak .html; accessed 26 May 2016):
Whether or not you need to speak standard English (as opposed to Singlish) depends on your personal circumstances. If you were representing your company internationally, attending major sales meetings in New York, London and Sydney, then you need to be able to communicate clearly in a way that best represents your company – if you are in this position, then hell no, you can't speak Singlish to foreigners who will not understand you. But if you are selling laksa in a hawker center in Ang Mo Kio, then Singlish will serve you just fine – the odds of an American, British or Australian tourist finding their way to a hawker center on Ang Mo Kio street 61 is extremely slim, so why the hell would that laksa hawker need to speak proper English (or even any English at all)?

I discussed at the beginning of this book (see the Introduction) that Singlish is a deeply entrenched cultural category because it is much debated in public discourse. But precisely because it is a highly debated category, the Singlish controversy is not just about linguistic issues; it is intertwined with identities of various sorts. What the foregoing examples all show is that the circulation and recirculation of recurrent ideas and images – especially via the media reporting of speeches, blogs and various websites – serve to establish and naturalize in public discourses specific indexical associations between Singlish and particular types of personas. Hawkers and taxi drivers are among the most commonly evoked characters and are treated as emblematic of a wider category of humble working-class Singaporeans, who are most comfortable just speaking Singlish and who cannot easily code-switch into Standard English. This is a characterological association between Singlish and identity that the government and the Singlitterati both seem happy to accept and propagate. I am by no means suggesting that there is a deliberate attempt to exclude the Singlish subaltern from public debates over Singlish: there is no conspiracy here. Rather, there is simply a presumption that the monolectal Singlish speaker needs to be and should be spoken for, not least because the debates concerning the merits of Singlish are conducted in the public sphere using Standard English. The result is that the monolectal Singlish speaker is essentially relegated to the status of a subaltern: spoken for, spoken about, but never directly speaking. In this regard, it is important to appreciate that this is not a situation that would be improved or remedied by inviting representations from the subaltern. That is, inviting the Singlish subaltern to make contributions to the Singlish controversy is not the answer to their voicelessness, for two reasons.

The first has to do with the fact that the debates are often conducted using what is generally recognized to be Standard English. Standard English is used because the debates are conducted in the public sphere and are assumed by both supporters and detractors of Singlish to carry significant implications for issues of national importance, such as the economy and national identity (see Chapter 2) – for why else would the issue of Singlish be of such lasting controversy? With this in mind, contributions using Singlish tend to lack gravitas and credibility unless the use of Singlish is seen as a matter of deliberate code-switching, rather than due to the lack of competence in the standard. Bourdieu (1991) describes this down-shifting into the less prestigious variety as a strategy of condescension, and it is this inability to employ the strategy of condescension that distinguishes the monolectal Singlish speaker from his or her better educated, more articulate and eloquent counterparts. Thus, despite the argument by the Speak Good Singlish Movement that ungrammatical and colloquial English should not be confused with each other (see Chapter 3), the reliance on the stereotypes regarding speakers of Singlish once again confuses the distinction. This lack of gravitas and credibility is also not helped by the fact that the stereotypes also entrench the indexical relationship between Singlish and a persona that is widely presented as clownish, humorous, and coarse (see the later examples).

The second reason concerns the specific issues to which the subaltern's experience with Singlish and English-language learning might be considered relevant. Two of the specific points of contestation are whether learning Singlish compromises or undermines a person's ability to learn Standard English and, relatedly, whether it is necessary to provide a social environment where the former is neither used nor encouraged. Recall that it is in relation to these points that the government has accused educated Singaporeans who champion Singlish of being irresponsible and not being considerate of their less-educated countrymen. There can be no individual subaltern who can claim that their use of Singlish does not adversely affect their ability to learn Standard English because, by the government's definition, no such individual would have both varieties in their repertoire. Competence in Standard English disqualifies an individual from having the status of a Singlish subaltern. Hence, any such individual's narration could take the form of a testament as to how their use of Singlish has been a liability that prevented them from learning the standard and therefore negatively affected their socio-economic prospects. The only possible Singlish subaltern is someone like a highly successful and wealthy hawker who might make the claim that the inability to speak Standard English has not been an impediment at all.[2] In both cases, the subaltern's narrative serves as 'unprocessed data' (Comaroff and Comaroff, 2012: 1), which the active debating parties can still interpret/theorize/spin to suit their own various stances vis-à-vis Singlish. In other words, someone else – better educated, more informed – would still have to speak for them. In this regard, it is interesting to consider the comments by bell hooks (1990: 343; italics added) on the relationship between the academic and the subaltern:

[There is] no need to hear your voice, when I can talk about you better than you can speak about yourself. No need to hear your voice. Only tell me about your pain. *I want to know your story. And then I will tell it back to you in a new way. Tell it back to you in such a way that it has become mine, my own. Re-writing you, I write myself anew. I am still author, authority.* I am still [the] colonizer, the speaking subject, and you are now at the center of my talk.

What is important to note from hooks's comments is that subalterns are deemed to be incapable of even knowing themselves unless their story has been refracted through the academic's way of telling. Only then does their lore/story/data acquire the status of knowledge/evidence/theory.

Shaping the Singlish Controversy

Let us remember that Singlish became controversial because the Singapore government was concerned that its increasing popularity was jeopardizing the ability of Singaporeans to learn Standard English. But the popularity of Singlish is not due to its use by the Singlish subaltern. Singlish was popularized in the

---

[2] The following story could be apocryphal. But apparently at a commencement ceremony some years ago in one of the local tertiary institutions, a prominent businessman was invited to give an address, which he delivered proudly in what many scandalized teachers in the audience later described as broken English. The businessman's message to the graduating students was that one did not need Standard English to succeed. Needless to say, he was never invited to speak again, and his story was quickly framed by the institution in question as an exception that nevertheless proves the rule.

mass media by early humorous publications such as Sylvia Toh Paik Choo's *Eh, Goondu!* (1982) and *Lagi Goondu* (1986)[3], by sitcom characters in the television series *Phua Chu Kang* (which aired from 1997–2007), and later by, among others, Colin Goh and Woo Yen Yen with their *Coxford Singlish Dictionary* (2009). On the other side of the Singlish controversy, the government's Speak Good English Movement provided a list of 'Singlish words which we need to avoid' (Kwan, 2003: 113) as well as various communicative scenarios for which it provides commentary. Kwan notes that one such scenario involves a conversation between a receptionist and visitor who is trying to arrange a meeting with her boss. The receptionist says things like 'Got appointment or not?', 'Must make appointment. He [her boss] very busy one.' The SGEM commentary then notes that 'the receptionist's use of Singlish gives the company a bad image. In Singlish, there is a tendency to leave out the subject in questions (e.g. "Got appointment or not?") and statements ("Must make appointment")' (37–38). The Singlish controversy, then, has been largely shaped by interventions from the government and the various popularizers of Singlish, and not by the Singlish subaltern.

The popularizers of Singlish have been successful in promoting Singlish precisely because they have been quite consistent in framing it as a variety that is used informally and in a humorous way. Here, for example, is Toh Paik Choo's description of the phrase 'rubbah-rubbah' (2011: 30, 35), with the accompanying cartoon illustration (Figure 2):

Rubbah/Rubbah-Rubbah
Malay, not surprisingly from 'rub'? Like the parent who didn't mind the daughter's boyfriend praising her in Spanish, German and Japanese, so long as he didn't praise her in Braille. To fondle, generally a good feeling all over!

And here is an explanation, both verbal and visual, for the word 'xiam' from *An Essential Guide to Singlish* (2003: 114–115; see Figure 3):

Xiam:
Get out of the way. Leave me alone. It can also mean 'excuse me' in the context that one wants to be avoided (when carrying a bowl of hot soup across a busy restaurant floor, for example.
Example: '*Xiam, xiam*! Let me pass before I spill this drinks all over you please, ah!'
Another meaing for *Xiam* is to take cover (or avoid responsibility).
Example: 'Eh, you better *xiam* before boss get back and arrow you to do this monthly reports what.'
Example: 'I must *xiam* now otherwise they kick me out, I did not remember the dress code.'

---

[3] Both books have recently been released as a single compilation, *Complete Eh, Goondu, The!* (2011), where the author is described on the cover as 'the Guru of Singlish'.

"Dey! No rubbah-rubbah!"

Figure 2. Illustration of 'rubbah-rubbah' by Toh Paik Choo

Notice that quite aside from the text, the cartoons accompanying the explanations make it very clear that these discussions of Singlish are intended to be light-hearted and humorous. This does not mean that there have been no works that discuss Singlish in a serious manner (see, for example, the discussion of Haresh Sharma's play about mental illness, *Off-Centre*, in Chapter 6). But in such works, Singlish as a variety per se is backgrounded in favour of more authentically portraying the situation as one marked by worries or concerns.[4]

---

[4] More interestingly, Goh (2016) suggests that Singlish has recently become more politically loaded and taken on more serious overtones as a consequence of its use as part of a wider

Figure 3. Illustration of 'xiam' by Miel in *An Essential Guide to Singlish*

In contrast, when the focus is on Singlish itself, humour and informality are the attributes that are highlighted. Thus, consider the following statements from C. Goh and Woo (2009: xix):

The beauty of Singlish lies in deliberate wordplay, so speakers should approach it with an irreverent sense of humour. Do not be afraid of mixing and matching words and phrases. Some of the most classic Singlish terms are an amalgam of different languages, e.g. 'buay tahan' or 'mana eh sai'. Also, feel free to bend the rules of proper English grammar by turning nouns into verbs or adjectives or vice versa, or even English tenses to non-English words, e.g. 'cabut-ed' or 'balik-ing'.

discourse about the politics of inclusion and exclusion to distinguish 'true' Singaporeans from migrants and new citizens. See Chapter 6 for further discussion.

It is no wonder, then, that such open calls to freely mix words and phrases, to 'bend the rules of proper English grammar' (even though changing grammatical categories is part of the grammar of 'proper English'), and to do so in the spirit of irreverence and playfulness can make the more linguistically conservative segments of the population, including government officials and other defenders of proper English, apoplectic.

In addition to the *Coxford Singlish Dictionary*, which has acquired a some-what authoritative status regarding Singlish words and phrases, Gwee's (2016) op-ed piece in the *New York Times* also happens to include 'A Singlish Primer' for American readers:

Pokkai (Pork-car-ai) Translates as "drop dead." Means to go broke, e.g. "Aditi shops at Gucci until she pokkai."
Bo hee hae ma ho (Boh-hee-hay-mar-ho) Equivalent to "Beggars can't be choosers," it means "When there's no fish, prawns are good too."
Gone case A lost cause.
Very the To say "very" in an incredulous way, e.g. "You know, you look smart but you talk very the stupid."
Buay tahan (BOO-ay tar-hun) Means that you cannot tolerate something, e.g. "I buay tahan the weather these days."
Kiasu (KEE-ya-soo) To behave in a competitive, self-serving way, e.g. "Those kiasu people have been outside the Apple shop since 3 a.m."

Contributions such as the *Coxford Singlish Dictionary* and Gwee's 'Singlish Primer' are internationalizing the profile of Singlish, so that understandings about Singlish are being shaped for both domestic and foreign audiences.

Bearing the preceding disussion in mind, I now explore in greater detail how the active contributions from the government and the various popularizers of Singlish and, by implication, the absence of contributions from the Singlish subaltern have served to shape the Singlish controversy. I focus on two issues: (i) who needs to learn Singlish and Standard English and why, and (ii) how should these varieties be learnt. The first issue concerns the motivation and choice of variety to be learnt, and the second concerns the mode by which such learning takes place.

The government's perspective, as already presented, is that all Singapore-ans need to learn Standard English for the instrumental purpose of making a living and that no Singaporean actually needs to learn Singlish. Those who can competently code-switch between Standard English and Singlish are the 'privileged' few – and they should not mistake their code-switching facility as something that easily extends to all Singaporeans. Especially for those Singa-poreans who are struggling to learn Standard English, any attempt to acquire both Singlish and Standard English will simply mean a poorer grasp of the lat-ter. On the other side of the controversy, the popularizers of Singlish do not dispute the instrumental value of Standard English, and so on this point, there is no disagreement between them and the government. The rift comes from the perceived value of Singlish: its popularizers believe Singlish needs to be protected and its use encouraged because it serves to solidify the bonds between Singaporeans regardless of their ethnic or class backgrounds.

What is largely missing from this shaping of the Singlish controversy is the question of whether the use of Standard English can also serve to bond Singaporeans. There have been tentative suggestions (see the earlier comments from Koh Tai Ann and note 4 in Chapter 1) regarding the development of a Standard Singapore English, but the possibility that this might serve to bond Singaporeans is never pursued in any detail. There is good reason for this, given that Singlish already exists as a prominent candidate to fill this role. In addition, there is a tendency to index any standard variety of English with a persona that can be variously described as more aloof, serious or elitist. Also largely missing from this shaping of the controversy is the question of whether Singlish might have any instrumental value at all. While the government has consistently dismissed this possibility as part of its rationale for discouraging the use of Singlish, the popularizers, too, have never really taken up this issue in any detail. There are indications, however, that Singlish is increasingly becoming more commodified (see Chapter 6); the popularity of books such as *Eh, Goondu!* and *The Coxford Singlish Dictionary* is itself evidence of this commodification.

Let us now consider the issue of how to learn the language varieties. It is assumed that Standard English is best learnt under the conditions of formal classroom instruction; that is, 'proper English' requires proper instruction. The external environment – the environment outside the classroom in this case – is then construed as either supporting or undermining classroom learning. The possibility that a more synergistic relationship might exist where activities and language use outside the classroom can transformatively enhance language learning if, say, learners were encouraged to be meta-linguistically sensitive to variations in use and to the reasons behind the choice of specific linguistic features, is lost in this way of construing the mode of learning for Standard English. Conversely, Singlish is presented as something that is learnt informally. While dictionaries and informal guides are available, the idea that Singlish can or should be formally taught is never seriously considered.[5]

Related to these assumptions about how Standard English and Singlish are learnt is a more general problem, which is that the government seems to adopt an ahistorical view of language learning, especially when it tries to discredit these supporters of Singlish. That is, the learning histories of these supporters themselves are erased or at the very least oversimplified. Recall that the

---

[5] This is not to say such formal classes in Singlish do not exist (see Chapter 6). Rather, their existence and relevance to the Singlish controversy are elided.

government's stance is that supporters of Singlish are making things difficult for Singaporeans who want to learn Standard English. Supporters of Singlish are creating an environment where Singlish is unnecessarily pervasive. Whereas these supporters can code-switch between Singlish and Standard English, learners of Standard English are apparently unable to do so or, at the very least, have great difficulty keeping the two distinct.

Such a stance, however, seems to completely ignore the learning histories of these supporters themselves. How did they come to acquire this facility to code-switch between Standard English and Singlish? Presumably, at least a fair number of them grew up in Singapore and experienced much the same kind of education system as those who did not acquire this facility. Their learning histories should in fact provide useful guidelines and ideas for how English-language education policy might be tweaked to better enable more students to code-switch between Standard English and Singlish. But rather than seeing these learning histories and experiences of these supporters as resources that could usefully inform education policy, the government has simply dismissed these individuals as irresponsible promoters of Singlish. In this regard, note that the government's rebuttal of Gwee's *New York Times* op-ed piece ignores Gwee's own history and efforts in becoming competent in both Standard English and Singlish. This personal linguistic biography is simply lumped together with the equally ahistorical characterization of those other Singaporeans who cannot speak Standard English and whose linguistic well-being is jeopardized because they need Standard English 'to earn a living'. Singaporeans are therefore either ahistorically characterized as needing to learn Standard English and living in an unhelpful environment where Singlish constitutes an obstacle to this learning objective, or they are already competent in both Standard English and Singlish and their insistence on using Singlish is a contributing obstacle to the learning objective of the first group.

Conclusion

Public understandings of what counts as Singlish are significantly shaped by active contributions from both the Singapore government and the popularizers of Singlish. It is these understandings of Singlish that form the ground, so to speak, upon which the merits or otherwise of Singlish get debated. In this regard, the absence of the Singlish subaltern voice means that the experiences and opinions of the monolectal Singlish speaker have little to no influence on the Singlish controversy except when portrayed and disseminated by the active contributors.

The remedy to such a state of affairs is not to provide the Singlish subaltern with a direct channel for voicing his or her views. As mentioned earlier, these views will more likely than not be categorized (as in fact they already are) as raw data that require theoretical processing in order to be treated as 'information' or 'knowledge' that might then have an impact upon the Singlish controversy. Under these circumstances, if taken-for-granted and deeply entrenched assumptions that currently inform the Singlish controversy are not themselves being subjected to critical examination, opening up a channel for the Singlish subaltern merely incurs the risk that his or her voice will be treated with condescension.

The more effective strategy, then, is to encourage a rethinking of precepts about Singlish and about the nature of language and identity more generally. While certainly a more challenging route to take, this strategy will provide longer-term benefit because it fosters a deeper and more critical appreciation of the nature of language ideologies. This longer-term benefit is increasingly important because social conditions are rapidly changing and becoming more complex. I return to this issue in the final chapter.

5   The Commodification of Singlish

Detractors of Singlish, including, most prominently, the Singapore government, have decried its use and popularity on the grounds that it lacks social and economic value and its continued usage will only serve to penalize those who speak it. There are obvious problems with this assertion, not least because if Singlish is conceded as being popular, then it must certainly possess at least some social value. As to the question of Singlish's economic value, its detractors concede (with some reluctance) that Singlish is probably useful when conducting commercial transactions in relatively 'humble' domains such as ordering food at hawker centers.

When these detractors criticize the use of Singlish and proclaim its harm, what they usually have in mind are contexts involving upward social and economic mobility: they are asserting that Singlish lacks value both in the educational system and the workplace. Students who speak Singlish will not be able to move upstream; workers, particularly professionals, who speak Singlish will not get promoted. But this assertion completely neglects that fact that, even in such domains, code-switching between Singlish and more standard Englishes does occur and it is such code-switching that can often facilitate the completion of various educational and professional tasks (Stroud and Wee, 2011). It also relies on a false choice, since the use of Singlish in no way precludes the use and learning of more standard Englishes (Siegel, 1999).[1] To put the matter in more linguistic anthropological terms, mplicit in these assertions about the supposedly deleterious effects of Singlish is the idea that Singlish – unlike its more prestigious linguistic counterparts – is neither a commodity nor is it commodifiable.

This chapter therefore focuses on the commodification of Singlish. This aspect of the Singlish controversy is not widely discussed, even though a

---

[1] This kind of prejudice against non-standard varieties is not uncommon. Honey (1983; 1997) is a well-known 'defender' of Standard English, arguing that allowing non-standard varieties into the educational system only serves to undermine students' ability to learn the standard and therefore compromises their future prospects. Honey's arguments have been criticized for their lack of serious scholarship (Crowley, 1999; Milroy and Milroy, 1999).

number of Singaporean films produced have been quite successful both commercially and critically. Singlish also features prominently in other creative forms, such as plays, novels, poems and even a book of photographs (discussed later). And as we already saw in Chapter 1, even the Singapore Tourism Board is keen to make use of Singlish in its attempts to attract tourists to Singapore. To varying degrees, Singlish has been commodified, particularly by the culture industries, and there are interesting comparisons to be made with its commodification by the non-culture industries.

I organize this discussion as follows. I first review the notion of commodification, contrasting the Marxist understanding of commodity as something that exists outside of and independently of the producer (after the production process has been completed) with the more neoliberal-influenced emphasis on human capital and skills development. Both these notions are relevant to our investigation of the commodification of Singlish, but in different ways. The neoliberal conception is more consistent with language skills as forms of embodied capital and hence not easily dissociated from the speaker. The Marxist understanding, in contrast becomes pertinent when, as tends to be the case with cultural products, a language performance is preserved, perhaps via being recorded and archived, such that it then exists independently of the speaker.

These different ways in which something can be commodified carry interesting and even surprising implications for the issue of authenticity and language ownership, implications that I explore in greater detail following the analysis of a number of examples involving Singlish.

Language, Commodification and Human Capital

Marx defines a commodity as follows:

A commodity is, in the first place, an object outside of us, a thing that by its properties satisfies human wants of some sort or another. The nature of such wants, whether, for instance, they spring from the stomach or from fancy, makes no difference. Neither are we here concerned to know how the object satisfies these wants, whether directly as means of subsistence, or indirectly as means of production. (Marx, 1887: Band I, Chapter 1, online version)

While Marx's definition of commodity 'aims to provide an understanding of consumer society and of capitalism per se' (Duchêne and Heller, 2012), it rather unfortunately also assumes that a commodity is necessarily a thing, 'an object outside of us'. This assumption may be appropriate in cases when the commodity is a physical object that has been cultivated or manufactured under the more traditional conditions of labor with which Marx was concerned. The assumption, however, becomes highly problematic when the analytical focus is on human capital and skills, as tends to be case in the new economy with its strong neoliberal orientation (Piller and Cho, 2013). As Agha (2011: 25, italics added) points out,

a focus on 'things that pass from hand to hand' during exchange, itself dubbed the 'circulation of matter' (Marx, 1967 [1867]:104), obscures the materiality of discourses that formulate commodities as social indexicals. *Yet exchange is simply one kind of 'use' among many; and commodities that merge use and users (such as skills) do not pass from hand to hand.*

Agha (2011: 25) also comments on the diversity of activities in which commodity registers participate in order to emphasize just how widespread and influential they are:

From the standpoint of registers, commodities mediate social life not through the "circulation of things" but through the recycling of commodity formulations and their fractions – diacritics and emblems, products and possessions, discourses and their objects, skills and penumbral personae – across diverse activity frames that recontextualize and transform them.

Thus, once we shift our focus to human capital, commodities qua skills have to be understood as 'embodied capital' (van Doorn, 2014: 357). Thus, van Doorn, citing Foucault, 2008: 224) emphasizes that labor can then no longer be seen as something separable from the worker because it now 'comprises a capital, that is to say, it is an ability, a skill':

As a result, the neoliberal analysis of labor effectively eviscerates the very concept of labor, instead positing a vision of economic conduct in which enterprise units perpetually seek to invest in their human capital in order to retain their competitive edge and thereby secure a future income in an insecure environment, whose variables are always in flux and thus remain opaque to each individual competitor on the market. (van Doorn, 2014: 357)

A skill, broadly defined, simply refers to a learned or acquired ability of some sort. Learned abilities cannot be divorced from the individuals who are in possession of the relevant skills, not least because individuals acquire skills to varying degrees of expertise or competence as a result of the interactions between aptitude, learning conditions and other life experiences. In the case of language learning, this is of course entirely consistent with a practice view of language, which emphasizes the variable and changing nature of language practices as a necessary correlate of language use (Park and Wee, 2012). Thus, the embodied nature of linguistic skills means that it is simply not possible to evaluate learned language abilities – and this extends to discourses concerning the commodity value of a language or its 'commodity formulations' – whilst bracketing out the speaker. But this bracketing out is exactly what does happen on a number of occasions, so that language competence often becomes ideologically constructed as a commodity in the more traditional Marxist sense –

being presented as something that exists 'outside of us'. And this construction has concomitant implications for language competence. If language has an autonomous existence, then language competence, too, can be construed as an absolute norm that is independent of speakers and against which the performance of speakers can be 'objectively' evaluated.

This more traditional understanding of language competence as commodity *a la* Marx exists in tension and contradiction with the neoliberal emphasis on the need for individuals to develop their own human capital. For example, the traditional Marxist view tends to downplay the individual worker and his or her skills in creating a product. The worker is seen as 'a fundamentally collective subject, whose living labor is rooted in cooperative practices whose value will always partly exceed economic calculation and measurement' (van Doorn, 2014: 357). In contrast, the neoliberal conception tends to emphasize the individuality of the worker and thus his or her ability (or lack thereof) in product creation.

Let me emphasize at this point that any tension or contradiction between these two views of language and language competence is a possibility rather than a necessary outcome. This is because both perspectives on the commodification of language are ultimately ideological and language ideologies are often partial. What this means is that any conflict between language ideologies is actually avoidable because of the effects of erasure (Irvine and Gal, 2000), as well as their tendency to be selectively applied. It is therefore best to treat these two views of commodity as different ideological framings and to exmaine when one view is appealed to or foregrounded and to what end. This will become clearer when, after a discussion of the commodification of Singlish in the culture industries, I provide a brief comparison with its commodification in the non-culture industries.

Singlish and the Culture Industries

The commodification of Singlish in the culture industries takes place in a variety of forms. To structure this discussion, I begin by describing a more personalized form of commodification in which the motivation behind the commercial project is personal and it is also highly local. I then move on to discuss examples that are increasingly less personal and where the market is increasingly more international in nature.

Consider the recent publication in 2015 of a coffee-table book by the Singaporean photographer Zinkie Aw. *Singaporelang – What the Singlish?* features forty photographs, each providing a visual depiction of a Singlish phrase.[2]

---

[2] Interestingly, partial funding for the book project was provided by the SG50 Celebration Fund. This is a government-supported fund, overseen by Minister for Culture, Community and Youth

The book can therefore be considered a kind of 'Visual Singlish Dictionary' (Aw, 2015). According to Aw (quoted in Lam, 2015), 'I was toying around with the idea of whether it is possible to transpose a language – particularly Singlish, which is (part of our) intangible local culture that gives me my sense of national identity – with something that I do best, photographing moments in a quirky manner.' Thus one reason why Aw embarked on this particular project is because Singlish is critical to her personal sense of being a Singaporean. Aw's project is clearly motivated by how crucially Singlish provides her with a personal sense of self.

Consider now some examples of the photographs and their accompanying Singlish expressions. One photo depicts a group of Singaporeans in a lift covering their noses, presumably because someone has just farted (the actual reason is left for the reader to infer). The photograph is accompanied by the word 'paiseh', which is Hokkien for 'embarrassed'. Another photograph (*'Singaporelang – What the Singlish?* by Zinkie Aw', posted 13 September 2015, culturepush.com; accessed 28 September 2015) shows a man clutching his stomach outside a public toilet, which he is unable to access because it is currently being cleaned. This photograph is accompanied by the phrase 'Buay tahan!', which contains the Hokkien word 'buay' (meaning 'unable') and the Malay word 'tahan' (meaning 'endure'). This Singlish phrase therefore refers to a situation that is extremely demanding or difficult to endure. At this point, it is worth recalling that Singlish is primarily associated with being uneducated, unpretentious, vulgar and humorous.

As a commercial project intended mainly for domestic consumption, the coffee-table book is also aimed at other Singaporeans, on the assumption that fellow citizens would enjoy expressing their national identity via Singlish. To enable them to do so, the book contains fifty-five speech-bubble stickers that readers can paste on the photos to create their own scenes. This means that while the photographs remain the same, readers can use the stickers to make their own linguistic contributions, adding their own Singlish phrases to the ones already provided by Aw. Because the photographs remain unchanged, the visual representations (recall the two examples involving the phrases 'Paiseh' and 'Buay tahan') are essentially light-hearted and humorous. Crucially, this means that even as Singaporeans readers, like Aw, are expected to enjoy the Singlish expressions and photographs as providing them with a sense of being Singaporean, the book *qua* circulated commodity does play up and contribute to the perpetuation of stereotypes about the kind of persona indexed by the use

Lawrence Wong, of about S$9 million to support projects initiated by citizens as part of the country's Jubilee Year celebrations. This funding support, again, points to an interesting and almost schizophrenic attitude towards Singlish on the part of the government, especially when there are possibilities for commodification.

of Singlish. That is, the idea of the Singlish speaker as someone who might be refined and have gravitas is largely absent.

Let us move on to the next example, the second edition of *The Coxford Singlish Dictionary* by C. Goh and Woo (2009). In their introduction to this second edition, C. Goh and Woo make the following statement (vii–viii):

After the first edition of the Coxford, we're even more convinced about how important Singlish is to Singaporeans' sense of who we are (especially when we're at ease and not trying to impress anybody)...
We've also personally seen the Coxford develop as a useful text for cultural exchange. In New York, where we're currently working, we met a Singaporean woman who had an inferiority complex about Singaporean culture as compared to American culture. But with the Coxford in her hand, she became much less diffident about being able to share her world, and was soon happily introducing her American friends to words like 'drama mama' and 'steady porn peep ee'.

Like Aw, C. Goh and Woo, too, express the view that Singlish is important to 'Singaporeans' sense of who we are'. They also provide an interesting anecdote of a Singaporean woman who managed to overcome her inferiority complex about Singaporean culture because of the *Coxford Singlish Dictionary*: presumably being the focus of a dictionary helps to bestow upon Singlish a sense of legitimacy. This latter point is worth elaborating. We are not told just how much Singlish the woman actually spoke, but that is irrelevant. The key point here is that the dictionary provided the woman with concrete evidence that she could show to her American friends that Singlish exists as a linguistic entity that is popularly accepted amongst Singaporeans and, moreover, is something that non-Singaporeans ought to become acquainted with if they want to better understand Singaporean culture. Having been the subject of a publication, Singlish now exists as an independently existing object, one that can be bought and sold, thus making knowledge of Singlish something that people are actually prepared to pay for (see the later discussion). And having its own dictionary means that Singlish is not linguistically ad hoc or haphazard; it is something that, to be properly spoken, requires guidance as to its norms and rules of usage even if this guidance is being provided humorously. In this regard, C. Goh and Woo (2009: viii) draw upon the highly prevalent ideology of the native speaker, one that privileges Singaporeans as the ones with the relevant linguistic expertise in Singlish, because 'it is a special part of who we are': 'Singlish is our knowledge, of which we are the experts. And we have the authority to teach others, because it is a special part of who we are.'

This privileging of native speaker knowledge is an extremely familiar ideological stance. Thus, C. Goh and Woo's dictionary entries and Aw's choice of Singlish phrases to accompany her photographs both derive their legitimacy from their status as Singaporeans and (therefore) as authentic speakers of Singlish. In this way, 'authenticity becomes a tool of power' because 'any group that insists on the authenticity of its own tastes in contrast to others' can claim moral superiority' (Zukin, 2010: 3). The 'moral superiority' in question arises from the fact these Singlish cultural products are produced by Singaporeans themselves, so that community and authenticity are positioned as working in concert to facilitate commodification (Budach, Roy and Heller, 2003: 604).

But we should also note that, for C. Goh and Woo, the evocation of this native speaker stance apparently does not result in any contradiction between the claim, on the one hand, that Singaporeans have 'special' knowledge of Singlish, and the assumption, on the other hand, that some Singaporeans are in a better position than others to provide authoritative guidance about Singlish usage. That is, the fact that knowledge of Singlish appears to be unevenly distributed amongst Singaporeans is not presented as a contradiction to the claim that links expertise in Singlish with being Singaporean. This contradiction is masked because of the ambiguity of the referent of 'others' (as in the phrase 'we have the authority to teach others'); it could either refer to other fellow Singaporeans or to non-Singaporeans. This ambiguity is increased by the fact that this statement comes immediately after the anecdote in which the Singaporean woman exposed her American friends to Singlish. Thus, even within the community of Singaporeans, some are apparently better 'connoisseurs of authenticity' (Zukin, 2010: 20) than others. Such 'connoisseurship' is the result of voice possibilities, where, as already observed (see Chapter 3), it is the better-educated and more articulate Singaporeans who are in a stronger position to influence public notions of what Singlish 'really' is.

Finally, the cover of the dictionary contains endorsements from American and British institutions, thus giving both Singlish in general and the *Coxford Singlish Dictionary* in particular the air of acceptance by traditional native speakers of more established varieties of English:

'Invaluable': *Times of London*
'Lovingly chronicles the comic eccentricities of Singapore's argot': *TIME Magazine*
'Humorous, with lots of cross-cultural wordplay': British Broadcasting Corporation

Such enthusiastic endorsements from non-Singaporean institutions can be critical in helping to foster a sense of pride in Singlish among Singaporeans themselves because they reflect back to them how much Singlish is valued or appreciated by the world at large ('others' in the sense of referring to non-Singaporeans), even if it might be domestically frowned upon by the Singapore government. In other words, these endorsements strengthen the perception that Singlish can indeed be a valued commodity despite what its detractors may claim. Therefore, even though the primary market of the *Coxford Singlish Dictionary* may be domestic, it is clear that there is also a secondary international market; as seen from the anecdote, C. Goh and Woo envisaged non-Singaporeans being exposed to the dictionary mainly via its purchase by Singaporeans, who then use it to introduce their international friends and colleagues to Singlish. Here, already, there is the potential for shifting from the view of language as a pre-existing object to the view that it is a form of embodied capital. As a transferrable skill that might also be learnt by non-Singaporeans, Singlish can be dissociated from its traditional native speakers, in this case, Singaporeans. As we see later when we discuss the non-culture industries, this is in fact what happens when non-Singaporeans, particularly expatriates who have spent time in Singapore, attempt to capitalize on their own knowledge of Singlish. Thus, the guarantee of authenticity or provenance that comes when Singlish is produced by native speakers appears to be less of a concern than in the culture industries.

For now, however, let us note that C. Goh and Woo are keen to cultivate a more international market, which can also be seen in their description of how audiences around the world, from Taiwan to Spain to America, were 'fascinated' by Singlish when they were promoting their film, *Singapore Dreaming* (see the later discussion). Their reference to films nicely leads us to consider yet another form in which the commodification of Singlish takes place. As mentioned, a number of Singaporean films have done relatively well at the local box office. One such early success includes *Army Daze* (1996), a comedy about the military experiences of a group of enlistees from a variety of socio-economic and ethnic backgrounds. This film used a great deal of Singlish to authentically reflect the speech patterns of their characters. Other films, such as Eric Khoo's *Mee Pok Man* (1995) and *12 Storeys* (1997), have enjoyed both local and international success. Both deal with themes of social alienation among working-class Singaporeans and also make use of Singlish, again to provide a realistic portrayal of the characters. *Mee Pok Man* was invited to be screened at more than thirty film festivals, and *12 Storeys* was featured at the Cannes International Film Festival.

More recently, C. Goh and Woo's *Singapore Dreaming* (2006), which portrays a Singaporean working-class family as they aspire towards a better life, became the first Singaporean film to win the Montblanc New Screenwriters Award at the 54th San Sebastian International Film Festival. It also won the Best Asian/Middle-Eastern Film Award at the 20th Tokyo International Film Festival. Ironically, given the film's international acclaim, its promotional trailer was banned from local free-to-air television by the government, due to what was deemed as the excessive use of Singlish. As C. Goh and Woo (2009: viii, italics in original) are keen to point out, many international audiences appreciated the film precisely because of its Singlish content:

When we were travelling around the world to promote our award-winning feature film, *Singapore Dreaming*, we found that audiences were fascinated by the Singlish dialogue.

There were questions about it at every single screening. In Taiwan, for example, youths in the audience began repeating some of the Singlish lines and expressed envy that we Singaporeans had such a developed vernacular English of our own. In Spain and America, audiences said they were surprised by how much they could relate to the inter-mingling of languages. After the screening of the film on American TV, an American viewer posted this message on the station's discussion board:

> *Singapore Dreaming showed me how the mixture of cultures on this small island have resulted in the most imaginative language/dialect: Singlish! It was the discovery of Singlish that made me understand just how 'globalized' Singaporeans really are AND because of its use in the film, the story and characters seemed more familiar to me.*

The success of these Singapore films contradicts the government's earlier asser-tions that Singlish not only lacks value but also that cultural products using Singlish will never find an audience overseas. In his 1999 prime minister's National Day Rally speech, Goh Chok Tong asserted,

Nicholas Lee, who plays Ronnie Tan in *Under One Roof*, wrote a letter in the *Straits Times* which hit the nail on the head. He had been criticized because Ronnie Tan did not speak Singlish. His reply was that the programme *Under One Roof* was shown over-seas as well as in Singapore. Programme series are very expensive to make. If they are only shown in Singapore, they will surely lose money. If the characters spoke Singlish, viewers overseas would not understand it.

Nicholas Lee cited one local production, 'Forever Fever', which could not be released in the US market because American audiences would not understand the Singapore English. So now they are considering removing the Singlish and dubbing 'Forever Fever' in English that Americans can understand. His conclusion was: 'We should all be aware that the only way forward is to look outward, and if the future of Singapore entertain-ment lies in 'Beng culture', then I am afraid it is a very bleak culture'. (http://stars.nhb.gov.sg/data/pdfdoc/1999082202.htm; accessed 5 September 2004)

The irony of the banning of *Singapore Dreaming*'s trailer grows even stronger given the Singapore government's recent 'cultural diplomacy project', launched under the auspices of the Ministry of Culture, Community and Youth and the Ministry of Foreign Affairs (MFA). According to an MFA statement, a 'travelling package of Singapore films' aims at 'profiling Singapore's cul-tural offerings abroad and developing international opportunities for our artists and institutions' (Heng, 2015). Among the films selected were Eric Khoo's *12 Storeys* and Jack Neo's *I Not Stupid*, and screenings have thus far been held in MFA missions in Berlin, Hong Kong, and London, with more planned.

Importantly, the ease and convenience with which Singlish can be conveyed are greatly facilitated by the use of digital technologies and social media. It is now much easier for commodified linguistic products to travel without the accompaniment of the speakers themselves. Videos about Singlish that have gone viral on YouTube are further illustrations of how the language can spread in the absence of any actual speakers. Consider the humorous YouTube video 'Sinful English (www.youtube.com/watch?v=fiYXiixlV0A), produced while

Barack Obama was the US president. In the video, young Americans are described as suffering from 'First World Communication Problems' because utterances in colloquial American English are too lengthy, leading to interactional issues. The 'remedy' proposed by the Black American president is 'Sinfully Speedy Syllable-Saving English' or 'Singlish'. This is followed by shots of the same young Americans now enjoying interactional efficacy because they are speaking Singlish. Other examples of the many humorous YouTube videos featuring Singlish are 'How to Speak Singlish' (www.youtube.com/watch?v=pxFYW8BBjXI), 'Caucasian Speaking Singlish Part 1' (www.youtube.com/watch?v=3HXqcoYdV5w), and 'Singlish Chat on Phone' (www.youtube.com/watch?v=NwhmJaWIU2M).

Finally, a number of Singapore texts are appearing on the reading lists of classes taught at overseas universities, usually as part of literature courses (Yuen, 2016). Examples include Alfian Sa'at's (1998) *Singapore You Are Not My Country* (University of York), Kirpal Singh's (1997) *To A Visitor to Singapore* (Sardar Patel University), Amanda Chong's (2006) *lion heart* (Cambridge International Examinations O-Levels/GCSE), Boey Kim Cheng's (2009) *Between Stations* (New York University at Sydney) and Stella Kon's (1989) *Emily of Emerald Hill* (School of Oriental and African Studies, University of London). Singlish is not necessarily the direct object of study, of course. Nevertheless, in studying theses texts, students and their lecturers discuss the language being used, and this includes lexical items and phrases that would be considered Singlish, such as 'chao ah beng' (Yuen, 2016). Stroud and Wee (2007) make a distinction between the direct consumption of languages as denotational codes and the indirect consumption of linguistic repertoires via being engaged in various activities such as wine tasting or listening to pop music. The inclusion of these texts on university syllabuses are instances of the latter.

In these examples described so far, even as the market for the consumption of Singlish moves from being more domestic to being more international, the legitimacy of many of these products derives from the producers themselves being native speakers of Singlish. These issues regarding the commodification of Singlish in the culture industries are nicely illustrated in the following case study of The Necessary Stage.

The Necessary Stage

The Necessary Stage (TNS) theatre company in Singapore makes for a particularly appropriate case study of the commodification of Singlish in the culture industries, for two reasons. The first has to do with the fact that Singapore's theatre scene has engaged in highly reflexive deliberations about the use of language, including Singlish. According to Shawn Chua (p.c.), a researcher with

TNS, there was in the late 1980s and early 1990s a concern with developing an appropriate voice and language for the theatre:

What recurs is the search for a local voice and identity, how the use of Singlish at that time was closely associated with humour (whether intended or not) or was too self-conscious, the ambivalent role of theatre as a tool of language instruction, how TNS was one of the pioneers committed to this exploration of an 'indigenous voice', as well as critical distinction between multilingualism and 'Singlish'.

In a 1997 newspaper article titled 'Finding the right language for stage', Gasmier quotes Alvin Tan as lamenting the 'linguistic insecurity' of actors. It was evidenced by them 'changing their way of speaking the moment they walked on to a stage' and 'made it necessary to work harder at getting them to speak in their natural tones'. As Tan (quoted in Gasmier, 1997) puts it,

We are still exploring what language we want to use . . . There is standard formal English, there is Singlish, there is English with a Singlish intonation but with correct grammar. And of course there is the Queen's English. We know definitely that we don't want the Queen's English but we are not sure what we want. Putting in an English intonation is not enough, we have to find a correct stage language. We have to find a language which can express our identity, our cultural background, who we are.

Lim Kay Siu, a professional actor, similarly expresses some ambivalence about how local English is being used in plays: 'I've seen plays where they use Singlish for the sake of using it – to draw cheap laughs. We've got to get over that stage' (Uekrongtham, 1988).

The difficulty of getting both actors and audiences comfortable with using Singlish on stage cannot be overstated. Alvin Tan recalls that when TNS first used Singlish onstage, there were uncomfortable giggles from the Singaporean audiences because 'some of them felt it wasn't acting because lines were not delivered in Received Pronunciation or Queen's English' (Chew, 2007). In a telling anecdote, Petersen (2001: 56) describes how the production of Robert Yeo's *One Year Back Home* was plagued by uncertainties about the use of English. Its director, Max Le Blond, accepted that some of the language being used was 'unnatural' and 'faults himself . . . noting that while in rehearsal, "blatantly against the facts and demands of the script, the tendency was to shift up through the gears of accent and settle at a level tangibly closer to the norms of received pronunciation"' (Le Blond, 1986: 117, quoted in Petersen, 2001: 56).

The second reason why TNS is such an appropriate object of study pertains to its status as one of the most established theatre companies devoted to Singapore-themed plays (Petersen, 2001: 58). TNS was formed in 1987 by Alvin Tan, who remains its artistic director. Haresh Sharma, the resident playwright of TNS, has written more than 100 plays. TNS is a non-profit theatre company, and according to its website (www.necessary.org/index.php/about-us; accessed 6 Dec 2015), its mission is to create challenging, indigenous and innovative theatre that touches the heart and mind ... Having presented more than 100 original plays in Singapore and abroad, TNS remains focused on breaking new ground in original local content and intercultural exploration ...

We are also committed to international exchange and networking between Singapore and other countries, through staging the company's plays abroad, inviting foreign works to be presented by the company in Singapore, through dialogues, workshops and training opportunities as well as creative collaborations leading to interdisciplinary productions.

TNS has also played an important role in helping Singaporean English become accepted as a natural aspect of local plays. As Petersen (2001: 63, 66) notes, 'The 1990s witnessed a proliferation of plays by Singaporean playwrights that reflected the rhythms of Singaporean English with increasing accuracy.' Alvin Tan and Haresh Sharma, together with other key figures in the Singapore theatre scene such as Kuo Pao Kun and Ong Keng Sen, 'have been leaders in putting before the public a range of plays that excavate the past while also reflecting the linguistic complexity that is still a part of daily life for many in Singapore'.

Four plays staged by TNS are worth noting because of how they reflect the evolution of Sharma's use of Singlish – from his early attempts to incorporate Singlish into his plays to his growing confidence that the use of Singlish, rather than working against the plays' internationalization, is in fact enhancing their reception. *Lanterns Never Go Out*, first staged in 1989, revolves around Kah Wei, a recent university graduate who stays in her room to avoid her relatives' nagging and unwanted advice. While in her room, she ruminates on her childhood, her various relationships, and her life choices. Birch (2007: 17) describes *Lanterns* as

an important, early, attempt by Sharma to explore the central structuralist/postmodernist theme of multiplicity and fragmented identity, and he did so by including a very confident use of Singapore English and Teochew. Realistic Singapore English was soon to become a major feature of much of Sharma's writings until the 2000s.

Talk 1 was staged in 1994. It is a play about the importance of communication that uses the format of a talk show. In his commentary on *Talk 1*, Birch (2007: 95) comments,

We also see in *Talk* some loosening up of language, given that restrictions on what could take place on stage were beginning to be a little more relaxed. Sharma is quite clearly seeing how far he might be able to go. He was always testing the waters, of course, but from 1993 on he was prepared to go further than he has previously. Furthermore, his now very confident use of Singapore English really does enable him to put Singapore and Singaporeans more firmly on the stage than has been done in the past, by anyone. The three characters in *Talk*, for example, switch from the more formal English they are required to use on television to the Singapore form of English they use themselves in everyday situations.

Still Building is a highly intimate play about the constraints and boundaries imposed by various kinds of relationships. According to Sharma's own notes to the play, 'the cast sits with you, the audience, speaks directly to you, asking you to see his/her point of view and draws you into their dilemmas and is affectionate in your midst. You have no choice but to become part of their world.' *Still Building* was first staged in 1992 and was the first of TNS's productions to be taken overseas, appearing at theatre festivals in Cairo, Glasgow and London. According to Birch (2007: 56), 'in *Still Building*, Sharma freely uses Malay, Hokkien and Mandarin, as well as realistic Singapore English, representing Singapore's extensive linguistic code-switching and mixing'. Around the time of its opening, Sharma was quoted in a local newspaper as saying, 'What's important now is that we get to test the universal appeal of the play. We have done a lot of Singaporean stuff and it's time to find out if this can be understood anywhere in the world or if we have over localized our work' (*Straits Times*, 27 April 1992).

As the following dialogue from *Still Building* shows, the characters from the play use Mandarin, as well as highly colloquial Singapore English. TNS even went so far as to compile a glossary for the audience explaining words such as 'hong yu' (Hokkien for medicinal oil) and 'jaga' (a security guard) (*The New Paper*, 20 May 1993):

MAY: (in Mandarin) How come so hot today?
JENNY: (in Mandarin) Ai yah, everyday also hot. (in English) Mr Razali. You not hot ah?
RAZALI: Hot.
MAY: But today . . . so hot like want to die already. I never sweat so much. See lah, my armpit all wet already. So embarrassing! Customers all can see. Mr Razali, you so good. You don't sweat ah?

May's question about the weather is entirely in Mandarin. Jenny's response to May is also in Mandarin, but her question to Razali is in colloquial Singapore English, as can be seen from the absence of any main verb and the use of the particle *ah*. Razali's monosyllabic answer, too, is phrased in colloquial Singapore English, being marked by the predicate and the absence of a subject. May's subsequent contribution indicates a switch from her earlier use of Mandarin to colloquial Singapore English: her response lacks a subject (*so hot like want to die already*) and a main verb (*you so good*) and contains various particles (*lah, ah*).

Birch (2007: 56) notes the positive international reception of the play: 'their [TNS's] interaction with other theatre companies was a very valuable experience enabling them to recognize that in fact their work was internationally approachable by much larger audiences who spoke English than were those productions delivered in the Cairo festival completely in French, Spanish or

Tagalog'. The positive reaction overseas was greatly encouraging for Alvin Tan, who is quoted as saying, 'It's very reassuring for us because we know how Singlish is condemned at home. It confirms how we felt, that this is a treasure' (*Straits Time*, 3 December 1994).

The fourth play, *Off Centre*, was staged in 1993. It is about the problems and prejudices faced by two former mental patients, Vinod and Saloma, which culminate in Vinod's suicide. The Ministry of Information and the Arts was concerned that the play 'presented a prejudiced view of mental disorder, its treatability and the therapists, besides ridiculing God, religion and national service' (Tan, 2015). The Ministry of Health even required that Sharma shift his original focus on schizophrenia to the less sensitive matter of common depression. Sharma's refusal to make this shift led to the withdrawal of funding support from the Ministry of Health, which had originally agreed to provide a grant of $30,000. This meant that TNS had to cover the costs from its own funds.

Birch (2007: 81, italics in original) emphasizes the level of sophistication and maturity exemplified by Sharma's use of language in *Off Centre*:

For the first time in Singapore we see, in a dramatist, a *consistent* and *sensitive* recognition and use of the language of Singapore, not simply to create effect, or to try and replace standard English on stage as some sort of postcolonial edging out of the language and discourse of colonial oppression, but as a recognition that language is more than words and syntax; it is the life and soul – the heart – the be all and end all – of what constitutes a social, cultural and personal identity. That is where Sharma makes one of his most important contributions in these first few years of his work.

These two issues – the sensitive and serious matter of the play and Sharma's use of language – have to be seen in relation to each other. In *Off Centre*, the varieties of English used are 'careful and realistic, ranging from the very formal to "Singlish"' (Birch, 2007: 81). In the piece of dialogue shown later, Vinod's English tends towards the standard variety, whereas Saloma's can be described as much more Singlish in nature, being colloquial and basilectal even. This variation is intended to reflect the differences in the characters' educational backgrounds. At the same time, Vinod's English also includes elements that might be considered Singlish, such as the absence of a grammatical subject and an indefinite article in the embedded clause (*I thought must have follow* up), the exclamatory 'Wah', the particle 'lah', and the absence of inflection (*He always force his views on me*). More to the point, the seriousness of the exchange between Vinod and Saloma means that the audience is expected to focus on the content of the discussion. The range of English used is not in itself the object of interest, which what allows the language to come across as natural. This is particularly noteworthy given that plays are what Coupland (2007: 148) calls 'high performance events':

They are scheduled events, typically pre-announced and planned, and therefore pro-grammed. They are temporarily and spatially bounded events, marked off from the rou-tine flow of communicative practice. They are co-ordinated, in the sense that they rely on specific sorts of collaborative activity, not least in that performers and audience members will establish themselves in these participant roles for the enactment of the performance.

High-performance events thus tend to be marked by greater self-consciousness about the use of language. This is one reason why Singapore theatre has engaged in such a deliberate and reflexive struggle with finding the 'right voice and language', and why (as noted several times already) Singlish, when it is used, tends to be stereotypically associated with humour to the point where it is often used for 'cheap laughs'. In this regard, Sharma's achievement in back-grounding or naturalizing the range of English found in Singapore so that it does not detract from but contributes to the poignancy of characters' emotional difficulties cannot be overstated.

VINOD: Do you still see a psychiatrist?
SALOMA: No.
VINOD: How come? I thought must have follow up.
SALOMA: I cannot pay. See doctor, buy medicine, stay at Woodbridge . . . my mother pay a lot of money already!
VINOD: Anyway, you're not missing anything. My psychiatrist only sees me for five minute. How are you? Fine thank you. Next! That's why my parents also make me see a therapist. Wah! Like New York right? But no use lah. Terrible, you know. He always force his views on me. And where are his views influenced from? [loud] The majority!! [soft] I'm a minority person. You know what he said? You must study, get a job, be the best, make a lot of money, but take it easy. Gimme a break!
SALOMA: Vinod, you smart. I am not smart. My best only 'N' level.
VINOD: Yah! What can you do with 'N' level . . . even if you don't have mental illness?

Importantly, since 2007, the Ministry of Education has included *Off Centre* in the GCE 'O' and 'N' level literature syllabus. It was in fact the first Singapore play to be offered as a school literature text. Thus, despite the initial appre-hensions of the government authorities, the play has since been accepted as a landmark in Singapore's theatre history.

Yet, TNS still remains conscious of and sensitive to the government's stance against Singlish. Sharma[3] points out that TNS still receives expressions of con-cern from teachers and students regarding the use of Singlish in some of his plays; they worry about the effect that it might have on students' English. He also explained that unlike the more 'elaborate' plays that TNS stages for the general public, he tries to avoid using Singlish in the shorter and simpler plays that are specifically created for the schools, saying, 'We don't bring Singlish to the schools'. Sharma laments that Singlish continues to be 'an easy target for

---

[3] Author's interview with Haresh Sharma conducted on 26 February 2016.

the government' because it is seen as 'a joke', by which he means that many of the examples of Singlish held up for vilification involve exaggerated uses of language and clownish behaviour. Sharma makes the important point here that the use of Singlish does not have to call attention to itself. If done 'properly' to reflect more authentic exchanges, Singlish would not be an issue because it would not even be noticed by the audience.

The TNS case study shows how the ambivalent attitudes towards Singlish that the company has had to deal with domestically contrasts with its plays' much more enthusiastic acceptance internationally. This more unequivocal international acceptance supports Brown-Saracino's (2009) suggestion that there appears to be a relatively widespread interest, especially among well-educated and affluent individuals, in the consumption of cultural products that provide them with some 'insight experience' into the culture of others. Brown-Saracino (2009: 192) refers to such individuals as 'cultural omnivores', referencing Peterson and Kern's (1996: 3) observation that the scope of cultural consumption amongst elites has widened 'from exclusionist snob to inclusionist omnivore' The cultural omnivore's inclusionist orientation is manifested in an 'appreciation for the underdog, which results in 'an ethos that values a sort of cultural democracy that embraces a familiarity with low-, middle-, and highbrow cultural objects alike – that celebrates the idiosyncratic character of people and place' underdog' (Brown-Saracino, 2009: 192). We can see how Singlish is attractive from a consumption perspective precisely because it suits the cultural omnivore's diet. It is positioned, albeit stereotypically, as a celebration of low culture that simultaneously indexes an authentically Singaporean experience. At the same time, if presented in sufficiently small doses or if accompanied by translations or glosses, Singlish does not become so unintelligible as to make the act of cultural consumption unnecessarily difficult.

Crucially, it is precisely because – from the cultural omnivore's perspective – encounters with Singlish are supposed to provide insights into authentic Singapore culture that the use of Singlish in a cultural product derives its legitimacy and appeal from the fact that it has been produced by a native speaker, in this case, the playwright Haresh Sharma. I suggest that we are looking here at commodification along the lines of both Marx's more traditional understanding of a product that exists 'outside of us' and the neoliberal emphasis on skill or capital. In this example, the products are the plays themselves as material objects in the form of scripts, as well as the performances that audiences pay to experience. The skill refers to the playwright's craftsmanship, in this case, Sharma's ear for authentic (Singaporean) dialogue and ability to create compelling characters. But if we abstract away from the individual producer (be this a dictionary maker, film-maker or playwright), then it is the Marxist view of commodity that dominates or gets foregrounded in the case of the culture industries. The issue here is not about whether Sharma is a better or more competent Singlish speaker than, say, C. Goh or Woo. Each might be individually judged on the artistic merits of his or her products (e.g. how Sharma's plays compare with those of other Singaporean playwrights or even how his recent plays compare with his earlier ones). But as far as the category 'native speaker' is concerned, membership in this category is treated, as per Van Doorn's (2014: 357) apt formulation, as a 'fundamentally collective subject'.

This is because in the culture industries, the native speaker of Singlish is critical as he or she is the producer who guarantees the provenance or authenticity of any cultural product involving the use of Singlish. That is, it is the producer's membership in this collective category – more so than his or her individual language skills – that gives the cultural product its imprimatur of authenticity. The product, once completed, is deemed to exist independently of the producer – for example, the *Coxford Singlish Dictionary*, various Singaporean films, TNS's plays – and is ready for consumption locally as well as internationally.

In contrast, as we now see, once we move to the non-culture industries, it is the view of commodification as human capital that dominates so that the link between Singlish and its native speakers slowly becomes uncoupled.

Singlish and the Non-Culture Industries

Consider an advertisement in a local newspaper for a workshop where one can learn 'Basic Singlish for daily use' (www.deal.com.sg/deals/singapore/really-meh-2-hr-singlish-workshop-199-stanford-language-centre-damn-shiok-man; accessed 25 May 2013). Notably, even the advertising text itself is in Singlish ('Really meh?...Damn shiok man' and 'Already 14 bought!'): 'meh' is a discourse-pragmatic particle that conveys skepticism, while 'shiok' is a Malay word used to convey delight. The ad also asserts that fourteen individuals had already signed up for the workshop. Thus, Singlish is not only being advertised as the content of the workshop; it is also being used as the medium of advertising itself in trying to attract participants. This is interesting because some defenders of Singlish have in the past relied on an argument involving situational code-switching to assure the government that Singlish speakers will know which situations are appropriate for the use of Singlish and which for the use of Standard English. The assumption underlying that argument was that Singlish will be used in private situations involving Singaporeans interacting among family and friends; more public and more formal situations, especially those involving foreigners, will require the use of Standard English. However, what the advertisement shows is that, as Singaporeans gain confidence and pride in Singlish, the rather simplistic correlations between varieties of English and use in specific situations – formulated along the formal/public-informal/private dimensions – are increasingly being violated.

In addition, while the participants in the workshop may include interested locals, the photograph in the advertisement shows a number of people with non-Asian features. This suggests that the advertisement is actually targeting foreigners, such as expatriates who may find knowledge of Singlish useful (and fun – according to the advertisement) as they spend prolonged periods of time living and working in Singapore.

It is at this point that we can start to see how knowledge of Singlish may be disconnected from Singaporeans themselves. There is no reason why those foreigners who have acquainted themselves with Singlish might not then try to pass on their own knowledge of the language to yet other foreigners. The cachet that such foreigners enjoy, despite not being native speakers, is that, as non-Singaporeans, they can better empathize with the challenges or difficulties involved in learning Singlish. For example, an Australian expatriate who goes by the name 'Aussie Pete' (he moved to the United States after spending ten years in Singapore) has a blog where he tries to provide a guide to Singlish for foreigners ('Singlish – A Guide for Foreigners', 28 May 2008, www.aussiepete .com/2008/05/singlish-language-guide-for-foreigners.html; accessed 2 October 2015). Aussie Pete's blog consists of brief explanations for various Singlish words and phrases, and he explains the need for his guide as follows:

As time goes by, and one spends much time living and interracting with the locals (especially outside of the tourist areas), it soon becomes apparent that English alone is not enough to fully converse on local topics.
    The intent of this post is to offer a guide to non-Singlish speaking people to perhaps better understand what is going on around them.

In yet another example, Benny Lewis ('The Irish Polyglot') offers language lessons on his blog, which claims to provide techniques that can help learners become fluent in various languages, including Singlish, in three months (www .fluentin3months.com/singlish; accessed 2 October 2015):

I'm Benny Lewis, a fun-loving Irish guy, a full-time globe trotter and international best-selling author. Since 2003, I've become a fluent and confident speaker of seven languages. And I'm able to have confident conversations in many others. I help people just like you to feel confident in speaking another language, even if they've only just started learning. My mission in life is *giving people permission to make mistakes*.

Finally, Cullen Hartley ('Education in Asia: 10 Singlish words to learn', www .cullenhartley.com/2009/05/10-singlish-words-to-learn; accessed 2 October 2015) tries to provide what he considers to be useful and stripped-down 'Basic Singlish' for expatriates:

If you're a soon-to-be expatriate planning a move to Singapore, you have undoubtedly heard of Singlish, the peculiar creole English spoken by most native Singaporeans. It is a mix of Malay, Chinese dialects, and English. Most people who bother to write about Singlish know it well, and they produce in-depth dictionaries cataloging the dialect's nuances. These books are an ever-present facet of every Singaporean bookstore, and if you want to learn more the material is definitely out there.

However, I feel the end result for most foreigners that pick up Singlish dictionaries is terminal information overload. People just don't learn much from picking up a dictionary. Even-tempered expats become overwhelmed and give up and the more adventurous look silly as they misuse and mispronounce words. (Excuse me, did you see that ang kat makaning char siew cheem bye? Lah-lor.)

I don't claim to be an expert on Singlish, but I will share ten words that I guarantee that you'll hear in Singapore.

The advertised workshop and blogs all point to a commodification of Singlish, where it is no longer just an in-group identity marker of solidarity but is also a cultural product that can be increasingly conveyed to non-Singaporeans *by* non-Singaporeans. Singlish can now be separated from Singaporeans and potentially even from the Singaporean identity itself. This is because anyone (Singaporean or otherwise) who professes a knowledge of Singlish might attempt to capitalize on that knowledge. Such a development may raise concerns amongst Singaporeans who might worry that 'their' cultural identity is being hijacked. But, as Budach, Roy and Heller (2003: 606–607) point out, this is a very real scenario when language is commodified in the new globalized economy:

In these conditions, the tight connection between language and identity is disturbed; language skills can have value independent of the "identity" of the speaker, and "identity" can be sold – in the forms of dance, music, museums, art, and so on – without the producers' having to be able to provide any of the historically related linguistic performances. Nonetheless, uncoupling does not always happen; groups understanding themselves historically as a community will use the notion of inheritance to legitimize privileged access to linguistic resources and to their new markets (see Rampton, 1995 on the notion of inheritance).

Since no single individual or group holds any proprietary claim to Singlish, even as some Singaporeans might object to the language becoming delinked from Singaporeans, other Singaporeans might actually celebrate its spread and embrace by non-Singaporeans.

Here, then, we have at work the neoliberal view of commodification, in contrast to that of Marx; this neoliberal conception understands commodification as embodied capital that is thus not easily dissociated from the specific language user or speaker. Each individual's linguistic skill therefore represents an investment in his or her own human capital, one that is open-ended enough that the individual may be spurred or even obligated to constantly improve on that skill. This continued investment in the self is what gives the embodied capital view of commodification its neoliberal character. As Feher (2009: 27) puts it,

an investor in his or her human capital is concerned less with maximizing the returns on his or her investments – whether monetary or psychic – than with appreciating, that is, increasing the stock value of, the capital to which he or she is identified. In other words, insofar as our condition is that of human capital in a neoliberal environment, our main purpose is not so much to profit from our accumulated potential as to constantly value or appreciate ourselves – or at least prevent our own depreciation.

What non-Singaporeans like Benny Lewis and Cullen Hartley are purveying are their own individual experiences with Singlish. They are not claiming to have any native speaker expertise in Singlish. In fact, Hartley is explicit in his disclaimer ('I don't claim to be an expert on Singlish'), and Lewis's goal is to get speakers to be comfortable with the idea of making mistakes. Nevertheless, they are claiming to have sufficient knowledge of and experience with Singlish that their guidance will be of value and relevance to other foreign visitors to Singapore.[4]

Conclusion: Implications for the Authenticity and Ownership of Singlish

In this chapter, I dealt with the commodification of Singlish in the culture and non-culture industries. The Marxist view of commodity as an independently existing object tends to be dominant in the culture industries, whereas the neoliberal view of commodity as embodied capital is more dominant in the non-culture industries.

At first blush, this state of affairs appears somewhat paradoxical. Why should non-native speakers of Singlish be keen to draw on the neoliberal notion of skills and human capital in contrast to their native-speaking counterparts? The answer lies in the fact that skills highlight the active process of learning and their value is situation-specific. In this regard, non-native speakers such as Benny Lewis and Cullen Hartley are foregrounding that their Singlish 'skill-set' is not just about the language but also – given their own experiences in

---

[4] This line of argument is familiar in English-language teaching contexts, in attempts to overcome the hegemonic status of the traditional native speaker. ELT scholars have argued that non-native speakers of English have their own roles to play, not least because they are more able to empathize with the linguistic realities of students for whom English is being learnt as a second or foreign language (Modiano, 1999: 23; Widdowson, 1994: 387).

learning the language – includes the kinds of situations and communicative difficulties that they and other foreigners to Singapore might experience. Language here is a skill that each speaker acquires to varying degrees of competence. And because the acquisition of language is partial and dynamic, it can continue indefinitely. Authenticity then becomes less of a concern than communicative efficacy since (i) each individual learns the skill anew and through the learning process willy-nilly introduces changes to the language practices, and (ii) each individual as a demonstration of his or her skill will have to be versatile and adaptable in deploying linguistic resources in response to new and different communicative demands.

In contrast, it would be odd for native speakers of Singlish such as Haresh Sharma or Colin Goh to highlight the situations and experiences by which they came to learn or acquire Singlish. The issue is not that this is impossible to do, but rather that it is ideologically at odds with the cultural model of native speakerism (Holliday, 2005). Native speakerism, as noted at the beginning of this chapter, takes it for granted that, simply by virtue of *being* a native speaker, one *possesses* a special insight into the language. In turn, the language and, by extension, the rules or norms governing how it is to be spoken (or written – although there has a been a historical tendency to privilege the spoken form as being a truer reflection of the language) are presumed to exist independently of the speaker. Hence, there is neither a reason for native speakers to highlight the specific details of their acquisitional experiences nor any need to qualify their level of language competence. Language is essentialized as a cultural heritage for which its speakers – as a representative of the community of native speakers – have special insight.

Linguistic products are thus detachable from individual native speakers *a la* Marx's understanding of commodity precisely because it is their community membership, rather than their individual skills, that guarantees its authenticity. There is nothing about the Marxist view, of course, that links language to the native speaker. But as a matter of historical default, the traditional influence of Marx's view of commodification and the tendency to think of language as a bounded autonomous system about which native speakers have some special intuition or knowledge have converged. Consequently, the native speaker, rather than representing an individual, represents instead a collectivity. The individual native speaker is a metonym for this collective cultural linguistic knowledge that is expected to be possessed simply as a result of one's racial characteristics (Rampton, 1995). There is some measure of irony in this. To metaphorically draw on Marx's economic discussion, one might say that the native speaker is analogous to an employee working for the 'right' company so that it is the company's brand that guarantees the quality of the product. In contrast, the non-native speaker is analogous to an individual manufacturer or craftsman who has to constantly demonstrate the relevant craftsmanship in order to attract and retain customers.

By way of closing, it is worth recalling Widdowson's (1994) remarks on the ownership of English. Widdowson was specifically concerned with the global spread of Standard English, and his key argument is that, as an international language, it is being used by various communities for multiple purposes, which 'transcend traditional communal and cultural boundaries . . . develop their own conventions [and] standard [so that] you do not need native speakers to tell you what [the standard] is' (382). Now, Singlish is most certainly not Standard English nor is it anywhere near as global or international. Nevertheless, being global or international is a matter of degree, rather than a binary property, and Singlish is certainly, thanks to the various industries involved in its commodification, becoming much more global than it used to be. As a consequence, the communal and communicative functions of Standard English that Widdowson (1994: 381–382) describes also apply to Singlish:

So when the custodians of standard English complain about the ungrammatical language of the populace, they are in effect indicating that the perpetrators are outsiders, nonmembers of the community . . .

I do not wish to imply that this communal function is to be deplored. Languages of every variety have this dual character: They provide the means for communication and at the same time express a sense of community, represent the stability of its conventions and values, in short its culture. All communities possess and protect their languages.

In the case of Singlish, while there are as yet no vocal or strident expressions of concern about its falling standards, ownership or appropriation by 'outsiders' – unlike the case of Standard English (Bex and Watts, 1999; Honey, 1997; Kachru, 1985, 1986, 1991; Milroy and Milroy, 1999; Quirk, 1990), it is not far-fetched to suggest that Singlish is at something of a crossroads. Those Singaporeans who are proud of Singlish and who wish to see it being more widely appreciated have to be aware that, as the language spreads and gains in popularity, the custodial role that Singaporeans presume to play as guardians of what counts as 'good/appropriate/correct Singlish' might well over time be lost.

In making these observations, I am not suggesting that Singaporeans qua custodians of Singlish are necessarily in any position to exercise agency over the matter. That is, Singaporeans, including key players in the culture industries such as local novelists, artists, playwrights, film-makers and dictionary makers, are not yet in a position to pre-empt or even remove Singlish's communicative value whilst ensuring that only its communal value survives. As Widdowson points out, these forms of value represent the dual character of language and are essentially different sides of the same coin. One does not exist without the other, and it is really a matter of the relative proportion of one to the other, rather than choosing one to the other's exclusion. The interesting complication, of course, is that as one grows in vitality, so does the other. The upshot is that, if the trajectory of Standard English is anything to go by, one strong indicator of Singlish's increasing vitality and value arising from its commodification will be arguments and controversies over who can be said to best represent 'real/authentic' Singlish.

6 Singlish, Migration and Mobility

In contemporary societies, integration and mobility force readjustments to taken-for-granted and comfortable assumptions about the stability of community boundaries, however such boundaries may be constructed. The stability of such boundaries is in any case already being challenged by rapid developments in transportation and communication technologies that make it possible for individuals to maintain, with relative ease, memberships in multiple communities and also with varying degrees of commitment. Nevertheless, migration and mobility remain matters of particular sensitivity vis-à-vis community boundaries because inward migration confronts the community with changes in daily patterns of interactions and even in infrastructure as new individuals, ethnic groups and cultural practices all make their presence felt. Likewise, though perhaps to a lesser extent, outward migration, depending on the reasons for why people are leaving and if left unchecked, can lead to a sense of loss as those left behind struggle to rejuvenate a community that appears to have lost its attractiveness for its members.

The readjustments to assumptions about the stability of community boundaries can take a number of forms. The most obvious, perhaps, is the tightening or (as the case may be) loosening of border controls. Border controls are implemented mainly at the level of the state (where concerns about the porous nature of borders are all too common), but migration and mobility also have impacts at the level of the city and neighborhood. Hence, having a more pervasive impact than border controls are issues of integration and solidarity in which social, cultural and linguistic shibboleths may be used to distinguish 'insiders' from 'outsiders'.

On all levels, the net effect of the continued mass movement of peoples is to heighten the awareness of community boundaries and, by extension, increase reflection about the nature of community identity, in the course of which such boundaries may shift and understandings of identities change. Completely dispensing with boundaries altogether is never a seriously considered option. One may wonder whether it would even be possible to eliminate boundaries and still retain some sense of identity. This seems unlikely given the relational nature of identity such that it needs a contrastive 'Other' to be defined, even if amorphously (Bucholtz and Hall, 2005). And so it is the need for a sense of identity that ultimately drives the establishment and re-establishment of boundaries, a point that Ulrich Beck, a sociologist and public intellectual (Slater and Ritzer, 2001: 266), seems to acknowledge when he remarks that boundaries will still be need to drawn even if they are 'fictive'.

In Singapore, inward migration is an important concern because of the government's foreign talent policy. Recall that Singapore has always been ethnically diverse, and the government has been very mindful that its language policy should reflect the country's multiracial character (see Chapter 1). It is for this reason that, in addition to recognizing the official ethnic mother tongues, the government granted English the status of an official language. The government envisioned that it would serve as an inter-ethnic lingua franca. But with rapid modernization and urbanization have come changes to marriage and reproduction patterns so that a nagging concern (certainly not unique to Singapore) has been the country's low fertility rate. And while the government has been actively encouraging Singaporeans to marry earlier and to have more children, it has also been aggressively trying to attract 'foreign talent' in the hope that such individuals will ultimately take up Singaporean citizenship and thus help to make up for the lack of reproductive productivity. At the same time, outward migration is also an issue because, as Singaporeans become better educated and more worldly, many are becoming much more mobile, and increasing numbers are working and living overseas. This has forced the government to devise strategies to foster and strengthen a globalized sense of what it means to be Singaporean, one that may no longer be defined by physically living within the country's territorial boundaries or, at the very least, is less reliant on such territorial boundedness.

Supporters of Singlish have actively championed Singlish as the language that can unite Singaporeans, as well as help to integrate new citizens. And while the government has seen fit to occasionally make use of Singlish, especially in trying to maintain contact with overseas Singaporeans, its official stance still remains strongly anti-Singlish (as we just saw in Chapter 5). This aspect of the Singlish controversy therefore raises fundamental questions about how language fits into nationalist imaginings, and I argue that both the supporters and detractors of Singlish expect the language that represents Singapore to bear an iconic relationship to the nationalist imagining. It is the difference in such imagining and interpretation of iconicity that leads to differences of opinion as to the suitability of Singlish, as I show later.

I organize this chapter's discussion as follows. I first focus on the issue of inward migration to show that Singlish is seen by a number of Singaporeans as a marker of successful integration into Singapore society. By the same token, it is used to distinguish non- or even 'inauthentic' Singaporeans from 'real' Singaporeans. I then address the issue of outwardly mobile Singaporeans. Here,

I explore how the government has made use of Singlish as it organizes activities to bond together overseas Singaporeans and remind them not to forget their Singaporean roots. I also explore the use of Singlish amongst overseas Singaporeans apart from any government-organized activity. Finally, I bring together the observations in these earlier sections to point out that there are different nationalist imaginings at work. Whereas the government is still clinging to an understanding of Singaporean diversity as a multiracial patchwork of distinct ethnicities – hence, its preference for multiple and distinct ethnic mother tongues to represent Singapore – supporters of Singlish are keen to emphasize the increasingly hybrid, fluid and boundary-changing nature of this diversity. For them, the linguistic amalgam that is Singlish is an ideal and iconic reflection of such hybridity and fluidity. Multiracialism and hybridity need not be mutually exclusive, of course. But in the context of globalization, patterns of diversity in Singapore are shifting from the former towards the latter – a fact that even the Singapore government recognizes albeit with some reluctance. As a result, not only is there is no reason why Singlish cannot co-exist with the official ethnic mother tongues but also it might actually be prudent from a language policy perspective for the government to start adopting a more accepting stance towards Singlish.

Inward Migration: Foreign Workers

While the Singapore government in the late 1960s was worried about overcrowding and overpopulation so that its population policy then was 'Stop at Two', by the 1980s, the new slogan was 'Have Three, or More if You Can Afford It'. According to a government website ('HistorySG: An Online Resource Guide', http://eresources.nlb.gov.sg/history/events/1d106f7e-aca1–4c0e-ac7a-d35d0772707d; accessed 8 June 2016), the fertility rate

decline began in 1977 when the TFR (Total Fertility Rate) dropped to 1.82 after registering 2.11 in 1976. Thereafter, the figure continued slipping and reached 1.74 in 1980; by 1986, the TFR was 1.42, which was the lowest in the decade of the1980s. The fall in fertility rate was attributed to various factors, including the two-child population policy and the lopsided procreation pattern in which better-educated married couples were delaying parenthood...

Previous anti-natalist measures, such as disincentives against the third child in school registration, were removed. These were replaced by new incentives designed to ease the burden of having a third child, such as tax rebates, childcare subsidies and the ability to use Medisave to cover the delivery costs of the first three children.

...

Over the years, the government regularly strengthened these pro-natalist incentives marked by the increase in tax rebates and childcare subsidies to encourage parents to have more children...Despite these measures, Singapore's TFR continued to stay well below the replacement level of 2.1 children, averaging 1.9 from 1990 to 1999, 1.4 from 2000 to 2009 period, and 1.2 from 2010 to 2013.

To compensate for this low population growth, the government decided to focus on attracting skilled foreign workers or 'foreign talent' (Yap, 2015: 28). Senior minister Goh Chok Tong elaborated on the importance of attracting talented foreigners in his 2000 National Day Rally speech:

Globalisation and technology have made the competitive environment a tougher one for us. For example, the Internet has removed geography as a barrier to competition. It will be the Silk Road of the world, bridging civilisations and distant places...In these growth sectors of the future, the key success factor is people. Talent and knowledge will decide who will be winners and losers. We must therefore change our mindset towards foreign talent. If we systematically recruit and welcome talent, and absorb them into our society, they will raise our know-how and competitive edge.

We have a lot to learn from the US here. The US economy is so vibrant largely because it is a talent-importing country. Throughout its history, it has attracted immigrants, including talent of all races and religiopns from many countries. These foreign talent have, over time, become American talent.

We cannot hope to attract the same range and depth of talent as Silicon Valley. But we can be a magnet for Asian talent. Even if we do not manage to get their very best, given the vast reservoir to draw from, the talent that does come will still be of high quality, and will contribute significantly to our development. I see foreign talent, or global talent, not as a quick fix to make up for the shortage of local workers. This is a long-term strategy to enable Singapore to sustain its vitality, competitiveness and prosperity. If we can absorb a steady inflow of global talent into Singapore, our ideas and outlook will stay fresh and vibrant, and we can be a competitive, global player.

There are a number of significant themes in this extract that have a bearing on Singapore's language policy. First, the foreign talent policy is not a 'quick fix', but a 'long-term strategy'. This is reflected in the government's establishment of a National Population and Talent Division that aims to support parenthood, engage talent, integrate new immigrants and also retain connections with overseas Singaporeans (www.nptd.gov.sg; accessed 8 June 2016).

Second, Goh uses the United States as an example of a place where immigrants have settled and in the process, become 'American talent'. The government is therefore not merely interested in attracting talent to work in the country; it also hopes to persuade such talent to ultimately take up Singaporean citizenship so as to become 'Singaporean talent'. Thirdly, although the United States has attracted 'talent of all races and religions from many countries', Goh's own vision (at least initially) for Singapore seems to be more restrictive and conservative: it is merely to be a 'magnet for Asian talent'. This final point is consistent with Singapore's ethnic mother tongue policy that, as we saw in Chapter 1, is intent on preserving an Asian identity and Asian values in opposition to Western ones (which is why English is not acceptable as an official mother tongue).

However, in the very next year, in the 2001 National Day Rally speech, Goh revisits the foreign talent issue, and while he makes essentially the same points, it is worth noting that he simply presents Singapore as a 'powerful magnet', thereby no longer restricting its pull to Asian talent: 'We, therefore, have to make Singapore a powerful magnet so as to be able to retain our own talent as well as draw in foreign talent. The more talent we have, the stronger our economic capability. Our companies will prosper. We will create jobs and wealth for all our people.'

As Wee and Bokhorst-Heng (2005) observe, this prioritizing of attracting foreign talent raises the possibility of bringing major changes to Singapore's demographic makeup, since the desired talent could very well come from a variety of ethnicities, not merely Asian ones. Indeed, the following quote from Prime Minister Goh Chok Tong's 1999 National Day Rally speech points to an appreciation of the possibility that Singapore could become 'less Asian' (see Chapter 1):

As Singapore becomes more international, there is an even greater need to preserve our Asian culture. Our bilingual policy becomes even more important. A good knowledge of our mother tongue will help us to retain our values, customs and culture. This will help us to foster close bonds with each other and to remain emotionally rooted to Singapore even when the Asian identity of our society is gradually diluted over time.

Goh's statement indicates that, while the government is aware that Singapore's demographics may change drastically in the near future, it is nevertheless digging in its heels by insisting that the ethnic mother tongues will be more important than ever.[1] His speech thus reflects the government's multiracial stance that holds that maintaining an ethnically diverse Singapore requires the recognition of and support for multiple mother tongues. This multiracial nationalist imagining motivated Singapore's historical departure from the Federation of Malaysia (see Chapter 1), and it remains largely unchanged even in the context of the foreign talent policy. But precisely because the extant language policy indeed 'becomes even more important', the question of how to reconcile a 'less Asian' Singapore with the need to 'preserve our Asian culture' is left unaddressed.

Goh likely did not address this question because the government's commitment to attracting foreign talent has created considerable unease among Singaporeans; therefore, the less said about its possible ramifications for the

---

[1] For an argument that the bilingual policy, which emphasizes English and an officially recognized ethnic mother tongue, will need to be modified to recognize individual mother tongues, including non-Asian ones, see Wee and Bokhorst-Heng (2005).

language policy the better. And while some Singapore citizens, such as the participants at various seminars held during a Singapore Student Symposium, are interested in how 'Singapore can help the foreigners to integrate into society and encourage these newcomers to sink their roots and set up homes here and ultimately become citizens themselves' (Chng, 2000: 3), there are also commonly expressed concern about those newcomers. A recent poll conducted in 2010 shows that these issues have not gone away (Lin, 2010). All these concerns continue. And at a government feedback session, a number of participants expressed their unhappiness that foreign men who become citizens were not required to perform the mandatory period of military service known as National Service, as well as their apprehension that the government was granting permanent residence status too easily to foreign talent who had yet to prove their commitment to the country (*The Straits Times*, 17 July 1998). All these concerns ultimately raise the question of what it means to be a Singaporean, especially if the government is seen to be privileging foreigners over its own citizens.

In addition to 'foreign talent', the government has also brought in lower-skilled foreign workers, such as domestic help and construction workers. Unlike the sought-after 'foreign talent' for whom immigration policies have been liberalized, the immigration of this latter group is restricted in a number of ways. They are subject to the

work-permit system, by which foreign workers are only allowed to work for the employer and in the occupation as reflected in the work permit, with employment contracts of a maximum of two years (subject to a one-off renewal), and therefore cannot gain access to the local labor market. Foreign workers are also subject to repatriation during periods of economic downturn, or in the case of females, upon becoming pregnant. Furthermore, they are not allowed to bring their spouses and children with them, nor can they marry Singaporeans or permanent residents (PRs). (Lim, 2010: 32–33)

The overall result of bringing in foreigners to work and live in Singapore – whether as 'foreign talent' or otherwise – has been an increase in the proportion of the nonresident/noncitizen population (Yeoh, 2007, cited in Lim, 2010: 31–32); the most rapid increase took place between 1990 and 2006, when this group grew by 170% from 248,000 to 670,000.

By 2011, perhaps unsurprisingly, the government's policy of bringing in foreigners had become a major source of tension. Prime Minister Lee Hsien Loong had no choice but to address it in a National Day Rally Speech, when he argued that even though this policy would have long-term benefits, there were in the short-term 'downsides':

One of these policies is foreign workers and immigrants. It is not easy because these are policies where the benefits are there but they are long term, whereas the downsides are immediate, the side effects are visible and people react to them and we have to respond to this. The foreign workers and immigrants we have taken have given us considerable benefits. Our economy has grown, our population has increased but over the last few years, the changes have been taking place quite fast and Singaporeans worry about the impact on them . . .

Unemployment is only about 2.2 per cent overall but still I know that Singaporeans worry about competition from foreigners.

The government paid a political price for its support for foreign immigration in the 2011 General Elections (Wee, 2015). The ruling political party, the People's Action Party, suffered significant setbacks despite winning enough votes to stay in power. One key setback was that the party won 'only' 60.14% of the vote, the lowest percentage since Singapore's independence. Another was the loss of a Group Representation Constituency (GRC) to the opposition for the first time in Singapore's electoral history. In a GRC, candidates from the same party stand as a group, which ranges in size from three to six individuals, at leas one of whom must come from an ethnic minority community (e.g. Malay or Indian). The group is voted into parliament as a unit. The PAP introduced the GRC structure as a means of ensuring minority representation in parliament. The popular belief was that the ruling party would never lose a GRC, but this was proven wrong in 2011. Even worse, one member of this losing GRC was a well-respected and popular minister, George Yeo. Speaking at a lunchtime rally, Lee Hsien Loong publicly acknowledged that there had been mistakes and that government interventions could have been better managed; he also recognized the deep unhappiness with 'higher housing prices and overcrowding on trains and buses caused, critics say, by lax immigration policies and an influx of foreigners' (Gopalakrishnan and Lim, 2011).

Singlish plays a curious role in the tensions raised by foreigners and their possible integration into Singapore. Goh (2016: 5) points out that a 2013 government white paper, which emphasized the continuing need for immigrants and foreign workers, 'provoked unhappy sentiments among many locals who felt that the policy outlined would worsen the crowdedness and quality of life of locals'. Moreover,

this growth in hot topics of complaint in Singapore everyday life was in turn exacerbated by the growing pervasiveness of social media, which permitted more local voices to express their views on big social media sites like Facebook, as well as local ones like *The Online Citizen* (theonlinecitizen.com) and *Sgforums* (sgforums.com), and via personal blogs.

It was in this period that Singlish moved subtly but noticeably from a discourse of playfulness in public culture, to an increasingly politicised discourse mobilised in angry social commentary especially in social media. (Goh, 2016: 5–6)

Because of the anxieties over immigration, the playful nature of Singlish has started occasionally to take on a somewhat more serious overtone, becoming a cultural shibboleth that distinguishes 'real' Singaporeans.

In effect, Singlish (among other indicators such as visible ethnicity, public behaviour, and class) has become a cultural-political shibboleth, mobilised in a project of defining and defending the space of the constructed 'Singaporean' from those perceived to be outsiders.

The following blog post demonstrates the kinds of sentiments described by Goh (2016). Chan, somewhat tongue in cheek, starts with the assertion that the use of Singlish serves to distinguish between 'two kinds of Singaporeans' but then suggests that there is actually 'only one kind' so that anyone who does not speak Singlish is basically a foreigner.

(1)   Chan Kai Chern, 'Singlish OK what. Why cannot speak leh?', 16 January 2014 (http://poachedmag.com/2014/01/16/singlish-ok-what-why-cannot-speak-leh/; accessed 26 May 2016):
There are two kinds of Singaporeans in Singapore. The first, that speaks and understands Singlish, and the second kind that does not . . . Wait a second. You know what. Screw that.
There is only one kind of Singaporean in Singapore. The kind that grows up communicating in the language of the Lion City. Singaporean-English, known now to the world collectively as Singlish.
What's that? You grew up here and you don't speak Singlish? You're a foreigner.

It would therefore seem that at least a number of Singaporeans use the ability to speak Singlish as a marker to distinguish locals from foreigners, as well as 'real' Singaporeans from their more elitist fellow citizens. Such sentiments become particularly interesting if not altogether curious when we juxtapose them with a recent survey conducted by the Institute of Policy Studies (IPS) of five thousand households (Mathew, Chiang and Zhang, in press). Only a small percentage of respondents indicated that Singlish was the language they identified with most. When asked which language they identified with most, 33.5% said it was the official mother tongue, 32.5% said it was English, 28.5% said it was some other heritage language, and only 4.4% said it was Singlish. Mathew, Chiang and Zhang (In press) further observe that, according to the survey, 13% of Singaporeans claim to be unable to speak Singlish.

The sentiments described by Goh (2016) and the findings of the IPS survey are not necessarily in contradiction with one another. This is because there is no reason why the same language should not be used for multiple purposes. Singlish is being used as a shibboleth in one case to help identify 'true' Singaporeans, whereas in the other case, when the formal identity of being Singaporean is not an issue, there is no obligation for a Singaporean citizen to identify with the language (notwithstanding the tongue-in-cheek jibe that 'If you grew up here, then how you not speak Singlish?'). However, if the linguistic trends observed by Goh (2016) and the IPS survey are put together, it would appear that Singlish is increasingly being positioned more as a means to establish the boundary between 'Singaporean' and 'non-Singaporean' than to foster a sense

of solidarity amongst members of the category 'Singaporeans' – despite claims
to that effect from the pro-Singlish camp.

Outward Migration and the Singaporean Diaspora

The issue of Singaporean global mobility is so interesting because, in the early
days of Singapore's independence, outward migration would have been tantamount to desertion. Now, however, the Singaporean diaspora is considered a
resource that the country can and should leverage, provided it can succeed in
persuading these overseas Singaporeans to retain a sense of affection, if not
loyalty, to their home country.

To see how official attitudes toward migration, mobility and the Singaporean
diaspora have changed over the years, consider the following extracts from the
country's National Rally speeches delivered each year by the prime minister in
observance of Singapore's independence (for a detailed discussion, see Brooks
and Wee, 2014). The 1974 and 1984 speeches were given by Lee Kuan Yew,
Singapore's first prime minister. The 1997 speech is by Goh Chok Tong, the
second prime minister.

In the 1974 speech by Lee Kuan Yew, he draws a clear boundary between
Singapore as a young country that has to withstand 'outside pressures' if it is
to develop a cohesive national identity:

We have given to us this small island . . . The crux of our problem is not lack of a huge
hinterland, oil, mineral resources. It would be nice if we could have these things. . . . But
that is not for us . . . Nature, geography and history decided that for us. The answer lies
within ourselves – the capacity to turn a people of largely immigrant stock into a people
with enough cohesiveness, with a national identity of their own, able to pursue their
national interests regardless of outside pressures. And we are going to have these outside
pressures. We've had them.

He also reminds Singaporeans that they cannot and should not be looking
back to the lands of their migrant ancestors. For example, Indian Singaporeans should not take special pride in the government of India and its leaders,
and the same applies to Chinese Singaporean vis-à-vis Chinese leaders. Thus,
even though ethnic diversity and distinctiveness remain a reality and 'primordial fact' (see Chapter 1), it should not be elevated above the need to cultivate
a more inclusive national identity (*we govern Singapore in the interest of all
Singaporeans regardless of race, language or religion*):

If I go to India and I am seen shaking hands with President Giri or Mrs. Indira Gandhi,
some Indians are happier. I have no doubts that if I were to take a picture with the leaders
of the PRC, there will be temporary euphoria amongst a section of the people. But is it
in our interest? But, without that, we are able to establish that we govern Singapore in
the interest of all Singaporeans regardless of race, language or religion.

This theme of the Singaporean national identity as being linked to the territorial boundary of the island is continued in 1984 where Lee asserts that modern Singaporeans are stuck on the island because they have nowhere else to go. Therefore, they should be making the best of their situation rather than be looking distantly outward, and certainly they should not be looking towards an ancestral location that no longer acknowledges them. The point of the 1984 speech is therefore to anchor Singaporeans physically to their island, especially through home ownership:

Where would you, a Singaporean, go if we suffer massive unemployment . . . ? . . . . You can no longer go back to China, India, Malaysia or Indonesia. Where will you go for a job . . . ? . . .

In 1964, this was just a gleam in the eyes of a few men. In 1984, it is a reality you can see and feel. There are also gleams in the eyes of 80,000 Singaporean families . . . who will add their names each year to the waiting list to be part of this home-owning society . . . We have a vital reason for ensuring that everyone owns at least one home. Homes are immovable property.

By 1997, however, Lee's successor, Goh Chok Tong has accepted that many Singaporeans are now travelling and working abroad, and even emigrating. Indeed, a later survey by Tan (2005: 89) suggests that 27% of Singaporeans have considered emigrating. In this speech Goh talks about 'Singapore communities in other cities' and no longer defines Singaporeans in terms of being located on the island. Goh thus appeals to a sense of national loyalty and familial ties they will feel (he hopes) *regardless* of where they may be:

In a very mobile world, more Singaporeans will go abroad to work . . . There are . . . sizeable Singapore communities in other cities – Sydney, Perth, London, Paris, Tokyo, Beijing, Bangkok, Manila . . . It is a facet of globalization and regionalization that we need to reflect on and address . . .

Abiding bonds to family and friends and deep loyalties to Singapore are crucial in this new situation. We must never forget that Singaporeans owe one another an obligation, and the more able ones, in whom Singapore has invested the most, have a special obligation to society. We must all join hands to keep Singapore together.

In his 1997 speech Goh thus recognized the reality of a Singaporean diaspora, but tied it to loyalty, responsibility and obligation to the country of origin.

To encourage overseas Singaporeans to maintain an emotional connection with their homeland, the government introduced two initiatives, the Overseas Singaporean Portal and Singapore Day, in the mid-2000s. The Overseas Singaporean Portal was launched in 2006 with these goals: providing overseas Singaporeans with information about events back home, making various government administrative services more easily available to them, and helping them to make contact with fellow Singaporeans. In his speech at the Regent Hotel in Shanghai marking this initiative's launch, then deputy prime minister and minister for home affairs, Wong Kan Seng, emphasizes the need to 'stay connected' to the 'Singapore spirit' (Wong, 2006):

There are now more than 140,000 Singaporeans spread across the world. The Overseas Singaporean diaspora is rich in its diversity of experiences, knowledge and networks. You add to the rich fabric of our nation. It is important for us to remain engaged with one other.

In an increasingly globalised world, many Singaporeans will follow in your footsteps to go overseas to study or work. Among you are some of our best and brightest talent. We want you to stay connected with Singapore, to know what is happening back home. At the same time, you can also share with fellow Singaporeans in other countries and Singapore what you are doing. Together, we can build a strong and interconnected Singaporean community that is not constrained by geographical limits or by Singapore's small size . . .

We will do well to harness this to our advantage – to use this tool to bring us closer together, to stay together as one people, overcoming the constraints of physical distance. It enables us to be united as one by the Singapore spirit, even though we may be physically apart. Let us celebrate our new found proximity and connection.

Wong's speech acknowledges that these overseas Singaporeans include 'our best and brightest talent' and reminds them that they have a contribution to make to Singapore's success ('Together, we can build a strong and interconnected Singaporean community'). The importance of maintaining a connection to the homeland was later reinforced by Grace Fu, then second minister for the environment and water resources, at the 2012 Singapore National Day Reception in Seoul. She describes the overseas Singaporeans as 'ambassadors' of the 'Singapore brand':

On a more serious note, Singaporeans and Singaporean companies are often known for reliability, competence, trust-worthiness, and a high standard for quality and safety. We deliver what we promise and are trusted. This Singapore branding is invaluable and has helped many Singaporeans and Singapore companies land job and business deals in many parts of the world. As our community in Korea, I urge each and every one of you to be the ambassadors of Singapore and help uphold the Singapore brand here.

With globalisation, the branding of Singapore is becoming ever important. Our karma is to live with our lack of resources including water and land. Our strategy is to keep a strategy of openness to investment and trade and be a liveable and vibrant city of choice in Asia. We are a hub, a shining red-dot, connected to the rest of the world. You are part of our connection to the rest of the world. There are now more than 190,000 Singaporeans, who are like you, spread across the world. The Overseas Singaporean diaspora is rich in its diversity of experiences, knowledge and networks. You add to the rich fabric of our nation and contribute much to our Singapore brand. It is important for us to remain engaged with one another. We want you to stay connected with one another and with Singapore, to know what is happening back home. A vibrant and connected Overseas Singaporean community around the world, with strong linkages to the family and friends in Singapore, will be an asset to the country.

Fu (2012) makes clear that overseas Singaporeans have undoubtedly benefitted from the 'Singapore brand', with its associated characteristics of reliability and competence. This branding has 'helped many Singaporeans and Singapore companies land job and business deals in many parts of the world'. Overseas Singaporeans therefore have an obligation to 'uphold' the brand, wherever they may be because they 'contribute much to our Singapore brand'.

To further strengthen this sense of connection (and, indeed, obligation) to Singapore, the government introduced Singapore Day in 2007. Singapore Day is a largely annual event organized by the Overseas Singaporean Unit (OSU), which comes under the Prime Minister's Office. The event is held in a different city each year. The first Singapore Day was held in 2007 in New York City, the second in 2008 in Melbourne, and the third in 2009 in London. There was no Singapore Day in 2010, possibly because the country was organizing the Youth Olympic Games that year, and having a Singapore Day would pose a strain on budgetary and other resources. In 2011 and 2012, the Singapore Day was held in Shanghai and Brooklyn, respectively, and in the years since in Sydney, London, Shanghai, San Francisco, and Melbourne.

According to the Singapore Day website, the goal is to bring 'a slice of home' to Singaporeans around the world (www.overseassingaporean.sg/c-event#sgday; accessed 28 October 2012):

Every year, Singapore Day travels to major cities around the world to bring to OS communities familiar sights, sounds and tastes. It's a mega get together!

Singapore Day is OSU's signature event where we organise a carnival in cities with a big concentration of overseas Singaporeans. We bring up the sights, tastes and sounds of Singapore, to give you a slice of home.

Singapore Day is an opportunity for the government to remind overseas Singaporeans that Singapore can be fun and enjoyable. Thus, the website describes the three 'key components' of Singapore Day as
– authentic hawker fare served by Singapore's celebrity hawkers,
– a concert by home-grown artistes, and
– a colourful experiential showcase of the latest cultural developments in Singapore
During the London Singapore Day in April 2009, occasional use was made of Singlish, such as the lexical item 'chope', which is used to indicate the reservation of a seat ('Singapore Day in London draws the crowds', *Sunday Times*, 26 April 2009). Here, the use of Singlish was, not unexpectedly, light-hearted, and crucially, the intended audience was not the 'less educated' subaltern, since most of the overseas Singaporeans are working professionals or university students pursuing a degree abroad. This use of Singlish was obviously a strategy intended to evoke a sense of being Singaporean, and it succeeded to the extent that it resonated with the associations with being back home and

interacting with fellow Singaporeans that the language holds for many overseas Singaporeans. For example, Aredi Alwis Tiang posted on the Singapore Day website that 'i attended singaporeday09london 3 days ago and had a unusually gleeful time to talk singlish with other singaporeans', to which londonchinese responded, 'You don't have to wait until the next Singapore Day to speak Singlish! There are several organisations in the UK catering for Singaporeans here. Come and join us and participate in some of our events!' (28 April 2009,   www.overseassingaporean.sg/public/forum/upload/index.php?/topic/ 2453-speaking-singlish-on-singaporeday09london; accessed 9 June 2016).

Recall that one of the arguments often put forward by proponents of Singlish is that many Singaporeans overseas use Singlish to express their national identity and to create a sense of community. This is clearly related to the notion of solidarity, and it is supported by londonchinese's invitation to Aredi Alwis Tiang to join the various UK-based organizations if he wanted to speak Singlish. An earlier study on Singaporean expatriates in Beijing (Kong, 1999) provided support for this argument. And my interviews (conducted in June/July 2013) with three Singaporean professionals working in a technology start-up in the San Francisco Bay Area corroborate it as well. All three stated that they used Singlish when interacting among fellow Singaporeans, with two qualifications. First, not surprisingly, their use of Singlish was sensitive to different kinds of situations and types of interactants. They avoided Singlish when they perceived the situation to be related to work or to be more formal, or when non-Singaporeans (American colleagues or other nationalities who might happen to be visiting) were present. This sensitivity arose after their American colleagues and friends who heard Singlish being spoken commented that it was difficult understand. These professionals made the conscious decision to avoid or reduce the use of Singlish when non-Singaporeans were present.

The second qualification to their use of Singlish was that, even among these Singaporean professionals, there was a cline of 'Singlish-ness', usually as a result of extended periods spent studying and working overseas. The three Singaporean professionals I spoke to were brothers; the two older ones studied in America and stayed on after graduation to work, and the youngest attended university in Singapore before joining his two older brothers in the Bay Area. The youngest of the three doubted if his older brothers spoke much Singlish. In contrast, the older brothers – who were both married to fellow Singaporeans also working in the Bay Area – claimed that they did use it, although they acknowledged that their use was probably more restricted than that of the youngest brother. All this is not too surprising, since 'Singlish' – like any other language name – is ultimately a label that, via meta-discursive regimentation (Makoni and Pennycook, 2007), may be attached to different language practices. As a result, there will be differences of opinion as to whether a given lexicogrammatical construction 'really' constitutes Singlish. So, while all three Singaporean brothers were willing to attach the label 'Singlish' to at least some of their language practices, the practices themselves were quite variable, given the differences in their social and educational experiences.

But perhaps of even greater relevance to the issue of migration was my interview with a fourth individual: a female Malaysian professional who worked in the same technology start-up as the three Singaporean brothers. She had spent a number of years studying and working in Singapore and readily claimed to be comfortable speaking both Manglish (the Malaysian counterpart to Singlish) and Singlish.[2] At the time of the interview she ws engaged to an American who, according to her, had picked up Singlish and spoke it naturalistically without any self-consciousness. Interestingly, she stated that even when they argued, her American fiancé would sometimes slip unself-consciously into Singlish. The linguistic trajectory of this couple is interesting from the perspective of the intersection between language and migration. This Malaysian female represents a case of migration into Singapore, as a result of which she readily counted Singlish as part of her linguistic repertoire. Her subsequent move into the Bay Area represents a case of migration out of Singapore. In addition, her interactions with her American fiancé indicate the acquisition of Singlish by a member of the host society. While this development may not be typical, it is not uncommon. In an earlier visit to Stockholm in March 2012, I encountered a female Malay Singaporean who was married to a Swede, and she also suggested that her Swedish spouse had picked up Singlish through regular interactions with her and other Singaporeans in Sweden. In this regard, the Singaporean interviewees working the San Francisco Bay Area, too, noted that some of their American colleagues would express interest in Singlish and would ask for demonstrations of this variety. This of course raises the issue of the commodification of Singlish and its marketing as an exportable cultural product (see Chapter 5).

Heartlanders and Cosmopolitans

It should be clear that the government has mixed feelings about the Singaporean diaspora. It certainly realizes that this is a phenomenon that it cannot hope to stem and that many Singaporeans may decide to sink their roots elsewhere, in a converse version of Singapore's own attempts to attract foreign talent. This is the basis for its exhortation to overseas Singaporeans not to forget their obligations to and connections with the home country.

---

[2] While there are some differences between Manglish and Singlish, the similarities are greater. This, again, points to the issue of meta-discursive regimentation. In any case, a detailed discussion comparing Manglish with Singlish is beyond the scope of this book.

Contributing to this governmental anxiety about the effects of the Singaporean diaspora if left unmanaged is the social, cultural and economic divide between this group of globally mobile educated professional Singaporeans and those who are less educated and less globally mobile. In his 1999 National Day Rally speech, Goh Chok Tong describes this divide as one between 'cosmopolitans' and 'heartlanders':

As Singapore becomes more international, two broad categories of people will emerge. One group I call the 'cosmopolitans', because their outlook is international. *They speak English* but are bilingual. They have skills that command good incomes in banking, IT, engineering, science and technology. They produce goods and services for the global market. Many cosmopolitans use Singapore as a base to operate in the region. They can work and be comfortable anywhere in the world.

The other group, the heartlanders, make their living within the country. Their orientation and interests are local rather than international. Their skills are not marketable beyond Singapore. *They speak Singlish.* They include taxi-drivers, stallholders, provision shop owners, production workers and contractors. Phua Chu Kang is a typical heartlander. Another one is Tan Ah Teck. (www.nas.gov.sg/archivesonline/speeches/view-html?filename=1999082202.htm; accessed 9 June 2016;, italics added)

Yet both groups are important: the cosmopolitans because they are 'indispensable in generating wealth for Singapore' and the heartlanders because they maintain 'our core values and our social stability'.

In a keynote speech one year later to the Community Development Council Seminar, Goh summarizes the relationship between the two groups in the following manner: 'The heartlanders nurture the cosmopolitans, while the cosmopolitans create opportunities that benefit the heartlanders. If cosmopolitans and heartlanders cease to identify with each other, our society will fall apart' (19 March 2000; www.nas.gov.sg/archivesonline/speeches/view-html?filename=2000031904.htm; accessed 9 June 2016).

Goh's cosmopolitan-heartlander distinction shows the persistence of language ideologies; it echoes the government's language policy, which is seemingly based on its inability to countenance the idea that English might possess for Singaporeans anything more than a purely instrumentalist or pragmatic value. The Singaporean cosmopolitans, though bilingual, ares English speaking, sophisticated and worldly and, because of these qualities, are in danger of losing their values. And while the official ethnic mother tongue is intended to serve as a cultural anchor that outweighs the potentially negative consequences of learning English, it may not serve this function for cosmopolitans when they are located overseas and are tempted by opportunities afforded outside of Singapore. In contrast, Singaporean heartlanders speak Singlish (= ungrammatical English that therefore lacks, according to the government, capital of any real value), are locally oriented by inclination, as well as by the lack of other, more international alternatives – but they are the keepers of Singaporean values. Goh's description of the 'heartlander' is of course the Singlish subaltern being evoked by proxy once again. Note his reference to stereotypical characters (taxi drivers and stallholders) as well as Phua Chu Kang and Tan Ah Teck, two television comedic characters.

The cosmopolitan-heartlander distinction brings to the forefront just how much notions of class are intertwined with the Singlish controversy. Recall that the reason why English has been recognized as an official language (but not an officially accepted mother tongue) is that it is supposed to facilitate communication across different ethnic groups. However, Goh's portrayal of the difference between these emerging categories of Singaporeans also suggests that there is a class division that correlates with the English-Singlish distinction. This view of Singlish as marking one side of the class division, that of the heartlander, obviously conflicts with the argument put forward by supporters of Singlish – that it is Singlish that can bridge class divisions.

Both positions are not without problems, however. The government's position is problematic because (i) the government itself occasionally uses Singlish to communicate with the cosmopolitans; (ii) cosmopolitans, whether overseas or back in Singapore, do make use of Singlish even among themselves, and (iii) therefore, if the heartlanders also use Singlish, then the government is wrong in downplaying the value of Singlish in bridging class divisions. The position of the Singlish supporters is problematic because (i) if Singlish is a language for fun, humour, and one where speakers are also encouraged to deliberately play around with linguistic conventions, then (ii) this is a highly restricted use of the language that does not take into account the so-called heartlanders' use of Singlish for other kinds of communicative purposes that may be much more serious or simply more mundane in nature, and (iii) neither does it acknowledge that, for many of these heartlanders, playing around with lexicogrammatical conventions requires first of all a sense of confidence and ease with Standard English, (iv) which they do not necessarily possess in the first place, which is why supporters of Singlish champion its use as a bridge across class.

These problems arise in no small part because of the incautious and cavalier use of the label 'Singlish', so that it becomes difficult to determine whether the various parties to the Singlish controversy can be said to actually be talking about the same thing. Even if we focus on a single group such as the government or supporters of Singlish, there are different and inconsistent notions of what counts as 'Singlish' within each group. Hence, it is important to ask whether they are drawing upon different and at times incompatible notions of Singlish. And if so, it is important to determine how these different notions might be related to one another, since it would be highly improbable that the various Singlishes have nothing in common except for the label. I discuss this question in detail in the concluding chapter of this book. To close this chapter, I highlight how, in addition to different notions of Singlish, there are also different and contested nationalist imaginings at stake.

Rocky Roads of Reflexivity and Nationalist Imaginings

One important debate in studies of nationalism has been the question of whether, as a result of the various processes associated with globalization, nation-states are inexorably moving towards an era of post-nationalism. It is not necessarily the case that we have already entered such an era, but comfortable assumptions concerning the homogeneous and bounded nature of identity, language and the nation-state may have been destabilized because these phenomena are themselves prone to being commodified under the globalized economy (Heller, 2011). Processes of commodification tend to encourage ironic and reflexive stances towards the phenomena that are being commodified, thus denaturalizing and detraditionalizing them (Giddens, 1990; 1991).

But reflexivity in and on itself does not guarantee a particular type of response. Heller's study of young Canadians notes a degree of ambivalence regarding the validity of traditional notions of nationalism rather than its outright rejection:

They are still tied to the identity categories with which they were raised, and they value the linguistic and cultural forms they were taught to associate with them, but they also recognize their historical situatedness. They reject the purist dimensions of older forms of nationalism, while retaining an affection for the authenticating practices that ended up being marginalized when francophone nationalism became institutionalized and an educated francophone bourgeoisie (themselves, really) got created and then commodified its authenticating practices...

We find social actors coming to grips with, and even embracing, the idea that it is time to reinvent francophone Canada in ways that blur boundaries and open up doors, others are concerned about what may be lost in the process. (Heller, 2011: 189)

Nevertheless, there is a tension between those who display such ambivalence and those for whom nationalism represents 'a permanent political project', rather than one based on historical contingency:

Here, I think, is the key. For many of the key producers of discourse on *la francité canadienne*, francophone Canada cannot be understood as a discourse produced under certain historical conditions and serving certain interests, a discourse that relies on those conditions for its reproduction and that requires a tremendous amount of work, on a daily basis, to reproduce. It must be understood as a permanent political project, one in which the nation is a value unto itself.

Heller's observations find resonance in the ways that Singlish has been positioned in Singapore's own nationalist discourse. For the Singapore government, for whom the country's independence was a reluctantly acquired status due to deep and fundamental disagreements with the Federation of Malaysia over how to manage and accommodate an ethnically diverse society, the articulation of multiracialism as a governing principle has been treated in almost ahistorical terms. The Singapore government views ethnic boundaries and distinctiveness as a 'primordial fact' (see Chapter 1) and therefore sees such boundaries as phenomena that are not likely to weaken, much less disappear, any time soon. As a consequence, the ethnic mother tongues are presumed to be necessary because of the further assumption that each ethnic identity needs to be correlated with a distinguishable language, both as a vehicle for the transmission of cultural values and as a marker of that distinct identity. A single language for inter-ethnic communication is still needed, of course. Yet it should be a language that carries no ethnic affiliation so that it can be ideologically positioned as ethnically neutral. The use of this inter-ethnic lingua franca is a matter of pure practical necessity, and hence the choice of English, which – on the same practical grounds – also provides its speakers with a linguistic resource that is advantageous in the arena of global economic competition.

Ethnic Enclaves and Housing Quotas

Indeed, the government has taken active and even highly interventionist steps to encourage interaction across the different ethnic groups. To foster inter-ethnic mingling and social integration, thereby preventing the creation of ethnic enclaves, particularly among members of the major ethnic communities, the state introduced in 1989 ethnic quotas in its public housing policy, known as the Ethnic Integration Policy. The quotas are supposed to roughly reproduce the proportion of ethnic communities at the national level so that the Chinese are allocated the highest quota, the Malays the next highest, and so on. Implementation is refined to the level of housing blocks and neighbourhoods. The ethnic quotas for March 2010[3] are shown in Table 3.

Table 3. *Ethnic Limits for Housing Development Board Flats*

Ethnic Group	Neighbourhood	Block
Malays (no change)	22%	25%
Chinese (no change)	84%	87%
Indians/Others[4]	12% (from 10%)	15% (from 13%)

[3] 'Policy changes to support an inclusive and cohesive home', Housing Development Board press release dated 5 March 2010, www.hdb.gov.sg/fi10/fi10296p.nsf/PressReleases; accessed 11 February 2011.

[4] Presumably the categories 'Indians' and 'Others' are combined to share the same quota because of the relatively small numbers within each group.

Once the quota for an ethnic group has been reached, no sale to a member of the same ethnic group is allowed. In this way, the ethnic classification of individuals affects their access to particular public housing locations.

Lee Kuan Yew spoke of the need to rely on such enforced communal inter-mingling because other possibilities such as affirmative action or forced mixed marriages between 'weaker' and 'stronger' ethnic groups as means of reducing social disparity were not feasible (quoted in Han, Fernandez and Tan, 1998: 185–187):

I do not believe that the American system of solving the problem stands any chance. First, they deny that there is a difference between the blacks and the whites. Once you deny that, then you're caught in a bind. All right, if we are equal, then why am I now worse off? You have fixed me. The system has fixed me. So they say, right, let's go for affirmative action. Lower marks to go to university, and you must have a quota for num-ber of salespersons or announcers on radio or TV. And so you get caught in a thousand and one different ways. And you say, since the army is now 30, 40 per cent blacks, you must have so many generals, so many colonels, and so on.
I don't know how they have got into this bind, but I think that is not realistic . . .
The only way we can all really be physiologically equal in brain power and every-thing else is to have a mélange. All go into a melting pot and you stir it. In other words, force mixed marriages, which is what the people in Zanzibar tried. The blacks wanted to marry all the Arab girls so that the next generation, their children, will be half-Arab. But I don't think that's a practical way nor will it solve the problem. And you can't do that worldwide, you can – maybe you can do that in Zanzibar. In the process, you diminish Zanzibar. Because whereas before you had some outstanding people who can do things for Zanzibar, now you have brought them down to a lower level.

The problems with affirmative action are well documented (Sowell, 2004) and I do not dwell on them here. Instead, I want to point out that Lee's objection to forced mixed marriages seems less grounded in the coercive nature of such relationships than in his view that the result would only serve to dilute the traits that characterize the 'stronger' group.

Hybridity in Singapore's History: The Eurasians and the Peranakans

Lee Kuan Yew's rejection of intermarriage as a means of fostering commu-nal intermingling reflected an undoubted element of erasure, because mixed marriages were a significant factor in Singapore's early history. Consider the case of the Peranakan community. The Peranakans are descendants of Chi-nese immigrants who adopted cultural practices associated with the Malay community. Under British colonial rule, many Peranakans occupied privileged positions in government administration and were relatively fluent in English (Lim, 2010). While some Peranakan families are ethnically mixed (part Chinese, part Malay), largely as a result of Chinese traders marrying Malay women, others are ethnically Chinese. The Peranakans demonstrate an interesting mix of cultural practices, with many continuing to practice the Chinese tradition of ancestral worship while speaking a variety of Malay, known as Baba Malay. Consequently, for the Peranakans, it is Malay or English rather than Mandarin that better reflects their ethnic heritage. However, the state's policy of assigning mother tongues along ethnic lines and deciding ethnic classification on the basis of the father's ethnicity means that most Peranakans are classified as Chinese and Mandarin is designated as their official mother tongue. That Peranakans represent an interesting hybrid of Chinese and Malay cultures is largely ignored.

Yet another case involves the Eurasian community, which was created as a result of ethnic mixing. In fact, the colonial bureaucracy coined the category 'Eurasian' to 'signify colonial subjects who were offspring of European fathers and Asian mothers' (Rappa, 2000: 157, 162). According to Gupta (1994: 37 citing Braga-Blake, 1992), 'families with Portuguese, British, and Dutch surnames, and Indian, Macao, Malacca, BencoolenBurmese, Siamese and Ceylon origins intermarried ... so that from disparate origins a unified, Christian, English-speaking community had emerged before the end of the nineteenth century.'

But although the Eurasians, along with the Chinese, Malays, and Indians, are considered among the 'founding races' in Singapore's history (Hill and Lian, 1995), they are categorized along with other minority groups under 'Others' because of their small numbers.[5] This has caused the Eurasian community to occasionally feel marginalized (Rappa, 2000), particularly because unlike the Chinese, Malays and Indians, they have no official ethnic mother tongue. This, again, is not surprising since the government designates mother tongues on the basis of the father's ethnic identity, and in the case of the Eurasians, the presence of European fathers would have meant recognizing a non-Asian language as an official mother tongue. For the Eurasian community, English represents the most plausible candidate for an ethnic mother tongue (Wee, 2002b; 2009), primarily because, since the time of British colonial rule, many Eurasians have grown up with English as their home language (Gupta, 1994: 19; Rappa, 2000: 168). However, as we already noted, English cannot be officially considered an ethnic mother tongue, and because English is also the medium of instruction

---

[5] Lee's remarks about ethnic mixing therefore sit rather curiously with his earlier remarks about uneven development between ethnic groups, where he includes the Eurasians as one of the groups that is doing well relative to the Malays.

in schools, it cannot be treated as the second language. Nevertheless, Eurasian children still have to meet the expectation of English-mother tongue bilingualism, in this case by learning one of the other languages as a second language (even though it may bear little connection to their ethnic identity and heritage).

In these cases of hybridity, we see that the government's response has been to insist that the relevant individuals fit one way or another into the existing system of classifying ethnic identities and allocating ethnic mother tongues. These problems of hybridity arise because the government's rationale for allocating English and the official ethnic mother tongues is informed by an ideology of monolingualism (Wee, 2007: 328), where each language is assumed to be a delimitable and self-contained system. Under Singapore's language policy, then a bilingual Chinese Singaporean, for example, is expected to be in possession of two separate language systems: one for Mandarin and one for English. Individuals and communities are expected to keep the systems separate, thus generating the expectation that proficiency in a particular language should be marked by a display of linguistic purity.

Hyphenated Ethnic Identities: A Policy Shift?

The ideology of monolingualism clearly is based on the assumption of ethnic primordialism. If different ethnic communities are intent on maintaining their cultural distinctiveness, they are also expected to maintain their historically affiliated languages. That is, cultural distinctiveness motivates the expectation of linguistic purity. As a consequence, certain languages, because of their historically established cultural affiliation with particular ethnic communities, are 'emotionally acceptable' in facilitating this need to preserve such ethnic distinctiveness. By the same token, other languages that have no such established historical and cultural affiliation (such as English) are not.

Singapore's policy of multiracialism and its consequent designation of official ethnic mother tongues to particular communities are thus also based on assumptions of ethnic primordialism. There is the belief that all ethnic communities possess a primordial 'instinct' to preserve ethnic distinctiveness. This is something that cannot change, and it must therefore be accepted as a starting point for policy formulation, whether it involves the allocation of public housing or ethnic mother tongues.

What was already a diverse (and hybrid) population to begin with looks set to become even more varied in its socio-linguistic profile in the twenty-first century, as citizens who have lived overseas return to the country and as foreign talent from different parts of the world take up Singaporean citizenship. All this raises the likelihood of hybrid identities emerging, especially if more Singaporeans marry foreigners. The number of Singaporeans with foreign spouses rose from 4445 in 1996 to 6359 in 2006; from 2004 to 2006, the most common male foreign spouses were from Australia, Bangladesh and Canada, while the most common female foreign spouses were from Australia, Brunei and Cambodia (www.filmo.com/sgspouse.htm; accessed 6 February 2011). This trend looks set to grow since the number of Singaporeans marrying foreigners has increased over a period of ten years from 30% to 40% in 2009 (Seah, 2010). One indicator is the increase in the Others category, which in 2000 constituted 1.4% of the population versus 3.3% in 2010. These statistics suggest that the numbers of Singaporeans who do not easily fall into the major ethnic categories of Chinese, Malay or Indian or even Eurasian will increase, especially if the government's policy to attract talented foreigner continues. Therefore, it will become more difficult to organize dynamics of Singaporean ethnolinguistic diversity along the lines of state-demarcated ethnically recognized identities.

In recognition of these demographic trends, the government decided in 2011 to officially recognize that some Singaporeans who, as a result of having mixed parentage, may want to claim double-barreled or hyphenated ethnic identities. That is, while many Singaporeans are still expected to be classified (or classifiable) as 'Chinese', 'Malay', or 'Indian, the state also realizes that some Singaporeans wish to be classified as, say, 'Chinese-Malay', 'Malay-Chinese', 'Indian-Chinese' or 'Indian-Malay'. Consequently, Singaporeans since 2011 have been able to officially opt for hyphenated ethnic identities.

In one sense, this initiative represents a significant and welcome policy shift since it no longer ignores the increasingly hybrid nature of Singaporean identities in a globalizing world. However, the initiative may not be quite as radical as it may appear. For one, part of the reason why the government was willing to allow hybrid identities is because it believed that the number of actual individuals who would insist on hybridity was small and therefore administratively manageable. Thus, Prime Minister Lee Hsien Loong said the following before the policy was implemented (Popatlal, 2010):

I don't think it will have a big impact on our . . . ethnic integration policies because the majority of the population will still be the major racial groups – the Chinese, the Malays, the Indians. And these are the other racial or ethnic groups who, in total numbers, will remain small for some time to come, and maybe for a very long time to come.

The government's confidence in this can be seen in the fact that it was even willing to make the policy retroactive so that individuals born before 1 January 2011 can also opt for a hyphenated identity.[6]

---

[6] 'Singapore to give multi-ethnic children double-barrelled race option', *China Daily*, 30 Dec 2010, www.chinadaily.com.cn/xinhua; accessed 22 Jan 2011.

Another reason why the implementation of hyphenated ethnic identities is not so radical is that the initiative still allows the government to cling to its primordialist view of ethnic distinctiveness and to maintain its policy of assigning ethnic mother tongues. This is because even hybrid Singaporeans are presumed to have a dominant ethnic identity, and this dominant identity is to be reflected as the first member of the hyphenated label. Thus, an individual who opts for 'Chinese-Malay' is someone who presumably feels mainly or primarily Chinese and to a lesser extent Malay. Consequently, for this person, his or her official mother tongue will be Mandarin, following from the government's assignation of Mandarin as the official mother tongue of the Chinese community. Conversely, an individual who opts for 'Malay-Chinese' is someone who presumably feels mainly or primarily Malay and to a lesser extent Chinese. This person's official mother tongue will be Malay, in accordance with the assignation of Malay as the official mother tongue of the Malay community. The two ethnic identities are not intended to be of equal status.

The status of Eurasian identity also raises interesting questions about the hyphenated ethnicity policy. While government officials have been quick to draw on 'Chinese-Malay' or 'Malay-Chinese' as examples of this official hyphenated identity, there has been little said about how the Eurasian identity might fit into this new scheme. Nevertheless, it appears possible for an individual to opt to be classified as, say, 'Eurasian-Malay' (Othman, 2010). With Eurasian as the dominant identity, any such Singaporean will then be considered for policy purposes as 'Eurasian', which raises the question about whether English can be acceptable as the ethnic mother tongue of the Eurasian community. But the status quo presumably remains unchanged: English is not an acceptable ethnic mother tongue, and so a child who is classified as 'Eurasian-Malay' will still have to opt for some other language to serve as a second language in the school system. This issue gains greater force since it appears that classifications such as 'Caucasian-Chinese' are also possible (Othman, 2010). This is despite the fact that such a classification confuses anthropological with ethnic categories, since from an anthropological perspective, 'Caucasian' includes peoples from parts of Asia and Africa. However, 'Caucasian' is also informally used, especially in the United States, to refer to someone who is 'white'. A Caucasian in this other sense might reasonably want to claim English as his or her mother tongue, which, of course, is infeasible because, for Singaporeans, only Asian languages are officially acceptable as mother tongues.

We can therefore see that this new initiative simply grafts a weak understanding of hybrid ethnic identity onto the already existing multiracial system that is grounded in ethnic primordialism. Hybridity has always been present in some form or other in Singapore, and the system of managing ethno-linguistic diversity has insisted on fitting individuals who might lay claim to a hybrid identity into the existing system: individuals of mixed parentage have always been expected to choose one parent's ethnic identity over the other. And individuals coming from a hybrid community such as the Eurasians have always been expected to adopt some other language as their second language in lieu of an ethnic mother tongue. The introduction of hyphenated ethnic identities still requires individuals to use these options and therefore can by no means be considered a sea change in the government's approach to the complexities of ethno-linguistic realities.

Trying to reduce hybridity to a version of mono-ethnicity creates a number of problems. First, the state's notion of hybridity assumes that individuals of mixed heritage have a combination of two different ethnic backgrounds. But this figure of two is arbitrary since there are individuals who might claim to have many more different ethnicities in their backgrounds. This is especially likely if individuals with hyphenated ethnic identities marry each other; their offspring might then reasonably claim to have triple or quadruple ethnicities in their heritage. Yet this more complex ethnic mix is considered too cumbersome to be allowed. According to Prime Minister Lee Hsien Loong, 'We allow double-barrelled names – well triple and quadruple that becomes not very practical' (Popatlal, 2010).

Second, the policy also requires siblings to have the same officially recorded ethnicity[7]. It is unclear at this point just how rigidly this aspect of the policy will be implemented, but it clearly does not allow for the possibility that siblings may have different subjective understandings of their hybrid backgrounds.

Third, for many individuals who are proud of their highly mixed ethnic backgrounds, being forced to choose one as dominant is not something that they may necessarily be comfortable in doing. Though the state's policy allows Singaporeans to change their ethnic identification twice in their lifetime, once before they reach the age of twenty-one and once thereafter[8], it is not implausible to suggest that many individuals with hybrid backgrounds will not want to be locked into a single ethnic identity, even when they reach middle age[9]. In this regard, consider this extract from a letter by Nurul Liyana Yeo a nineteen-year-old Singaporean student whose father is Chinese and mother Malay ('My thoughts', *The Straits Times*, 5 March 2011): 'As someone who is half Chinese and half Malay, I would have to choose which comes first. It is a real problem: I love my parents equally. How can I decide if I am more Chinese or more Malay?'

Fourth, we have seen that the state's management of ethnic diversity is linked to its allocation of public housing and official mother tongue. This creates, not

---

[7] Ibid.   [8] Ibid.
[9] Consider this non-Singaporean example: a South African academic in her early forties proudly declared that she was part Khoisan, part Asian and part White. More significantly, she was happily undecided about what to consider herself ethnically.

surprisingly, awareness among Singaporeans that the decision of which member of the hyphenated identity is to be the dominant one can carry important implications for access to various resources. Once again, Nurul Liyana Yeo provides interesting insights into how an individual of hybrid background might weigh various considerations in deciding which particular ethnic identity to privilege as dominant:

> But money is an issue forcing me to look for bursaries and scholarships . . . being a Chinese Muslim in a place that assumes all Malays are Muslims and all Muslims are Malays makes it tough; the promotion of the Malay-Muslim community takes precedence over my lack of funds.
>
> And as for applying to Chinese organizations, the forms insist that I fill up my mother's non-existent Chinese name, and her dialect group.

In Nurul's case, there are obviously no clear-cut answers. But what is relevant is her indication that her decision whether to identify as 'Chinese-Malay' or 'Malay-Chinese' will be significantly influenced by which option increases her chances of obtaining financial support from various Chinese or Malay-Muslim organizations.

Conclusion

Since the desire of ethnic communities to preserve their distinctiveness is taken as a given and any indication of hybridity tends to be downplayed, government policy has focused, not surprisingly, on how this desire might be accommodated while maintaining ethnic harmony in an ethno-linguistically diverse society. As a consequence, little consideration has been given to hybridity as a growing phenomenon in its own right. This is because, by definition, any such consideration essentially presumes that the preservation of ethnic distinctiveness has been breached.

In contrast, for proponents of Singlish as a language that can represent the national identity, the concern is less with the demarcations that separate distinct ethnicities than with reflecting the view that Singapore society, taken as a whole, is a mélange of diverse ethnic groups, some of which have mixed (through intermarrying or simply adopting cultural practices of different ethnic affiliations) to a greater degree than others. The argument in favour of Singlish is not necessarily a push for or towards hybridity. Rather, it would appear that the rationale for supporting Singlish is based on the belief that it can simultaneously accommodate the country's traditional ethnic boundaries *as well as* the blurring of those boundaries. That is, the language is seen to be sufficiently flexible and inclusive because it does not require an abandonment of traditional ethnic or linguistic boundaries, but neither does it take such boundaries too seriously.

The specific concerns vis-à-vis the appropriateness of Singlish as a national language marker, then, revolve around what kind of nationalist imagining is at stake. A more traditional imagining, as exemplified by the government, is that ethnic distinctiveness is a reality that is not likely to go away anytime soon. And there are undoubtedly communal concerns about the need to preserve such distinctiveness that the government has to heed and manage. The danger represented by Singlish, in this regard, is that it is linked to a cultural worldview that, while laudably liberal, tends to underestimate the power of communalism.

However, the traditional view of diversity as organized along ethnic lines fails to take into account the fact that, even within any given ethnic or national identity, there are already differing statuses reflecting differences in educational qualifications, professional expectations, hopes and desires regarding the likelihood of future migratory trajectories, among other factors. And such 'non-traditional' forms of diversity pose increasingly significant policy challenges for the creation and maintenance of social cohesion and integration (Vertovec, 2006: 28). When combined with the hybrid identities resulting from inter-ethnic marriages, the global mobility of Singaporeans, and ethnic identities traditionally construed, the result is what Vertovec (2006, 2007) has memorably labeled 'superdiversity'. Superdiversity poses important challenges for our understanding of language, culture and identity, setting the stage for the discussion in the next chapter.

7   What Is Singlish? Language, Culture and Identity in a Globalizing World

We have seen that the Singlish controversy revolves mainly around the question of whether Singlish can be considered a national liability or a national asset. One position is based on the claim that the use of Singlish undermines attempts to learn Standard English, which is assumed to be more valuable and useful in the global economy. The fear in this case is that if Singaporeans were to be unable to speak Standard English because of the supposedly contaminating presence of Singlish, there would be severe repercussions for the country's economic prosperity and competitiveness. The other position, in contrast, focuses on the unifying role that Singlish can play in fostering cohesion and solidarity across ethnic and social divides, including helping to integrate newly minted Singapore citizens.

Throughout the public debates over the merits of Singlish (or lack thereof), globalization tends to be represented as an external force to which the country needs to respond. That is, globalization is understood as something that exists 'out there' and Singaporeans have to make a decision as to whether Singlish actually has a useful role to play in grappling with globalization. However, if globalization in fact involves a re-arranging of social relations at multiple levels (Giddens, 1990; see Chapter 1), then globalization is already 'in here' as well as 'out there', and the question has to be confronted about the extent to which the distinction between 'in here' and 'out there' is at all meaningful. In much the same vein as Giddens' emphasis on how social relations are affected across various levels, Held, McGrew, Goldblatt and Perraton (1999: 16; see also Held and McGrew, 2003: 3) describe globalization as embodying 'a transformation in the spatial organization of social relations and transactions – assessed in terms of their extensivity, velocity and impact – generating transcontinental or interregional flows and networks of activity, interaction and exercise of power'. The views of globalization presented by Giddens and Held et al. are summarily described by Scholte (2000: 46) as affecting 'the nature of social space', though it should be emphasized that 'social space' is intended to refer to both temporal and spatial properties.

This way of thinking about globalization, one that rejects a simple 'in' versus 'out' dichotomy, undergirds Sassen's (2006) analysis of how globalization is destabilizing the traditional state assemblage of territory, authority and rights. Historically established complexes of territorial boundaries have long been associated with the sovereignty of states, and it is within these linkages of physical location and political autonomy that residents – in particular, citizens – are recognized as enjoying specific rights. Sassen's point is that globalization has forced a loosening, restructuring and, in some cases, outright delinking of these historically constructed assemblages. She is careful not to suggest that the state is necessarily obsolete; rather, the actual outcomes of globalization depend on how specific states differentially negotiate its spatio-temporal impacts (Sassen, 2006: 227). In this regard, recall the discussion in the Introduction where I noted that a traditional conceptual assemblage of language X, culture X and identity X is treated as being essentially distinct from another assemblage between language Y, culture Y and identity Y. In this way, Chinese language, culture and identity constitute a naturalized package that must be kept separate from other similar packages. As with Sassen's observations regarding the assemblages of territory, authority and rights, globalization, too, has consequences for traditionally inherited assemblages involving language, culture and identity. It would be simplistic to assume that such inherited assemblages are automatically rendered obsolete by glob-alization, just as it would be inaccurate to treat them as being completely unaffected. Rather, there are likely to be varying degrees of restructurings that occur within the set of resources that we may think of as constituting 'language', 'culture' and 'identity', as well as in the relations between these sets.

Though Sassen (2006, 5) uses the term 'assemblage' in her argument, she also insists that her use is intended to be purely descriptive rather than theo-retical: 'I simply want the dictionary term. I locate my theorization elsewhere, not on this term.' Nevertheless, as I show later in this chapter, approaching the notion of an assemblage in theoretical terms can be extremely fruitful. For now, I want to highlight another effect of globalization – what might be called reflexive modernization (Beck, Giddens and Lash, 1994). As Coupland and Kelly-Holmes (in press) point out, 'virtually all cultures that are subject to accelerated flows of people and things, but also to accelerated flows of mediated cultural forms, representations and relativizations, are increasingly unable to function non-reflexively. It becomes less possible to just "live out" inherited social formations, deterministically.' That is, rapid transformations in spatio-temporal arrangements and relations also have the effect of forcing those affected to respond adaptively. The result is reflexive modernization, an increased awareness of the inherited nature of social formations in the course of which it becomes inevitable that the foundations of the traditional arrangements and relations are variously defended, modified or rejected altogether. Larner and Walters (2004: 507, italics added) elaborate on this concept by explicitly linking reflexive modernization to globalization and emphasizing 'a reflexive moment' in the discursive nature of how communities and individuals construct themselves:

Globalization can be understood in terms of a historical ontology – *a reflexive moment in the discursive construction of ourselves where knowledge of the subject is produced in terms of its interconnectivity, mobility, sovereignty.* We are produced as global subjects, emerging from a past of nation-state-focused political struggles. Globalization discourse could thus be seen as a moment of reflexivity, a 'fold' in which another dimension of human existence is opened up. Less a force that impinges upon subjects; more a site in the production of particular kinds of subjectivity and experience: 'be global!'; 'think global!' Our argument, then, is that globalization is not necessarily global and not simply 'out there' ... We are suggesting that globalization is not so much a new epoch as it is a way of imagining human life.

Transformations in spatio-temporal arrangements and reflexive modernity clearly have significant effects on language, culture and identity. Yet, these effects are seldom explicitly taken into account in attempts to provide a theoretical understanding of Singlish, much less in the public debates over Singlish. In what follows, I discuss a number of such attempts.

Static Approaches to Defining Singlish

Nobody disputes that Singlish is the result of influences from multiple languages. Perhaps unsurprisingly, then, one early attempt to make sense of Singlish draws upon work in the study of pidgins and creoles. Platt (1975) proposes treating Singlish as a creoloid, as a way of acknowledging that it demonstrates creole-like properties while not necessarily having originated from a pidgin.

The notion of a creoloid is largely out of favour since it describes a problem (within a specific understanding of how creoles originate) without actually solving it. What is instructive here, however, is that arguments over whether Singlish is in fact a pidgin, a creole or creoloid partake of an objectivist orientation (Lakoff, 1987). By this I mean that these concepts are assumed to refer to autonomously existing linguistic types, so that the goal becomes trying to decide under what specific kind of linguistic object Singlish should be categorized. This same objectivist orientation is found also in Platt's (1975): 366) discussion of the lectal continuum, which locates Singlish towards the basilectal end of the continuum based on the properties that he discerns as diverging significantly from the acrolect.

Rejecting the lectal continuum approach because it treats Singlish as resulting from a lack of competency in other languages rather than from a strategic desire to communicate more effectively, Gupta (1994) proposes a diglossic approach, with Standard Singapore English as the H and Colloquial Singapore

English (Singlish) as the L. The shift between Standard Singapore English and Colloquial Singapore English is thus recast as a matter of interactional choice, rather than a reflection of a speaker's limited competence (Low and Brown 2005). However, as Leimgruber (2013: 18) observes, appealing to diglossia is problematic because 'diglossic speech communities do not normally code-switch between H and L intrasententially, the two codes being distributed functionally'. Yet the problem with the diglossic approach goes beyond merely redefining the concept to accommodate the Singapore situation – and, of course, the redefinition of diglossia is not without precedent, given that Fishman (1967) famously redefined Ferguson's (1959) original definition. We have seen that there are different and conflicting understandings of what Singlish is – quite aside from what relationship it is supposed to bear as a putative L to a H – and these multiple interpretations of Singlish cannot be accounted for even by a modified definition of diglossia.

Finally, consider Kachru's three circles model of World Englishes (Kachru, 1985, 1986; Kachru and Nelson, 1996). To account for the changing distribution and functions of the English language as it spreads across the globe, it distinguishes between inner, outer, and expanding circles of countries. Countries within a given circle represent specific 'types of spread, patterns of acquisition and the functional domains in which English is used across cultures and languages' (Kachru, 1985: 12). The inner circle countries (such as the United States, the United Kingdom, New Zealand, Australia, and Canada) are primarily places where the traditional monolingual native speakers of English are located. Countries in the outer circle are those with a history of colonialism by English-speaking countries (such as Singapore, Malaysia, and India) and where the language has been retained after de-colonization to serve various institutionalized functions. In the outer circle countries, then, English may have an official status and is moreover the first language of many speakers in that it is acquired in the home environment. The variety spoken often shows varying degrees of influence from contact with local languages. Finally, the expanding circle consists of countries (such as South Korea, Japan, and China) where English has no or a restricted official status; it is essentially a foreign language, used mainly for international communication rather than serving major domestic functions.

Kachru's model has come under significant criticism of late (Bruthiaux, 2003; Jenkins, 2003; Pennycook, 2003, 2008; Rajadurai, 2005). As Park and Wee (2009: 390) observe,

Most of these charges suggest that the model does not adequately capture the heterogeneity and dynamics of English-using communities: it cannot accommodate hard-to-classify cases such as Egypt and South Africa; it does not allow for the possibility of countries moving from one classificatory circle to another; it is too oriented towards the nation-state; and (ironically) it perpetuates the very inequalities and dichotomies that it otherwise aims to combat, such as the distinction between native and nonnative speakers.

One problem with the model, then, is that it underestimates the range of variation in uses of English both within and across nation-states. It underplays the political and ideological factors that go into creating such linguistic realities, which is ironic given Kachru's (1991) intention of combating discriminatory attitudes towards different varieties of English. In the case of Singlish, while the controversy surrounding it can be treated as corroborating the claim that an outer circle variety such as Singlish is plagued with ambivalence regarding its legitimacy (see Chapter 3), the model nevertheless is also (as with the diglossic approach) unable to come to grips with the fact that there are different understandings of what constitutes Singlish. For the model to be able do this, it needs to be re-conceptualized as a representation of the 'ideological forces that delimit local creativity and utility of English in the world' because 'understanding the dynamics and interrelations of World Englishes requires more explicit attention to the complex set of language ideologies that not only shapes local language politics, but also global relations among Englishes in different contexts' (Park and Wee, 2009: 393–394). As I noted in the Introduction, the identification of what counts as a variety is by no means a straightforward matter, and it is often the controversies surrounding the legitimacy of a putative variety (including questions about whether it in fact exists) that can contribute to its ontological robustness.

These foregoing attempts to explain what Singlish is are all therefore too static. This is because their analytical goal is one of trying to provide a determinate classification of Singlish within an adopted framework (creolistics, diglossia, three circles). But Singlish is part of a complex involving culture and identity that is changing as a result of globalization. This means that models that aim to explain the nature of Singlish have to be much more dynamic.

Towards Greater Dynamism

Schneider (2007: 13) is well aware of the problems with the three circles model and even with his own dynamic model, which focuses on the emergence of postcolonial Englishes; his model aims to show that 'despite all obvious dissimilarities, a fundamentally uniform developmental process, shaped by consistent socio-linguistic and language-contact conditions, has operated in the individual instances of relocating and rerooting the English language in another territory, and therefore it is possible to present the individual histories of PCEs as instantiations of the same underlying process' (5). The scope of Schneider's model therefore is deliberately limited to Englishes in the equivalent of Kachru's inner and outer circles, and he admits that it is 'not well suited to grasp the vibrant developments of the Expanding Circle' (Schneider, 2014: 9).

The dynamic model comprises five phases: foundation, exonormative stabilization, nativization, endonormative stabilization, and differentiation. The key feature of the final phase is 'internal differentiation', in which 'differences within a society and between individuals ... can be given greater prominence' (Schneider (2007: 53). It is because of this internal differentiation that Schneider describes phase 5 as 'a turning point from which something new springs: the stage of dialect birth':

New varieties of the formerly new variety emerge, as carriers of new group identities *within the overall community*: regional and social dialects, linguistic markers (accents, lexical expressions, and structural patterns) which carry a diagnostic function only *within the new country* emerge. (2007: 54, italics added)

The analytical endpoint of the dynamic model is internal social differentiation (internal to the nation-state and marked by the emergence of multiple speech communities along social, regional and other lines) and internal linguistic differentiation (marked by the emergence of dialects). However, linguistic evolution and dynamism obviously do not end there, and there is a need to conceptualize the developments in the spread of English beyond phase 5. Schneider (2007: 317) acknowledges that 'the glocalization of English will continue' and suggests two factors as being of particular importance in shaping the wider applicability of the model (310–311):

One is demography, the relative proportion between STL and IDG stream members who interact at any given point in time ...
    The other factor is a society's primary motivation for the use of English, the role which the language has assumed in a given community. As a tendency, its evolution has been most vigorous if it was adopted as a means of community solidarity. This process usually works subconsciously, and it entails covert prestige for indigenous varieties of English, typically against the official promotion of a formal (and often external) norm.

STL and IDG, respectively, refer to the 'settlers speech community' and the 'indigenous speech community', and it is the interaction between these two communities that, according to Schneider, will continue to be a major factor influencing the kind of English that emerges. The other factor has to do with the reason why a community uses English, and here, Schneider identifies solidarity as being of particular importance. Foregrounding these two factors reminds us of the 'basic principles' underlying the dynamic model: 'human beings of different origins who stay together need to get along with each other, and therefore they will accommodate in the long run; and they are likely to give expression to this convergence by linguistic means' (Schneider, 2007: 311).

In his discussion of the development of English in Singapore, Schneider (2007: 153) suggests that 'the evolution of English ... is far advanced ... and appears likely to go all the way along the cycle, given the linguistic dynamics that can be observed'. He goes on to argue that Singlish is likely to flourish, despite the official attempts at discouraging its use, because 'the willingness of the population to defend and stick to Singlish is remarkable, especially so in the light of the government's stern rejection of this speech variety' and there is considerable pride in Singlish, with many Singaporeans seeing it as 'an icon of national identity' (Schneider, 2007: 160, citing Rubdy, 2001: 347).

However, as we have seen from the discussion in the preceding chapters, the use of Singlish in the context of inward and outward migration – in particular, its use by Singaporean professionals living and working overseas, as well as its acquisition by non-Singaporeans – brings the discussion about the spread of English outside the boundaries of the nation-state. This is a necessary step if our analyses of English are to go beyond phase 5 of the dynamic model. Migration in today's globalized world cannot always be easily categorized along the lines of settler speech community versus indigenous speech community. While there are undoubtedly cases where the settler-indigenous distinction is still relevant, it is not obvious that the social conditions under which expatriate profession-als enter a host society would qualify them as 'settlers', and conversely, it is also doubtful that the members of the local community with whom these pro-fessionals interact (many of whom are professionals in their own right) can be adequately described as 'indigenous'. We have also seen from the presence of Singlish in YouTube videos, Singaporean movies, and other cultural produc-tions that it is becoming increasingly commodified and, as a consequence, is acquiring the status of an exportable cultural product. Commodification lends a different dynamic to language practices such that the impetus for using a lan-guage variety becomes less reliant on solidarity considerations. Thus, increased linguistic reflexivity and sophistication; migration, especially of professionals, across nation-states; and the commodification of Singlish are factors that are not easily accommodated by the dynamic model, nor was that necessarily ever its intention. Instead, the model envisages connections with ongoing macro socio-linguistic changes in terms of notions such as settler and indigenous speech community interactions and solidarity within the community.

The central claim of the dynamic model is that it is consistent with various socio-linguistic precepts. But the issue now is whether or not these precepts are themselves problematic, so that abiding by the principle of consistency may now require a re-evaluation of the precepts. As Heller (2008: 505) remarks,

Indeed, if we are asking questions about what it means these days to try to understand what language and social process have to do with each other, it is not because the goal now seems meaningless, but rather because the tools we have inherited are encounter-ing some of their built-in limitations in current confrontations with the way things are unfolding in the world around us, confounding our attempts to understand them.

Similarly, Rampton (2006: 14–15) argues that the view of speech communities as 'objective entities' that were 'empirically identifiable' has 'broken down', leading to an interest in 'communities of practice', with a concomitant emphasis on more micro and dynamic approaches to social interaction. This newer approach is wary of assuming at the outset the relevance of social categories (such as gender, age or educational level) in defining the community being investigated. By the same logic, this also means that the dynamic model's central reliance on 'the speech community . . . as its sociolinguistic unit of description' (Schneider, 2007: 313) may have to be reconsidered, since categories such as 'settler speech community' or 'indigenous speech community' cannot be identified objectively nor their relevance to any data set be taken for granted. Instead, the analyst must be prepared to allow the social categories to emerge from an observation of the practices in which the community members themselves engage. There may therefore be a need to recognize that the broader macro socio-linguistic landscape (both in terms of the phenomena that need to be accounted for and the conceptual tools being used by linguists) has changed significantly. This change is often described as the shift from modernity to late modernity, and it carries implications for how we understand notions such as community, identity, and even language itself – an issue that I address next.

A model that is arguably even more dynamic is Alsagoff's cultural orientation model (COM). Alsagoff (2007: 42) recognizes that the label 'Singlish' has been used in ways that obscure the distinction between its being an educated and 'uneducated variety' and emphasizes that the COM is specifically concerned with the former rather than the latter. But to place this restriction on the COM is to already accept the distinction as pre-given, rather than to ask the ideologically more interesting questions of who makes the distinction, on what grounds and how it is being sustained. For example, given that users of Singlish describe what they are saying as 'ungrammatical' sometimes and as 'colloquial' at other times, the COM has to also recognize how the speakers make this distinction and what kind of cultural orientation is implicated by it.

Having restricted the COM to the 'educated' version of Singlish, Alasgoff (2007: 38) then suggests that the variation in Singapore English (between Singlish and more standard English constructions) reflects an ongoing negotiation between different cultural orientations:

At one end are practices and orientations representing a globalist perspective, and at the other those associated with the local(ist) perspective. COM posits that speakers of Singapore English vary their style of speaking by negotiating fluidly within a multidimensional space framed by these two bipolar cultural perspectives. Thus, speaking in degrees of Singlish . . . indicates a symbolic shift towards a local(ist) orientation, while adopting the varietal feature of StdE . . . indicates a move towards a global(ist) orientation; where the degree or extent of use of the features uniquely associated with the respective varieties can be seen as a measure of the strength of the orientation.

The COM seems to take as axiomatic that the relationship between Singlish and Standard English is one of tension and conflict. The use of 'bipolar' in that extract conveys this conflict, as do references to a 'conflict between "being global" and "being local" (Alsagoff, 2007: 34), and to 'English being "pulled" in two different directions' (38). To reflect this tension, Alsagoff prefers to use the terms 'International Singapore English' and 'Local Singapore English' for 'Standard English' and 'Singlish', respectively.

But it is not clear that decisions about whether to use Singlish or Standard English are necessarily plagued by such angst. Moreover, the COM is also focused on the use of Singlish and Standard English within what may be described as the domain of interpersonal communication; it seems to have little to say about more public and more commodified uses of Singlish, much less the use of Singlish by non-Singaporeans (see, for example, the reference to *Orange Is the New Black* in the Introduction). It is also not clear that shifts between Singlish and Standard English can be adequately captured by relying on a polarity that is characterized in terms of a global-local orientation, since this suggests that (i) Singaporeans who use Standard English, even amongst themselves, are engaged in a globalist perspective; (ii) conversely, Singaporeans who use Singlish are automatically engaged in a localist perspective; and (iii) more fundamentally, it leaves unaddressed the thorny question of who decides that the practices are meta-discursively categorizable as 'Standard English' or 'Singlish'. This third question is critical because assumptions underlying the COM appear to rely on the 'degree or extent of use of the features' associated with the different varieties in order to make claims about the relevant orientation. The point here is not that the COM is off the mark; rather, it is that the COM may be too narrow in its focus, since the use of Singlish for interpersonal communication, when Singaporeans have to consciously decide how localist or globalist they want to be and to modify their linguistic practices accordingly, is just one part of a much wider set of issues involving Singlish. Finally, it is not clear just how general the COM is intended to be as a model that aims to account for language practices and orientations. That is, is the model generalizable to cases involving other varieties, or is it only specific to the Singapore context?

While appreciating the relevance of cultural orientation, Leimgruber (2013: 63, 107) nevertheless notes that it is just one part of a wider range of social meanings that can be indexed by use of the features associated with Singlish or Standard English. Leimgruber also sees the COM as problematic because it treats two distinct varieties, Standard English and Singlish, as serving different cultural orientations (52), whereas 'an indexical approach would ... leave the definition of distinct varieties aside' (58). Indexicality highlights that the meanings of linguistic features are tied to specific contexts of usage. Importantly, recent works by Silverstein and Eckert, among others, have emphasized that newer meanings may be created based on existing ones, so that there can be different orders of indexicality resulting in the formation of an indexical field, 'a constellation of meanings that are ideologically linked' (Eckert, 2008: 464).

Leimgruber (2013) suggests that the notion of indexicality (Eckert, 2008; Silverstein, 2003) can provide an important conceptual point of departure for the description of what he prefers to refer to generally as 'Singapore English'.[1] The idea of investigating Singapore English via the conceptual lens of indexicality is an extremely exciting one since – as Leimgruber (2013: 13, 26) shows in his review of earlier and more contemporary models of Singapore English – it demonstrates that notions of a post-creole continuum, diglossia, clines of formality and proficiency, and cultural orientation are all problematic in different ways. Importantly, Leimgruber makes the following observation:

> Features of Singlish include, but are not restricted to, discourse particles, existential constructions with *got*, the *where got* collocation, non-inflected verb phrases and noun phrases, pro-drop, BE-deletion, and the absence of conjunctions introducing conditional clauses. Features that mark StdE in Singapore include inversion in interrogatives, the use of certain auxiliaries, and the presence of verb and nominal inflexions. *While these features are seen, in this new [LW: indexical] model, as being indicative of Singlish and StdE, respectively, that is, as 'belonging' to their respective codes, they do not, by their mere occurrence in a given utterance, mark that utterance as being 'in Singlish' or 'in StdE'. This is an important point, as it solves the issues encountered in previous models with regard to speakers using separate homogeneous codes and constantly switching from one to the other:* this model suggests that features recognized as diagnostic of Singlish and StdE are potentially used consciously by speakers in order to index a particular social meaning. (2013: 104, italics added)

The key issue, then, is whether it still makes sense to assume that the targeted language or variety is a 'separate homogeneous code' or whether the attempt to treat languages/varieties as ontologically stable objects of analysis is itself the result of indexical practices arising from ideologies relating to meta-discursive regimentation (Makoni and Pennycook, 2007). Leimgruber takes up this issue in his concluding chapter and, citing Blommaert (2010: 126, italics in original), suggests that there is a need to 'move away from distinct "varieties" ... towards

---

[1] Alsagoff (2014) criticizes Leimgruber for using indexicality in a much different way than Eckert, pointing out that he seems to at times talk about indexicality in relation to a variety such as Singlish or Singapore English and at other times he discusses indexicality in relation to individual features. The latter use cleaves more closely to Eckert's use of indexicality, whereas the former raises the question of how meaningful it is to talk of the indexicality of a variety when Leimbgruber himself has criticized variety-based models. The confusion arises from Leimgruber not being consistent in his expressions, rather than from any fundamental problems with his approach or his use of indexicality. As Leimgruber (2013: 104; see the later discussion in the main text) makes clear, he is talking about the various features that are associated with a named variety, which means that his focus is on the features themselves. Any direct reference to a variety appears to be shorthand for the features that speakers meta-linguistically associate the named variety.

linguistic *resources*, which may originate from any imaginable language or variety, but which are, in production, used for their social meaning'.

The idea of using indexicality to understand Singlish is certainly promising. Indexicality is closely linked to style (including non-linguistic style systems relating to dress, location, among others) and is influenced not only by ideologies that pertain to language but also by others i that are more broadly socio-political in nature (such as commodification, identity and neoliberalism, to name just a few). As a consequence, once a linguistic (or non-linguistic, for that matter) feature becomes highlighted as a potential resource (or liability), that very act of highlighting itself can 'change the meaning both of the resource and of the original style, hence changing the semiotic landscape' (Eckert, 2008: 457). All these considerations point to the properties of linguistic features being open-ended and ever changing. And while these considerations may be less of an issue when linguists focus on individual features, such as Campbell-Kibler's (2007; see the later discussion) work on 'ING', they are in much more urgent need of addressing when the focus is on putative varieties such as Standard English and Singlish.

Indexicality and Assemblages

The intellectual origin of indexicality is traceable to C. S. Peirce's conception of the sign as a triadic relation between sign, object and interpretant, as opposed to de Saussure's work, which focuses on the signifier-signified dyad (Deely, 1990: 115). While the interpretant is itself yet another sign (Sebeok, 1994: 12), it comes about as a result of the interaction between an earlier sign and the activities of a user of this earlier sign. It is the notion of an interpretant that crucially allows relations between signs to be understood as an ongoing, possibly never-ending, process of semiosis, where signs do not merely exist but also dynamically give rise to yet more signs (cf. Deely, 1990: 23). But as signs give rise to other signs, the relationships between them are hardly random or arbitrary, and this leads to various discussions about how to best understand these relationships.

Silverstein's (2003) indexical order represents one such proposal, where a first-order indexical gives rise to a second-order indexical, and so on. As an example, Eckert (2012) discusses Labov's (1963) study of how the diphthong /ay/, marks the speaker as coming from Martha's Vineyard. This would constitute a first-order indexical. But while some Vineyarders lowered the nucleus of the diphthong so as to converge more closely to the pronunciation of the mainlanders, others reversed this pronunciation trend so as to avoid a lowering of the nucleus. This would constitute a second-order indexical, where the speaker is projecting her identity not just as a Vineyarder but also as a specific kind of

Vineyarder, as someone who is arguably more authentic than those other Vine-yarders whose pronunciation more closely resembles that of the mainlanders (Eckert, 2012: 88). And, of course, there is no reason why the indexical order should stop only at two, so that multiple indexical orders are not only possible but typical.

This growth in indexical orders led Eckert (2008) to introduce the notion of an indexical field to highlight the association of a linguistic feature with 'a constellation of ideologically linked meanings, any region of which can be invoked in context' (Eckert, 2012: 94). An example of an indexical field is found in Campbell-Kibler (2007) who shows that the velar variant (as in "talking") tends to be associated with intelligence, formality, and sophistica-tion, whereas the non-velar version (as in "talkin'") tends to be associated with the absence of these attributes (see also Eckert, 2012: 97). Another example comes from Eckert (2008: 469), who notes that the indexical field of /t/ release can include meanings such as 'being a school teacher', 'being British', 'being formal', 'being emphatic', 'being exasperated', 'being educated', 'being ele-gant' and 'being a gay diva'. Some of these are social types ('British', 'school teacher', 'gay diva'); others are relatively stable attributes ('educated', 'artic-ulate'); while yet others are stances that can change quite quickly and easily ('exasperated', 'emphatic'). More importantly, these categories should not be taken as representing hard distinctions within the indexical field. Rather, the relations between them are highly fluid (Eckert, 2008: 469), which is why it is useful to speak of an indexical potential (Eckert, 2012: 97), where in any instance of the feature being used, a number of the categories could be activated rather than just a single determinate category. And speakers may not always have a clear or determinate sense of which specific category/categories is/are being 'activated' by the use of the feature.

Finally, Blommaert (2005: 4, see also the discussion in Chapter 4) has intro-duced the notion of orders of indexicality to capture the fact that indexical meanings 'occur in the form of stratified complexes, in which some kinds of indexicalities are ranked higher than others'. Thus, there are clusters of index-ical meanings that, individually as well as collectively, indicate prestige as opposed to stigma, or rationality as opposed to emotion, among other qualities. What this means is that the indexical fields described by Eckert are themselves stratified, so that it is possible to speak of a group of indexical fields that, for example, happen to be ranked higher than a different group because the former is a complex of fields that happen to be associated with prestige while the lat-ter is a complex of fields that happen to be associated with stigma. Often the source of these orders of indexicality is 'real or imagined actors perceived to cause to emanate the authoritative attributions under which one should orient', including various centring institutions such as the peer group, family members, schools, the church and the state (172). In this way, 'indexicality is one of the points where the social and cultural order enters language and communicative behavior' (ibid.).

Given this discussion, let us now consider some examples relating to Singlish. Lee, Ling and Nomoto (2009) note that, in Singlish, *got* can be variously used as an existential marker (1) and to indicate realis (2), and it can also occur as part of the expression *Where got* to signal disagreement (3).

(1)   I got two brother, one sister.

(2)   I got go to Japan.

(3)   A: This dress very red.
             'This dress is very red'
         B: Where got?
             'Is it? I don't think so'

In addition, Leimgruber (2013: 79) presents an excerpt from the satirical blog *MrBrown*.com, where the writer is criticizing the government's optimistic outlook on the economy; he notes that *Where got* can also index a stance of sarcasm, especially given the deliberate shift from Standard English in the initial part of the excerpt to Singlish, as signaled by *Where got inflation?* (4). Commenting on (4), Leimgruber suggests that the use of *where got* indexes a first level of sarcasm, 'as well as, at a second order, a Singlish (localist) orientation. A potential third-level (or 'higher'-level) index would reference an unspoken criticism of government communicative strategies' (79).

(4)   My bowl of bak chor mee [a noodle dish] at the coffee shop nearby recently
         upped their prices from $2 to $2.20. Some have even upped it to $2.50. And
         don't even talk about aircon food court prices. Inflation? Where got
         inflation? Singapore economy booming what.

An indexical field for Singlish *got* would therefore comprise meanings such as existential marking, realis and disagreement – although, of course, it is not the lexical item per se that carries these meanings, but rather the item's participation in a variety of grammatical constructions (Goldberg, 1995). Moreover, the higher indexical orders remind us that *got* signals not merely traditional linguistic meanings but also more socio-pragmatic meanings relating to stance and cultural orientation. In this regard, it is relevant to note that, among the higher indexical meanings being signaled in (4) via the switch to Singlish, is not only a cultural orientation towards a more Singaporean or local identity but also a meta-linguistic one in that the writer is also signaling a pro-Singlish stance. That is, the writer clearly has the capacity to avoid using Singlish since he competently makes use of Standard English in the initial part of the excerpt. The later switch, then, is deliberate and strategic, and the decision to utilize linguistic features that are known to be associated with Singlish therefore also signals a stance or attitude that is positively oriented towards that variety. This meta-linguistic signaling need not always involve a clear switch from one variety to another (such as from Standard English utterances to Singlish utterances). I reproduce next an example discussed in Chapter 2:

(5)   It's si beh condemn that as Chinese peepur, our standard of Chinese am not as powderful as our Engrand.

In (5), the deliberate mispronunciations of 'people', 'powerful' and 'English', as well as the use of the Hokkien intensifier *si beh*, are flouts of Standard English conventions and, as with (4), signal a positive disposition towards Singlish.

It is at this point that Blommaert's insights concerning orders of indexicality become especially pertinent. Because the use of Singlish constructions, such as those in (4) and (5), can signal a meta-linguistic stance that favours Singlish, such usage threatens to destabilize established orders of indexicality – in this case, orders of indexicality relating to the positioning of Standard English's prestige vis-à-vis Singlish stigma – by flouting them (Blommaert 2005: 173). The important point to keep in mind is that this higher-order meta-linguistic stance need not always be signaled by the use of ostensibly Singlish constructions. Thus, while the uses in (1–3) can be described as being associated with meanings such as 'being a Singaporean', 'being informal' and perhaps even 'not being competent in Standard English' (depending on one's knowledge of the speaker's background, as well as of the kinds of other utterances produced by her), (4) and (5) are different because there is a clear and deliberate switch from using Standard English into using Singlish or the intentional use of nonce Singlish constructions (i.e. constructions that are marked as deliberation violations of the linguistic conventions associated with Standard English). It is because of such deliberate switches or violations of Standard English conventions that a higher indexical order concerning the meta-linguistic stance can be invoked.

This also allows us to account for the different understandings of what is Singlish. Since the same linguistic feature or construction may or may not invoke higher order indexical meanings, the use of any feature on its own underdetermines the kinds of meanings being invoked. It is possible therefore to categorize a given feature under the same language name 'Singlish' (or 'Standard English', for that matter) while attributing different understandings to both the name and the feature. One important factor in this regard is the degree to which a linguistic feature has become conventionalized or routinized as a Singlish feature so that it is no longer seen as a nonce formation and its use does not necessarily imply that the speaker is deliberately aiming to speak Singlish. This may sound paradoxical, and so some elaboration is warranted. Consider the difference between the uses of *got* in (1–3), which, as already noted, may signal that the speaker is a Singaporean or is being informal, but do not necessarily signal that the speaker is intentionally or deliberately using Singlish. Contrast (1–3) with 'powderful' in (5), which, while also categorizable as a Singlish linguistic feature, is highly marked as a deliberate violation of Standard English pronunciation; hence, its use inevitably signals the speaker's desire to be seen and identified as not just a Singaporean or being informal, but, reflexively, as a proud and playful speaker of Singlish. The differences between (1–3) and (5) are accounted for in terms of Coupland's (2007) continuum from mundane to high performance (see Chapter 3). The more conventionalized a linguistic feature is as a Singlish feature, the less likely will its use, *mutatis mutandis*, invoke the higher-order indexical meanings associated with meta-linguistic reflexivity. So, unless and until 'powderful' becomes routinized as a conventional Singlish way of pronouncing 'powerful', a speaker who uses it cannot but be seen as invoking – and knowingly so – an identity as someone who is happy and willing to use Singlish. This is why it is possible for the same linguistic features to be classified as Singlish qua 'broken or ungrammatical English' and as Singlish qua 'colloquial English playfully performed by highly educated speakers who are also competent in Standard English'. More importantly, because neither the boundaries of a indexical field nor the meanings 'within' it are sharply delimited, it is possible for one and the same speaker to slip between these difference understandings of Singlish without necessarily being aware of having done so.[2]

Thus far, we have been privileging language in our discussion of indexicality. The notions of semioisis and indexicality are, however, presumed to be relevant to all kinds of signs and not only linguistic ones. We therefore need a perspective that does not necessarily accord language a central role since there are clearly non-linguistic matters such as notions of ethnic and national identity, as well as economic progress, that bear on the Singlish controversy. That having been said, we nevertheless need to be able to recognize that concepts such as language, the economy, and the community all tend to be accorded their own ontological integrity and distinctiveness, even if they are based on questionable assumptions regarding their presumed essential natures. That is, there is no analytical or conceptual payoff if we discard the distinctiveness accorded

---

[2] These observations add nuances to Makoni and Pennycook's (2007: 2) notion of meta-discursive regimes or socially invented understandings of language, in particular, conceptualizations of varieties as 'separate and enumerable categories'. The language names themselves may be delimitable linguistic objects, but these names, as well as the linguistic features that are classified under them, are all associated with indexical meanings that are fluid. And while meta-discursive regimentation may be aided by the orders of indexicality so that complexes of features are kept separate by being organized into strata, this by no means guarantees the lack of seepage between the various strata. The likelihood of such seepage occurring may even be increased by deliberate floutings of established orders of indexicality.

to these concepts in favour of some unorganized morass of signs and indexicalities. This is where Deleuze's notion of an assemblage is useful, which he defines as follows: 'What is an assemblage? It is a multiplicity which is made up of many heterogeneous terms and which establishes liaisons, relations between them, across ages, sexes and reigns – different natures. Thus, the assemblage's only unity is that of co-functioning: it is a symbiosis, a "sympathy"' (Deleuze and Parnet, 2002: 69).

An assemblage, then, is a contingent mix of practices and things, where this contingent ensemble of physical and non-physical objects – broadly characterizable as 'semiotic' – is distinguished from yet other contingent ensembles in being 'selected, organized, stratified' and hence demarcated from an otherwise endless flow of circulating signs (Deleuze and Guattari, 1987: 406). In other words, an assemblage is patently an entity whose boundaries are semiotically constructed and demarcated by making use of various resources. Assemblages are therefore 'always coming together and moving apart' (Wise, 2005: 77). The conceptual value of thinking in terms of an assemblage is that it recognizes the important role that boundedness plays, even if there happen to be multiple boundaries and the nature of these boundaries is contested and shifting.

Assemblages can establish 'liaisons' with other assemblages, so that we can have coalitions of assemblages as well as nested assemblages or assemblages within assemblages (DeLanda, 2016: 20). When a linguistic assemblage (bearing a name such as 'Singlish' or 'Standard English') is linked to some other assemblage, such as a range of national practices that are seen as constituting the Singaporean identity (e.g. being born in Singapore, enjoying local cuisine, espousing support for multiracialism), then we have a liaison between two assemblages. When the linguistic assemblage 'Singlish' is further sub-divided into phonological, lexical, morphological, semantic and other components (as linguistic assemblages are sometimes wont to be), then we have assemblages within assemblages.

This assemblage approach represents a 'radical' way of viewing the construction of reality, as Haggerty and Ericson (2000: 608) emphasize: 'To dig beneath the surface stability of any entity is to encounter a host of different phenomena and processes working in concert. The radical nature of this vision becomes more apparent when one realizes how any particular assemblage is itself composed of different discrete assemblages which are themselves multiple.' Haggerty and Ericson are certainly correct in emphasizing the radicalness involved when thinking in terms of assemblages and, indeed, when taking seriously the assemblage nature of objects. This radicalness arises from the realization that things that are typically assumed to have an internal unity and thus (by virtue of this unity) a built-in or naturally endowed boundary as well – such that this boundary serves to externally and 'naturally' distinguish one thing from some other – are, in fact, heterogeneously constituted internally. By extension, then, the boundaries that we otherwise often take for granted as unproblematically bestowing 'thingness' are themselves contingent. What this means is that properties and processes hitherto considered external to the thing in question could on other occasions conceivably become incorporated as internal to and therefore part of the thing instead. Conversely, internal elements could under different circumstances become exteriorized or expelled from the erstwhile unity of the thing to then be treated as separate from the thing proper.

In making these points, Deleuze and Guattari are therefore drawing attention to the fact that different kinds of phenomena and processes are always being constituted and then reconstituted and, hence, assembled and reassembled as one (temporarily) discretely bounded stable entity. Such re-arrangements are ongoing so that even as we examine a single assemblage, we have to be aware that there are assemblages within assemblages. This recursivity of assemblages follows from the internal heterogeneity and contingently constituted nature of objects. Returning to the examples mentioned earlier, the boundaries between the linguistic assemblage known as 'Singlish' and the set of national practices indexing the Singaporean identity are fluid rather than hard ones, as are the lines that demarcate the sub-divisions within the linguistic assemblage of 'Singlish'. These boundaries are not fixed but shiftable.

The reason for this, as DeLanda (2006: 10–11, italics in original) explains, is that component parts of assemblages bear relations of exteriority rather than relations of interiority to one another:

Today, the main theoretical alternative to organic totalities is what the philosopher Gilles Deleuze calls *assemblages*, wholes characterized by *relations of exteriority*. These relations imply, first of all, that a component part of an assemblage may be detached from it and plugged into a different assemblage in which its interactions are different.

Relations of interiority assume a natural fit between the components, often to the point of invoking some form of essentialism (e.g. '"Lah" is a Singlish particle because it so fundamentally captures or reflects the Singaporean identity' or 'If you are Chinese, then you must obviously speak Mandarin'). Relations of exteriority, in contrast, make no assumptions about how changes to the component parts necessarily serve the larger totality. Rather, the component parts only bear a contingent relationship to the totality, and indeed to other component parts, because 'the parts that are fitted together are not uniform either in nature or in origin... the assemblage actively links these parts together by establishing relations between them' (DeLanda, 2016: 2). Needless to say, relations of exteriority are often misrecognized (Bourdieu, 1980; 1984) as relations of interiority.

Returning to the concept of a language once again, it is worth appreciating the value of thinking in terms of assemblages: doing so encourages us to further examine prevailing assumptions about the ontology of language. Why, for example, should we limit language's material dimension to words (whether spoken or written)? On what grounds do we exclude the speakers/writers or the mode of communication (phone, book, blog)? Consider what we understand by graffiti. It is 'outlawed literacy' or 'criminalized' (Conquergood, 1997: 354–5) precisely because its appearance on public surfaces is 'deemed a threat to property, propriety and pristine walls' (Pennycook, 2008: 137). Once abstracted from the public surface on which words and pictures may have been illegally painted, the language used no longer constitutes graffiti. Thus, as noted earlier, what might be taken to constitute a language or a proper manifestation of that language (which is much the same thing) and even what might be considered the relevant community of speakers can shift. Decisions about how to bound a language from a range of material and non-material phenomena – that is, decisions about how to lift out and demarcate to therefore 'assemble' a language that is 'yours' as opposed to 'theirs' – are very much dependent upon the social and political goals of the actors involved.

The concept of assemblages also has implications for the tendency to invoke linguistic scales, a common rhetorical strategy in much of the discourses involving language rights. This can be seen from distinctions that are often made between 'global languages' and 'minority languages', where the former are usually also 'killer languages' held responsible for the demise (imminent or foregone) of the latter (Farías, 2010). A key aspect of the stasis on which this rhetorical stance is grounded is the infolding of scales into languages themselves, so that certain languages can then – with considerable oversimplification – be categorized as 'global' and others as 'minority' or 'small'. But the point to be emphasized here is that once we start appreciating the assemblage nature of language (and indeed, other phenomena as well), then scales have to be recognized as epiphenomena that emerge from the ways in which different assemblages happen to be constructed, rather than as properties of languages themselves. From an assemblage perspective, 'scalar structuration and clustering are rejected as underlying structural processes and consequently as analytical categories' (Farías, 2010: 17). Thrift (quoted in Farías, 2010: 116–117) highlights the dangers arising from an uncritical adoption of scales:

One of the problems you do get into if you decide that there are scales is that you start allocating things to one scale or another, to one territory or another. Once you start doing that you almost predetermine the conclusions in ways which are really quite problematic. They are problematic in terms of the distinctions you use: big or small, flow or static, all these kinds of distinctions. Once you start using scales you start to foreground conclusions. I can agree with the literature on scalar shift to the extent that sometimes I think there are ways in which an operating system goes from being of one size to being of another size. I can see that; I can see that the boundaries are important. But that's not quite the same thing as scale. For me, it is a term we can do without.

This is not to suggest that scales are unimportant. Rather, it is to emphasize that they are the result of how assemblages are put together at different times and in different ways by different actors (Latham and McCormack, 2010: 65). As Thrift points out, boundaries are important, but they are not the same as scales. Drawing boundaries is how assemblages are constructed, and so it would be inconsistent to argue for the conceptual value of thinking in terms of assemblages while at the same time arguing that boundaries are inconsequential. Rather, the important thing is to acknowledge the 'fictive' nature of boundaries (Beck, in Slater and Ritzer, 2001: 266); that is, to acknowledge that boundaries are always in the process of being drawn and redrawn. And it is as a result of boundaries being drawn differently that scalar properties emerge so that a system 'goes from being of one size to being of another size'.

In the case of language, for example, this means that it is critical to ask just how specific understandings of language have been assembled and to what ends. Labels like 'global language' or 'minority language' are drawn with boundaries specified by their respective pre-modifiers. And we have seen in the Singlish controversy the uncritical use of such labels, especially from those opposed to Singlish who assert that, in contrast to Standard English, Singlish is not and can never be a global language. But, as should be clear by now, whether a language is global or otherwise has nothing to do with some intrinsic scalar property of the language. It is a matter of how the language has been assembled. In this regard, assemblage theory is perfectly consistent with an understanding of globalization as involving the rearranging of social relations on multiple levels (Giddens, 1990; Held, McGrew, Goldblatt, and Perraton, 1999; see the earlier discussion). Globalization is not some external phenomenon that threatens the gates of a community; it is about how ideas concerning language, culture and identity – and the relationships between them – have to be re-evaluated; hence, it involves an evermore reflexive awareness of the fictive boundaries that delimit such assemblages and of the relations of exteriority that hold the component parts together. As an illustration, consider the commodification of Singlish, its concomitant circulation overseas and its consumption by Singaporeans and non-Singaporeans. Here, at multiple levels, we find Singlish being re-assembled (it is being constructed under the rubric of creative works as opposed to being produced under relatively more 'naturalistic' conditions of actual communication) for different markets (tourists, local audiences and international audiences at film or theatre festivals). Along with this re-assembly of the linguistic package are re-adjustments to the package's liaisons with other assemblages such as those pertaining to identity and communicative purposes.

Such restructurings of the component parts of assemblages, as well as the links between erstwhile distinct assemblages, are historically constrained, of course. DeLanda (2016: 17–18, italics in original) refers to such constraints as 'downward causal influence':

But in the majority of cases the component parts come into being when a whole has already constituted itself and has begun to use its own emergent capacities *to constrain and enable* its parts: most people are born into communities that predate their birth, and most new government agencies are born in the context of an already functioning central government. Nevertheless, the ontological requirement of immanence forces us to conceive of the identity of a community or of a central government as being continuously produced by the day-to-day interactions between its parts. So we need to include in a realist ontology not only the processes that produce the identity of a given social whole when it is born, but also the processes that maintain its identity through time. And we must also include the *downward causal influence* that wholes, once constituted, can exert on their parts.

This explains why re-structurings to the components of assemblage do not necessarily entail a shift in how the assemblage itself is being perceived. Components are inserted and fitted into extant assemblages such as Singlish or Standard English. Lexical and phonological innovations may occur, indexical fields may expand or contract, and all of this takes place as the actual individuals who constitute the affiliated group of 'native speakers' or 'linguistic community' die and are replaced by different individuals. But the commitment to immanence encourages, as a matter of ideological default[3], the view that the assemblage *qua* constituted whole retains a structural integrity that is unaffected by changes to its component parts. Even events like the launch of SGEM are not so much reactions to Singlish as much as formations that re-constitute and concretize the notion of Singlish in various ways. Therefore, even though there is no doubt that the label 'Singlish' is commonly used by the various participants in the Singlish controversy and therefore refers to a robust cultural category, there is no reason to assume that this category actually describes a well-defined linguistic variety, much less a unified category. The label has been used by the various parties to refer to different things at different times: a colloquial variety, ungrammatical English, a shibboleth, a solidarity marker. And rather than insist that there must an underlying Singlish essence that courses through these multiplicities, there is greater value in appreciating these multiplicities as describing different socio-linguistic objects or linguistic assemblages. Singlish, then, needs to be understood as a 'multiple object [that is] enacted at different moments and sites' (Farías, 2010: 13). It has to be stressed, as Farías (2010: 13, citing Mol, 2002)

---

[3] While Deleuze and Guattari are known to have criticized the very notion of ideology, there is in fact no incompatibility in combining ideological analysis with that of assemblage (Massumi, 2002: xvi).

does, that all these enactments 'are not to be understood epistemologically as different perspectives on the object, but ontologically acknowledging that different realities are being enacted here and there, now and then'. The privileging of a 'purely' linguistic assemblage, where the linguistic is separated out from other assemblages that it may be a part of, is ultimately an ideological issue, one that often relies on the erasure of non-linguistic elements.

In public debates over Singlish, the different ways in which Singlish has been assembled relies, often implicitly, on indexical links between linguistic elements and elements relating to persona and even broader macro sociopolitical phenomena. This is by no means unusual. In Thailand, for example, the labels 'Tinglish' and 'Thaiglish' are taken to refer to an established variety or varieties of English. There are multiple websites that assume that the existence of Tinglish or Thaiglish can be taken for granted. For example, Stewart (2013) states that 'Tinglish' 'can also be know (sic) as Thaiglish' and is 'the non-standard form (on) English used by native Thai speakers due to language interference'. Another site, www.into-asia.com (accessed 31 January 2015) describes 'Tinglish' as the 'Thai version of English' where sentences 'are simplistic but still easily understandable':

For instance, 'I didn't want to go yesterday' would likely be said instead as 'Yesterday I not want go'. There's also the doubling of a few English words where it happens in Thai e.g. 'same same', 'near near' etc.

And the website www.theknowledge.in.th (accessed 31 January 2015) asks rhetorically:

Ever heard of the word *Tinglish* or *Thaiglish*? They are the unofficial terms used to describe the fusion of the Thai language with the English language often producing a new word with a meaning that may or may not be grammatically correct... When a Thai person says that *'These pants are fit'*. What they really do mean is that, *'These pants are too small'*. *Fit* is Thaiglish for *small*.

In contrast, Lee and Nadeau (2011: 1123) suggest,

Tenglish (pronounced 'tinglish') is characterized as the English spoken by Thais, while Englithai refers to the Thai spoken by Anglophones, or native English-speakers. The third form, Thaiglish, is characterized as a bonfide hybrid language, which conflates the Thai and English language structure and vocabulary...

Tenglish is merely an adaptation of English and will generally lack particles, articles and/or correct grammar conjugation...

Thai Americans will often try to speak in the Thaiglish form, which adapts the Thai language rhythm, tone, and pattern. Thaiglish speakers will retain Thai pronunciation, tonality, and question tags like 'na' and 'ja' and particles like 'krub' and 'ka' to soften their tone, indicate respect, a request, encouragement or other moods... Another characteristic of Thaiglish is adding suffixs (sic) like '-ing' when words cannot be directly translated or clearly described in one English word. For example, the term 'wai-ing' as in 'I am wai-ing my aunt' is often used amongst Thai Americans when one is referring to the traditional Thai form of greeting someone.

Here, we have assemblages of 'Thaiglish', 'Tenglish' and 'Tinglish', with varying degrees of overlaps. And these assemblages are not purely linguistic in nature, despite the ostensible concern with language. The identification of the named variety is dependent on identity of the speaker. Thus, for Lee and Nadeau (2011), 'Tenglish' is spoken by native Thais, whereas 'Englithai' is spoken by Anglophones or native English speakers. In contrast, Stewart (2013) treats 'Tinglish' and 'Thaiglish' as interchangeable labels for the variety of English spoken by native Thais.

This is why debates over whether Singlish is an asset or a liability grossly underestimate the complexity of the issues involved, not least because the debating parties are not necessarily always arguing over the same thing. Even among those who support the use of Singlish, different assemblages are involved depending whether Singlish is being celebrated as the playful flouting of the conventions associated with Standard English or as the language that bonds Singaporeans from different social and ethnic backgrounds. And among those who decry the use of Singlish, different assemblages, too, are involved depending on whether Singlish is being highlighted as the obstacle that prevents the learning of Standard English or as the language that tourists might find enhances their experience of Singapore.

Because the Singlish controversy involves different assemblages and because 'the assemblage's only unity is that of co-functioning' (Deleuze and Parnet, 2002: 69; see the earlier discussion), the way to understand the Singlish controversy is to ask what kinds of functions or, in this case, socio-political agendas, are served by the different assemblages. The different parties involved in the controversy need to be confronted with their various assemblages and the various goals they are pursuing. The purpose here is not to determine with any finality who is 'right' or who is 'wrong'. It should be clear by now that any attempt to make such a determination completely misses the point of assemblages. Instead, if the debating parties can agree that some of their goals are not too dissimilar, then that becomes a good start to examining the ways in which their respective understandings of Singlish (qua assemblages) might also be in need of revision if these goals are to be realized. Such a move is especially important because Singlish is itself part of yet other assemblages relating to national identity and culture that are themselves changing.

Future Directions for Linguistic Work

While I have focused primarily on Singlish, an assemblage approach is obviously of much broader significance and holds promising directions for future linguistic work.[4] Let me therefore close by considering four such directions.

First of all, it seems clear that an assemblage approach carries strong resonances with integrationism. As Harris (2016) points out:

> The term integrational alludes to the recognition that the linguistic sign alone cannot function as the basis of an independent, self-sufficient form of communication, but depends for effectiveness on its integration with non-verbal activities of many different kinds. These include all those that do not depend in any way on being able to speak or write; i.e. most of the basic activities needed for everyday living (eating, drinking, bodily movement, standing up, lying down, walking, fetching and carrying, avoiding obstacles, using elementary tools, paying attention to objects and happenings in the immediate environment, etc.) . . .
> The integrated character of linguistic and non-linguistic practices is so fundamental for human beings as to make it difficult to separate out any purely linguistic component. However you try to tackle the problem, there is no universal dividing line between the linguistic and the non-linguistic.

Harris goes on to contrast integrationism with segregationism:

> Such an analysis stands in marked contrast to traditional semiology, where the reigning assumption is that there must already exist established systems of signs (e.g. languages), without which communication would be doomed to failure. Thus integrationism (as opposed to 'segregationism', i.e. any approach which assumes that systems of communication are independent of their potential users or of the contexts in which they can operate) denies the existence of context-free signs. Signs, including linguistic signs, are products of the communicational process, not its prerequisites.

There are, however, issues with the way in which integrationism contrasts itself with segregationism that might benefit from an assemblage approach. The first is intregrationism's rejection of the assumption that already established systems of signs exist. But as the earlier discussion of downward causality indicates, even if the system (linguistic or otherwise) is constantly being re-constituted and re-structured, this does not imply that it is not meaningful to speak of assembled and pre-existing wholes into which more recent components have to

---

[4] DeLanda (2016: 57) has sketched the implications of assemblage theory for the evolution of languages, treating words and sentences as biological replicators along the lines of memes that spread across populations. Such an approach has, however, been already developed in much greater detail by Croft (2001: 366), who argues for 'lingueme replication' as the process where 'replication is subject to all the vagaries of communication and social context':

> A speaker replicates linguemes in the way intended by her; the hearer understands those replications based on the context of the discourse situation, and his experience of prior replications of those structures – an experience which may not be the same as the speaker's, and which may involve misunderstandings and negotiations of meaning. But the production of any utterance involves a speaker replicating existing morphosyntactic structures to encode the current experience, and the hearer using his knowledge to map the morphosyntactic structures onto a conceptual structure.

fit. The second concerns the distinction between different assemblages. Assemblage theory certainly rejects the ideas that the linguistic and the non-linguistic can be divided in any way that is universal since the constituents of any assemblage bear relations of exteriority to each other. However, it is clear that the linguistic signs that speakers make use include meta-linguistic ones such as 'variety', 'code' and 'language'. So, integrationism has to at the very least find some way of accommodating speakers' own ideological assumptions that languages are ontologically stable and delimitable entities, such that speakers' own sign interpretation behaviours are informed by this assumption. Once again, assemblage theory may be of some value by allowing integrationism to maintain its anti-segregationist stance while recognizing the emic validity and ideological influence of the distinction between the linguistic and the non-linguistic. In fact, there may be good reasons to do so given the robustness of this distinction. One might even, to adapt a phrase from Mitchell's (2000) discussion of modernity and capitalism, ask if language is possibly a piece of non-disposable fiction. The phrase 'non-disposable fiction' captures nicely the highly entrenched nature of the notion of language (and even affiliated concepts such as dialects and registers) and why it is extremely difficult if not altogether impossible to do without it.

Second, an assemblage approach highlights the need to engage with language as a material phenomenon given that an assemblage can involve heterogeneous phenomena. While the materiality of language has been recognized in linguistics, particularly in the field of linguistic landscape studies (see also Blommaert, 2013; Scollon and Scollon, 2004; 2008), its consequences have yet to be fully appreciated and theorized. Thus it is important to be prepared to de-centre the notion of language and recognize that language is but one (and not always the most important) semiotic resource being used. The workings of language have to be understood in relation to other modalities, such as spatial markers of time and place, visual gestural accompaniments such as the use of color or font size, and the kinds of materials being utilized (cardboard, metal, among others). What we recognize to be 'language' cannot easily be separated from its material manifestations, including its social settings. Our conception of language also has to extend to include the various technological developments that change the ways in which communication is conducted, since 'tools exist only in relation to the interminglings they make possible or that make them possible' (Deleuze and Guattari, 1987: 90). These different agencies and technologies allow for different enactments and realizations of language. For example, in a BBC travel show, an English speaker travelled across China using a translation app on his mobile phone to communicate with locals. His English utterances were translated by the app, with varying degrees of communicative success into Mandarin, which would then play the translated version for his Chinese interlocutors. In this regard, we have to seriously consider that the

Mandarin 'spoken' by the app in the phone is not the same Mandarin as that spoken amongst the Chinese.[5] We also have to consider that the English-speaking traveller is a kind of Mandarin 'speaker' when using the app, so that the app becomes an (occasional) extension of the speaker, a hybrid entity that we might characterize as a linguistic cyborg along the lines of Haraway (1991).

Third, the phenomenon of superdiversity or the 'tremendous increase in the categories of migrants, not only in terms of nationality, ethnicity, language, and religion, but also in terms of motives, patterns and itineraries of migration, processes of insertion into the labor and housing markets of the host societies, and so on' draws attention to how communicative resources are increasingly mobile (Blommaert and Rampton, 2016: 22–23). As Blommaert (2010: 197) points out, mobility creates unpredictability (Blommaert 2013: 8) because language gets dislodged from its traditional settings, and its traditional functions become distorted by the processes of mobility as language gets inserted into new settings. This process of insertion therefore changes – in ways that are both subtle and not so subtle – both the new settings and the language itself. If this is so, then it becomes pertinent to enquire further into the relationship between circulation and sharing. Does the circulation of a language and the distortions that may result mean that it is not at all possible to talk about the language being shared? And if a language can indeed be shared, then what are we to make of the distortions entailed by its circulation?

As we have seen from the discussion of Singlish throughout this book (and somewhat more briefly from the discussion of Thaiglish and Tinglish), the perceived unity of a language – as encapsulated in the name given to that language – is really an abstraction of many different linguistic items of varying sizes (word, phrase, entire sentence level constructions) that are also polysemous to varying degrees. This is a point that Rymes's (2014: 10–11) diversity principle nicely sums up: 'The more widely circulated a communicative element is, the more highly diverse the interactions with it will be'. Rymes gives the follow example:

To illustrate this principle, consider the Hindi/Urdu word *Jaan-e-man*. In a Bollywood film, the heartthrob might use this word (loosely translated, 'sweetheart') to refer lovingly to his girlfriend. But now, Hindi-speaking Bollywood fans in Philadelphia (among

---

[5] This scenario is of course somewhat reminiscent of Searle's (1980) Chinese Room Argument. Searle's point in that paper was to suggest the inadequacy of the Turing Test, since syntactic rules and symbolic strings may be manipulated to give the appearance of communication even in the absence of actual understanding. Searle's argument is complex and has undergone subtle revisions in response to counter-arguments from critics, but the key issue is that Searle was leaving out the role of any user of the computational system (since the individual who occupies the room has been reduced to being nothing more than a symbol manipulator). And this is precisely the point being emphasized in the present chapter about the dangers of reifying language to the point where speaker activity and its role in not just interpreting linguistic symbols but also changing what the symbols mean as a consequence of the activity itself have been bracketed out.

many other cities, globally), and in one English classroom they used it jokingly among themselves. Soon, other students (non-Hindi-speakers) began to use it too. '*Jaan-e-man*' was no longer being used as a term of endearment, like 'sweetheart', but more as a way of semi-ironically getting someone's attention, as in '*Jaan-e-man*, hand me a computer' ... the way people use *Jaan-e-man* is likely to continue to expand to more social groupings and functions anew in more diverse interactions. The new uses ... are not incorrect. They are simply new. And, in illustration of the Diversity Principle, people are not robotically repeating Bollywood phrases, they are embedding them in highly diverse interactions, creating unique nuances of meaning and functionality.

That is, the circulation of language necessarily results in a wider and more diverse range of interactions. At the same time, however, this diversity can be assembled and re-assembled according to different communication functions and agendas, and even under the same language name such as 'Singlish'. Assemblage theory therefore provides a theoretically useful way of accounting for how it is that a language can be seen as common/shared even as we recognize that circulation involves fragmentation and increased diversity. That is, different understandings of 'Singlish', 'Tinglish', and so on, are already different re-assemblings of languages, and the fact that these differences are *not* highlighted for explicit discussion allows them to be perceived (and what is in effect the same thing) and function as common/shared. Explicit arguments about how to properly define 'Singlish' will only serve to foreground the different assemblages involved. And this nicely leads us to the final direction for linguistic work.

A more applied direction for linguistic work concerns public understandings of language and language-related matters. We have seen, via an in-depth examination of the Singlish controversy, that arguments or concerns about language are seldom, if ever, just about language alone. Language is tied up with assumptions about appropriate social behaviour, social justice, status, mobility, and of course identity – especially ethnic and national identities. It is ironic, however, that despite its importance to society, the nature of language is not sufficiently discussed or debated. This is all the more critical when our assumptions about the nature of language can affect the ways in which language policies are formulated and, ultimately, the kind of society we live in.

One common assumption is that language names unproblematically refer to something that exists objectively outside of human experience. Another assumption is that, to the extent that human agency is relevant, this is usually in the form of traditional native speakers, who are construed as the appropriate authorities to consult regarding what might be grammatically correct or appropriate. These assumptions lead to a number of other related ones. For example, if there is this thing called 'English' that exists independently of human activity, then it must have properties that can be determined independently of what people think or do. Thus, questions and assertions about grammatical rules, meanings of words or notions of correctness are often phrased as though human intervention is irrelevant. This is why it is not uncommon to encounter questions and assertions like the following:[6]

'What is the REAL meaning of the word *bead*?'
'Proper English has no redundancies. African American Vernacular English (AAVE) has redundancies (*I ain't no marksman*). Therefore, AAVE is not proper English.'

But while linguists are themselves now appreciating that much of what we assume to be timeless or intrinsically correct rules about proper usage are ultimately conventions, public understandings about language – and its relationships to identity and culture – still tend to be based on outmoded and problematic assumptions. In this regard, it is interesting to note that Cambridge University has a Professor for the Public Understanding of Risk and Oxford University has a Professor for the Public Understanding of Science. Here is the description of the Simonyi Professorship for the Public Understanding of Science at Oxford:

The task of communicating science to the layman is not a simple one. In particular it is imperative for the post holder to avoid oversimplifying ideas, and presenting exaggerated claims. The limits of current scientific knowledge should always be made clear to the public. Once done so, however, there is also a role for presenting speculative ideas, which can convey to non-scientists some of the excitement of doing true science. The Professor should communicate scientific ideas through a variety of media, in order to reach a wide range of people. These include, but are not limited to, public lectures, writing articles and books, and television and radio appearances.

Analogously, the field of linguistics needs to urgently start addressing public understandings of language and its liaisons with other assemblages. The effects of globalization are leading to increased social diversity, with the demographic profiles of many communities altering drastically as a result of inward and outward migration. These changes to the demographic and cultural makeup of a community are intensified by rapid advances in telecommunications and transportation that make interconnections between ostensibly separate and distinct communities easier to cultivate, sustain and, as a result, harder to ignore. To minimize and even pre-empt the likelihood of increased tensions and conflicts as populations become more diversified, many old assumptions – about language names or labels as referring to linguistic systems that must be kept distinct, as being associated with a distinct and traditional group of speakers – have to be re-evaluated.

---

[6] Where human agency is considered relevant, then answers to questions about language can be found by checking with traditional native speakers. Unfortunately, this confuses linguistic competence with racial characteristics.

Conclusion

In this book, I argued that a study of the ideological underpinnings of the Singlish controversy provides us with a window to many issues that pertain not only to the spread of English and the emergence of distinct varieties but also to the very nature of language itself. This was made possible by my focus not just on the publicly contested issues regarding whether Singlish is an asset or a liability but also by my use of these contestations as a stepping-stone to uncover the different understandings of what Singlish is – and, from there, highlighting the value of thinking of Singlish in terms of an assemblage. Furthermore, I also showed that, *qua* assemblage, Singlish (and language in general) has to be better appreciated as a material phenomenon, with the implication then that we have to be prepared to de-centre language as but one of the many resources being drawn upon, even when the assemblage in question is ostensibly a linguistic variety. Finally, I suggested a number of future directions for linguistic work arising from my study of Singlish. The notion of an assemblage is still fairly new to linguistics, and I have little doubt that it holds great potential for theorizing about the nature of language, a potential that I believe can easily expand beyond the directions I laid out in this chapter.

References

Agha, A. (2011). Commodity registers. *Journal of Linguistic Anthropology*, **21**(1), 22–53.

Alsagoff, L. (2007). Singlish: Negotiating culture, capital and identity. In V. Vaish, S. Gopinathan and Y. Liu, eds., *Language, Capital, Culture*. Rotterdam: Sense Publishers, 25–46.

Alsagoff, L. (2010). English in Singapore: Culture, capital and identity in linguistic variation. *World Englishes*, **29**, 336–348.

Alsagoff, L. (2014). Book review of Singapore English: *Structure, Variation and Usage* by Jakob Leimgruber. *Journal of Language Contact*, **7**(2), 441–445.

Alsagoff, L. and Ho, C. L. (1998). The grammar of Singapore English. In J. A. Foley, T. Kandiah, Z. M. Bao, A. F. Gupta, L. Alsagoff, C. L. Ho, L. Wee, I. S. Talib and W. Bokhorst-Heng, eds., *English in New Cultural Contexts: Reflections from Singapore*. Singapore: Oxford University Press, 127–151.

Anderson, B. (1991). *Imagined Communities: Reflections on the Origin and Spread of Nationalism*. Revised edn. London: Verso.

Andreas, P. (2014). Dialogue of the deaf: Scholars, policymakers and the drug war in US foreign relations. In A. F. Lowenthal and M. E. Bertucci, eds., *Scholars, Policymakers, and International Affairs: Finding Common Cause*. Baltimore: Johns Hopkins University Press, 74–87.

Ansaldo, U. (2004). The evolution of Singapore English. In L. Lim, ed., *Singapore English: A Grammatical Description*. Amsterdam: John Benjamins, 127–149.

Aw, Z. (2013). *Singaporelang – What the Singlish?*. Self-published.

Baetens, B. H. (1986). *Bilingualism: Basic Principles*, 2nd edn. Clevedon: Multilingual Matters.

Bao, Z. M. (1998). The sounds of Singapore English. In J. A. Foley et al., eds. *English in New Cultural Contexts: Reflections from Singapore*. Singapore: Oxford University Press, 152–174.

Bao, Z. (2005). The aspectual system of Singapore English and the systemic substratist explanation. *Journal of Linguistics*, **41**, 237–267.

Bauman, R. and Briggs, C. (1990). Poetics and performance as critical perspectives on language and social life. *Annual Review of Anthropology*, **19**, 59–88.

Bauman, Z. (1992). *Institutions of Post-Modernity*. London: Routledge.

Beck, U., Giddens, A., and Lash, S., eds. (1994). *Reflexive Modernization: Politics, Tradition and Aesthetics in the Modern Social Order*. Oxford: Polity Press.

Bell, A. (2013). *The Guidebook to Sociolinguistics*. Oxford: Wiley-Blackwell.

Benjamin, G. (1976). The cultural logic of Singapore's 'multiracialism'. In Riaz Hassan, ed., *Singapore: Society in Transition*. Kuala Lumpur: Oxford University Press, 115–133.

Betts, R. (1975). *Multiracialism, Meritocracy and the Malays of Singapore*. PhD diss., Massachusetts Institute of Technology.

Bex, T. and Watts, R. J. (1999). Introduction. In T. Bex and R. J. Watts, eds., *Standard English: The Widening Debate*. London: Routledge, 1–12.

Birch, D. (2007). *Interlogue: Studies in Singapore Literature, vol. 6: Haresh Sharma*. Singapore: Ethos Books.

Blom, J. and Gumperz, J. J. (1972). Social meaning in linguistic structures: Code switching in Northern Norway. In J. J. Gumperz and D. Hymes, eds., *Directions in Sociolinguistcs*. New York: Holt, Rinehart and Winston, 407–434.

Blommaert, J. (1999). The debate is open. In J. Blommaert, ed., *Language Ideological Debates*. Berlin: Mouton de Gruyter, 1–38.

Blommaert, J. (2005). *Discourse*. Cambridge: Cambridge University Press.

Blommaert, J. (2010). *The Sociolinguistics of Globalization*. Cambridge: Cambridge University Press.

Blommaert, J. (2013). *Ethnography, Superdiversity and Linguistic Landscapes: Chronicles of Complexity*. Clevedon: Multilingual Matters.

Blommaert, J. and Rampton, B. (2016). Language and superdiversity. In K. Arnaut, J. Blommaert, B. Rampton and M. Spotti, eds., *Language and Superdiversity*. New York: Routledge, 21–48.

Blommaert, J. and Verschueren, J. (1998). *Debating Diversity: Analyzing the Discourse of Tolerance*. London: Routledge.

Bloom, D. (1986). The English language in Singapore: A critical survey. In B. K. Kapur, ed., *Singapore Studies: Critical Surveys of the Humanities and Social Sciences*. Singapore: Singapore University Press, 337–458.

Bokhorst-Heng, W. (1998). *Language and Imagining the Nation in Singapore*. PhD diss., University of Toronto.

Bokhorst-Heng, W. (1999). Singapore's Speak Mandarin Campaign: Language ideological debates and the imagining of the nation. In J. Blommaert, ed., *Language Ideological Debates*. Berlin: Mouton de Gruyter, 235–265.

Bokhorst-Heng, W. (2005). Debating Singlish. *Multilingua*, **24**, 185–209.

Bourdieu, P. (1980). *The Logic of Practice*. Stanford: Stanford University Press.

Bourdieu, P. (1984). *Distinction: A Social Critique of the Judgement of Taste*. London: Routledge.

Bourdieu, P. (1988). *Homo Academicus*, P. Collier, trans. Stanford: Stanford University Press.

Bourdieu, P. (1991). *Language and Symbolic Power*. Cambridge, MA: Harvard University Press.

Braga-Blake, M. (1992) Eurasians in Singapore: An overview. In M. Braga-Blake and A. Edbert-Oehlers, eds., *Singapore Eurasians: Memories and Hopes*. Singapore: Times Publishers, 11–23.

Brooks, A. and Wee, L. (2014). *Consumption, Cities and States: Comparing Singapore with Asian and Western Cities*. London: Anthem Press.

Brown-Saracino, J. (2009). *A Neighborhood that Never Changes: Gentrification, Social Preservation and the Search for Authenticity*. Chicago: University of Chicago Press.

Bruthiaux, P. (2003). Squaring the circles: Issues in modeling English worldwide. *International Journal of Applied Linguistics*, **13**(2), 159–178.

Bruthiaux, P. (2010). The Speak Good English Movement: A web-user's perspective. In L. Lim, A. Pakir and L. Wee, eds., *English in Singapore: Modernity and Management*. Hong Kong: Hong Kong University Press, 91–108.

Bucholtz, M. and Hall, K. (2005). Identity and interaction: A sociocultural linguistic approach. *Discourse Studies*, **7**(4–5), 585–614.

Budach, G., Roy, S., and Heller, M. (2003). Community and commodity in French Ontario. *Language in Society*, **32**, 603–627.

Cai, H. (2011). From dialect to Mandarin and English. *Straits Times*, 15 January 2011.

Cameron, D. (1995). *Verbal Hygiene*. London: Routledge.

Campbell-Kibler, K. (2007). Accent, (ING) and the social logic of listener perceptions. *American Speech*, **82**, 32–64.

Castells, M. (2012). *Networks of Outrage and Hope: Social Movements in an Internet Age*. Cambridge: Polity Press.

Cavallaro, F., Ng, B. C., and Seilhamer, M. (2014). Singapore Colloquial English: Issues of prestige and identity. *World Englishes*, **33**(3), 378–397.

Chan, B. (2016). Singlish all abuzz. *Sunday Times*, 22 May 2016.

Chan, B. C. (2014). Singlish OK what. Why cannot speak leh? *Poached Mag*, 16 January 2014. http://poachedmag.com/2014/01/16/singlish-ok-what-why-cannot-speak-leh/; accessed 26 May 2016.

Chew, D. (2007). Getting out of the cultural desert. *TODAY*, 15 January 2007.

Chew, P. (2005). Change and continuity: English language teaching in Singapore. *Asian EFL Journal*, **7**(1), 4–24.

Chng, H. H. (2003). 'You see me no up': Is Singlish a problem? *Language Problems & Language Planning*, **27**(1), 45–62.

Chong, Terence. (2011). *The Theatre and the State in Singapore: Orthodoxy and Resistance*. London: Routledge.

Chua, B. H. (1995). *Communitarian Ideology and Democracy in Singapore*. London: Routledge.

Comaroff, J. and Comaroff, J. (2012). *Theory from the South*. New York: Routledge.

Conquergood, D. (1997). Street literacy. In J. Flood, S. B. Heath and D. Lapp (eds.), *Handbook of Research on Teaching Literacy through the Communicative and Visual Arts*. New York: Simon & Schuster: 354–375.

Coupland, N. (2007). *Style*. Cambridge: Cambridge University Press.

Coupland, N. and Kelly-Holmes, H. (2017). Making and marketing in the bilingual periphery: Materialization as metacultural transformation. In J. R. Cavanaugh and S. Shankar, eds., *Language and Materiality: Ethnographic and Theoretical Explorations*. New York: Cambridge University Press.

Croft, W. (2001). *Radical Construction Grammar*. Oxford: Oxford University Press.

Crowley, T. (1999). Curiouser and curiouser: Falling standards in the standard English debate. In T. Bex and R. J. Watts, eds., *Standard English: The Widening Debate*. London: Routledge, 271–282.

De Costa, P., Park, J., and Wee, L. (2016). Language learning as linguistic entrepreneurship: Implications for language education. *Asia-Pacific Education Researcher*, **25**(5), 695–702.

Deely, J. (1990). *Basics of Semiotics*. Bloomington: Indiana University Press.

198   References

de Kock, L. (1992). "Interview with Gayatri Chakravorty Spivak: New Nation Writers Conference in South Africa." *ARIEL: A Review of International English Literature*, **23**(3), 29–47.

DeLanda, M. (2006). *A New Philosophy of Society: Assemblage Theory and Social Complexity*. London: Continuum.

DeLanda, M. (2016). *Assemblage Theory*. Edinburgh: University of Edinburgh Press.

Deleuze, G. and Guattari, F. (1981). Rhizome. *Ideology and Consciousness*, **8**, 49–71.

Deleuze, G. and Guattari, F. (1987). *A Thousand Plateaus: Capitalism and Schizophrenia*. Minneapolis: University of Minnesota Press.

Deleuze, G. and Parnet, C. (2002). *Dialogues II*. New York: Columbia University Press.

Deterding, D. (2011). Language in Brunei: Woodleigh. *Brunei Linguistics*, 11 July 2011. http://brunei-linguistics/blogspot.sg/2011/07/woodleigh.html; accessed 20 September 2012.

Duchêne, A. (2008). *Ideologies across Nations: The Construction of Linguistic Minorities at the United Nations*. Berlin: Mouton de Gruyter.

Duchêne, A. and Heller, M. (2012). Multilingualism and the new economy. In M. Martin-Jones, A. Blackledge and A. Creese (eds.), *The Routledge Handbook of Multilingualism*, London: Routledge: 369–383.

Eckert, P. (2008). Variation and the indexical field. *Journal of Sociolinguistics*, **12**, 453–476.

Eckert, P. (2012). Three waves of variation study: The emergence of meaning in the study of sociolinguistic variation. *Annual Review of Anthropology*, **41**, 87–100.

Farías, I. (2010). Introduction. In Ignacio Farías and Thomas Bender, eds., *Urban Assemblages*. New York: Routledge, 1–24.

Feher, M. (2009). Self-appreciation; or, the aspirations of human capital. *Public Culture*, **21**(1), 21–41.

Ferguson, C. (1959). Diglossia. *Word*, **15**, 325–340.

Fishman, J. A. (1967). Bilingualism with and without diglossia; diglossia with and without bilingualism. *Journal of Social Issues*, **23**, 29–38.

Foley, J. A. (1998). Language in the school. In J. A. Foley et al., eds., *English in New Cultural Contexts: Reflections from Singapore*. Singapore: Oxford University Press, 244–269.

Fong, V., Lim, L., and Wee, L. (2002). Singlish: Used and abused. *Asian Englishes*, **5**(1), 18–39.

Foucault, M. (1977). *Discipline and Punish*, A. Sheridan, trans. New York: Pantheon.

Foucault, M. (1984). Truth and power. In Paul Rabinow, ed., *The Foucault Reader*. New York: Pantheon, 51–75.

Foucault, M. (2008). *The Birth of Biopolitics: Lectures at the Collège de France, 1978–1979*, G. Burchell, trans. Basingstoke: Palgrave MacMillan.

Fu, G. (2012). National Day speech to Singaporean community in Seoul, Korea. http://app.mewr.gov.sg/web/contents/contents.aspx?contid=1703; accessed 26 October 2012.

Gal, S. (1989). Lexical innovation and loss: The use and value of restricted Hungarian. In N. Dorian, ed., *Investigating Obsolescence: Studies in Language Contraction and Death*. Cambridge: Cambridge University Press, 313–331.

Gal, S. and Irvine, J. T. (1995). The boundaries of languages and disciplines: How ideologies construct difference. *Social Research*, **62**, 967–1001.

Gao, S. (2015). Multilingualism and good citizenship: The making of language celebrities in Chinese media. Paper presented at the Sociolinguistics of Globalization Conference, 3–6 June. Hong Kong University.

Gasmier, M. R. (1997). Finding the right language for stage. *Straits Times*, 7 September.

Gee, J. P. (2001). Educational linguistics. In M. Aronoff and J. Rees-Miller, eds., *The Handbook of Linguistics*. Oxford: Blackwell, 647–663.

Giddens, A. (1987). *Social Theory and Modern Sociology*. Cambridge: Polity.

Giddens, A. (1990). *The Consequences of Modernity*. Cambridge: Polity.

Giddens, A. (1991). *Modernity and Self-Identity*. Cambridge: Polity

Giddens, A. (2002). *Runaway World: How Globalization Is Reshaping Our Lives*, 2nd edn. London: Profile Books.

Goh, C and Woo, Y.Y. (2009). *The Coxford Singlish Dictionary*, 2nd edn. Singapore: Angsana Books.

Goh, R. (2009). Uncertain locale: The dialectics of space and the cultural politics of English in Singapore. Paper presented at the workshop on 'The Politics of English' in Asia, 4–5 August. Asia Research Institute, National University of Singapore.

Goh, R. (2016). The anatomy of Singlish: Globalization, multiculturalism, and the construction of the 'local' in Singapore. *Journal of Multilingual & Multicultural Development*, **37**(8), 748–758.

Goldberg, A. (1995). *Constructions: A Construction Grammar Approach to Argument Structure*. Chicago: University of Chicago Press.

Gopalakrishnan, R. and Lim, K. (2011). Singapore PM makes rare apology as election campaign heats up. *Reuters India*, 4 May. http://in.reuters.com/article/2011/05/04/idINIndia-56766220110504; accessed 24 October 2012.

Gupta, A. F. (1994). *The Step-Tongue: Children's English in Singapore*. Clevedon: Multilingual Matters.

Gupta, A. F. (2010). Singapore Standard English revisited. In L. Lim, A. Pakir and L. Wee, eds., *English in Singapore: Modernity and Management*. Hong Kong: Hong Kong University Press, 57–90.

Gwee, L. S. (2016). Do you speak Singlish? *New York Times*, 13 May.

Hagens, S. A. (2005). Attitudes toward Konglish of South Korean teachers of English in the Province of Jeollanamdo. PhD diss., Brock University, Canada.

Haggerty, K. D. and Ericson, R. V. (2000). The surveillant assemblage. *British Journal of Sociology*, **51**(4), 605–622.

Han, F. K., Fernandez, W., and Tan, S. 1998. *Lee Kuan Yew: The Man and his Ideas*. Singapore: Times Editions.

Haraway, D. (1991). *Simians, Cyborgs, and Women: The Reinvention of Nature*. New York: Routledge.

Harris, R. (2016). Integrationism: A very brief introduction. www.royharrisonline.com/integrational_linguistics/integrationism_introduction.html; accessed 26 August 2016.

Held, D. and McGrew, A. (2003). The great globalization debate: An introduction. In David Held and Anthony McGrew, eds., *The Global Transformations Reader*. Cambridge: Polity, 1–50.

Held, D., McGrew, A., Goldblatt, D., and Perraton, J. (1999). *Global Transformation*. Cambridge: Polity.

Heller, M. (2008). Language and the nation-state: Challenges to sociolinguistic theory. *Journal of Sociolinguistics*, **12**(4), 504–524.

Heller, M. (2011). *Paths to Post-Nationalism*. Oxford: Oxford University Press.

Heng, J. (2015). Diplomatic missions screening Singapore films in cultural push. *Straits Times*, 21 December 2015. www.straitstimes.com/singapore/diplomatic-missions-screening-singapore-films-in-cultural-push; accessed 5 September 2017.

Hill, M. and Lian, K. F. (1995). *The Politics of Nation Building and Citizenship in Singapore*. London: Routledge.

Hoe, Y. N. (2009). Insistence on bilingualism in early years of education policy was wrong: MM Lee. *Channel NewsAsia*, 17 November. www.channelnewsasia.com/stories/singaporelocalnews/view/1018826/1/html; accessed 18 November 2009.

Holliday, A. (2005). *The Struggle to Teach English as an International Language*. Oxford: Oxford University Press.

Holmes, J. (1984). Modifying illocutionary force. *Journal of Pragmatics*, **8**(3): 345–365.

Holmes, J. (2013). *An Introduction to Sociolinguistics*. London: Routledge.

Honey, J. (1997). *Language Is Power: The Story of Standard English and Its Enemies*. London: Faber and Faber.

Honey, J. (1983). *The Language Trap: Race, Class, and the Standard Language Issue in British Schools*. Middlesex: National Council for Educational Standards.

hooks, b. (1990). Marginality as a site of resistance. In R. Ferguson, M. Gever, Trinh T. M., and C. West, eds., *Out There: Marginalization and Contemporary Cultures*. Cambridge, MA: MIT Press, 341–343.

Hopper, P. J. (1998). Emergent grammar. In M. Tomasello, ed., *The New Psychology of Language*. Mahwah, NJ: Lawrence Erlbaum, 155–175.

Hussain, Z. (2011). More English in Malay, Tamil homes. *Straits Times*, 15 January.

Irvine, J. T. and Gal, S. (2000). Language ideology and linguistic differentiation. In Paul Kroskrity, ed., *Regimes of Language*. Santa Fe: School of American Research, 35–83.

Jack, G. (2010). Languages and the market. In H. Kelly-Holmes and G. Mautner, eds., *Language and the Market*. Houndmills: Palgrave, 7–19.

Jaffe, A. (1999a). Locating power: Corsican translators and their critics. In J. Blommaert, ed., *Language Ideological Debates*. Berlin: Mouton de Gruyter, 39–66.

Jaffe, A. (1999b). *Ideologies in Action: Language Politics on Corsica*. Berlin: Mouton de Gruyter.

Jaworski, Adam, and Thurlow, Crispin. (2010). Introducing semiotic landscapes. In Adam Jaworski and Crispin Thurlow, eds., *Semiotic Landscapes: Language, Image, Space*. London: Continuum, 1–40.

Jenkins, J. (2003). *World Englishes: A Resource Book for Students*. London: Routledge.

Jing, X. and Zuo, N. (2006). Chinglish in the oral work of non-English majors. *CELEA Journal*, **29**(4), 15–20.

Juris, J. S. (2012). Reflections on #Occupy Everywhere: Social media, public space, and emerging logics of aggregation. *American Ethnologist*, **39**(2), 259–279.

Kachru, B. B. (1982). *The Other Tongue: English Across Cultures*. Urbana: University of Illinois Press.

Kachru, B. B. (1985). Standards, codification, and sociolinguistic realism: the English language in the Outer Circle. In R. Quirk and H. G. Widdowson, eds., *English in the World: Teaching and Learning the Language and Literatures.* Cambridge: Cambridge University Press, 11–30.

Kachru, B. B. (1986). *The Alchemy of English: The Spread, Functions and Models of Nonnative Englishes.* Oxford: Pergamon Press.

Kachru, B. B. (1991). Liberation linguistics and the Quirk concern. *English Today,* 7, 3–13.

Kachru, B. and Nelson, C. (1996). World Englishes. In S. McKay and N. Hornberger, eds., *Sociolinguistics in Language Teaching.* Cambridge: Cambridge University Press, 71–102.

Kennedy, P. (2001). Introduction: Globalization and the crisis of identities? In P. Kennedy and C. Danks, eds., *Globalization and National Identities: Crisis or Opportunity?* New York: Palgrave, 1–28.

Koh, J. (2016). Singlish in the skies on Aug 9? Must be Jetstar, lah. *Straits Times,* 2 August.

Kok, M. (2012). 'Double confirm' more catchy than 'confirm confirm'. *Straits Times, Life!,* 18 August.

Kong, L. (1999). Globalization and Singaporean transmigration: Re-imagining and negotiating national identity. *Political Geography,* 18(5), 563–589.

Kroskrity, P. V. (2000). Regimenting languages: Language ideological perspectives. In P. V. Kroskrity, ed., *Regimes of Language.* Santa Fe: School of American Research, 1–34.

Kwan, M. Y. (2003). The Speak Good English Movement: A debate of the Englishes. MA thesis, National University of Singapore.

Labov, W. (1963). The social motivation of a sound change. *Word,* 18, 1–42.

Lakoff, G. (1987). *Women, Fire and Dangerous Things.* Chicago: University of Chicago Press.

Lakoff, G. (1993). The contemporary theory of metaphor. In Andrew Ortony, ed., *Metaphor and Thought,* 2nd ed. Cambridge: Cambridge University Press, 202–251.

Lam, L. (2015). Singlish brought to life in new photo book. *Asia One,* 21 September 2015. www.asiaone.com/singapore/singlish-brought-life-new-photo-book; accessed 31 August 2017.

Larner, W. and Walters, W. (2004). Globalization as governmentality. *Alternatives,* 29, 495–514.

Latham, A. and McCormack, D. P. (2010). Globalizations big and small. In Ignacio Farías and Thomas Bender, eds., *Urban Assemblages.* London: Routledge, 53–72.

Lazzarato, M. (2009). Neoliberalism in action: Inequality, insecurity and the reconstitution of the social. *Theory, Culture & Society,* 26(6), 109–133.

Le Blond, M. (1986). Drama in Singapore: Towards an English language theatre. In Peter Hyland, ed., *Discharging the Canon: Cross-Cultural Readings in Literature.* Singapore: Singapore University Press, 112–125.

Lee, Jonathan and Nadeau, Kathleen. 2011. Thai Americans: Vernacular language, speech and manner. *Encyclopedia of Asian American Folklore and Folklife,* Vol. 3. Santa Barbara, California: ABC-CLIO.

Lee, Kuan Yew. (1970). The twain have met. Dillingham Lecture, East-West Center, Honolulu, Hawaii, 11 November 1970.

Lee, Kuan Yew. (2012). *My Lifelong Challenge: Singapore's Bilingual Journey.* Singapore: Straits Times Press.

Lee, N., Ling, A. P., and Nomoto, H. (2009). Colloquial Singapore English *got*: Functions and substratal influences. *World Englishes*, **28**, 293–318.

Lee, P. (2016). English most common home language in Singapore, bilingualism also up: Government survey. *Straits Times*, 10 March.

Lee, S. H. (2011). British or American, it's still English. *Sunday Times*, 2 October.

Levinson, S. (1992). Activity types and language. In P. Drew and J. Heritage, eds., *Talk at Work: Interaction in Institutional Settings*. Cambridge: Cambridge University Press, 66–100. Originally published in *Linguistics*, **17**, 356–399.

Li, W., Saravanan, V., and Hoon, J. N. L. (1997). Language shift in the Teochew community in Singapore: A family domain analysis. *Journal of Multilingual and Multicultural Development*, **18**(5), 364–384.

Leimgruber, J. (2013). *Singapore English: Structure, Variation and Usage*. Cambridge: Cambridge University Press.

Lim, L. (2004). English in Singapore and Singapore English. In L. Lim, ed., *Singapore English: A Grammatical Description*. Amsterdam: John Benjamins, 1–18.

Lim, L. (2009). 'Peranakan English'. In D. Schreier, P. Trudgill, E. Schneider, and J. Williams, eds., *Lesser Known Varieties of English*. Cambridge: Cambridge University Press, 327–347.

Lim, L. (2010). Migrants and 'mother tongues': Extralinguistic forces in the ecology of English in Singapore. In L. Lim, A. Pakir and L. Wee, eds., *English in Singapore: Modernity and Management*. Hong Kong: Hong Kong University Press, 19–54.

Lin, R. (2010). Singaporeans split on issue of foreigners' presence: Poll. *Straits Times*, 28 June 2010.

Lo Bianco, J. (2004). Language planning as applied linguistics. In A. Davies and C. Elder, eds., *Handbook of Applied Linguistics*. Oxford: Blackwell, 738–762.

Loh, D. (2010). Speak Good English Movement spreads message creatively. *Channel NewsAsia*, 13 September 2010. www.channelnewsasia.com/stories/singaporelocalnews/view/1080953/1/.html; accessed 29 October 2012.

Loh, D. (2015). Singapore's environment favours entrepreneurship, startups: Venture capitalists. *Channel News Asia*, 21 April. www.channelnewsasia.com/news/business/singapore/singapore-s-environment/1798640.html; accessed 15 May 2016.

Low, E. L. and Brown, A. (2005). *English in Singapore: An Introduction*. Singapore: McGraw-Hill.

Makoni, S. and Pennycook, A. (2007). Disinventing and reconstituting languages. In S. Makoni and A. Pennycook, eds., *Disinventing and Reconstituting Languages*. Clevedon: Multilingual Matters, 1–41.

Marx, K. (1967 [1887]). *Capital: A Critique of Political Economy*, vol. I, S. Moore and E. Aveling, trans. New York: International Publishers.

Massumi, B. (2002). *Parables for the Virtual: Movement, Affect, Sensation*. Durham: Duke University Press.

Mathew, M., Chiang, W. F. and Zhang J. (in press). *Language Proficiency, Identity and Management: Results from the IPS Survey on Race, Religion and Language. IPS Exchange Series*. Singapore: National University of Singapore.

Mauzy, D. K. and Milne, R. S. (2002). *Singapore Politics under the People's Action Party*. London: Routledge.

Meyers-Scotton, C. (1993). *Duelling Languages: Grammatical Structure in Code-Switching*. Oxford: Clarendon Press.

Meyers-Scotton, C. (2002). *Contact Linguistics: Bilingual Encounters and Grammatical Outcomes*. Oxford: Oxford University Press.

Miel. (2003). *An Essential Guide to Singlish*. Singapore: Talisman Pu.

Milani, T. (2007). Debating Swedish: Language politics and ideology in contemporary Sweden. PhD diss., Stockholm University.

Miles, W. (1998). *Bridging Mental Boundaries in a Postcolonial Microcosm: Identity and Development in Vanauatu*. Hawaii: University of Hawaii Press.

Milkman, R., Luce, S., and Lewis, P. (2013). *Changing the Subject: A Bottom Up Account of Occupy Wall Street in New York City*. New York: City University of New York.

Milroy, J. (2001). Language ideologies and the consequences of standardization. *Journal of Sociolinguistic*, **5**(4), 530–555.

Milroy, J. and Milroy, L. (1999). *Authority in Language*. London: Routledge.

Mitchell, T. (2000). The stage of modernity. In T. Mitchell, ed., *Questions of Modernity*. Minneapolis: University of Minnesota Press, 1–34.

Modiano, M. (1999). International English in the global village. *English Today*, **15**(2), 22–28.

Muniandy, M. K., Nair, G. K. S., Shanmugam, S. K. K., Ahmad, I., and Noor, M. N. B. (2010). Sociolinguistic competence and Malaysian students' English language proficiency. *English Language Teaching*, **3**(3), 145–151.

Nash, R. (1970). Spanglish: Language contact in Puerto Rico. *American Speech*, **45**, 223–233.

Norton, B. (2000). *Identity and Language Learning: Gender, Ethnicity and Educational Change*. Harlow: Pearson.

Ong, A. (2006). *Neoliberalism as Exception*. Durham: Duke University Press.

Ong, A. (2006). *Neoliberalism as Exception: Mutations in Citizenship and Sovereignty*. Durham: Duke University Press.

Othman, Z. (2010), Double-barrelled race system to start on Saturday. *Today Online*, 30 December 2010. www.todayonline.com/Hotnews/EDC101230-0000209/Double-barrelled-race-system-to-start-on-Saturday; accessed 30 December 2010.

Pakir, A. (1992). English-knowing bilingualism in Singapore. In B. K. Choon, A. Pakir and T. C. Kiong, eds., *Imagining Singapore*, 2nd ed. Singapore: Times Academic Press, 254–278.

Pakir, A. (2000). Singapore. In W. K. Ho and R. Y. L. Wong, eds., *Language Policies and Language Education: The Impact in East Asian Countries in the Next Decade*. Singapore: Times Academic Press, 259–284.

Park, J. (2009). *The Local Construction of a Global Language: Ideologies of English in South Korea*. Berlin: Mouton.

Park, J. and Wee, L. (2009). Three Circles redux: A Market-theoretic Perspective on World Englishes. *Applied Linguistics*, **30**, 389–406.

Park, J. and Wee, L. (2012). *Markets of English*. London: Routledge.

Park, J. and Wee, L. (2013). Linguistic baptism and the disintegration of ELF. *Applied Linguistics Review*, **4**(2), 339–359.

Pennycook, A. (2003). Global Englishes, Rip Slyme and performativity. *Journal of Sociolinguistics*, **7**(4), 513–533.

Pennycook, A. (2008). Multilithic English(es) and language ideologies. *Language in Society*, **37**, 435–444.

Perrons, D. (2004). *Globalization and Social Change: People and Places in a Divided World*. London: Routledge.

Peterson, R. A. and Kern, R. M. (1996). Changing highbrow taste: From snob to omnivore. *American Sociological Review*, **61**(5), 900–907.

Petersen, W. (2001). *Theatre and the Politics of Culture in Contemporary Singapore*. Middleton, CT: Wesleyan University Press.

Philips, S. U. (2000). Constructing a Tongan nation-state through language ideology in the courtroom. In P. V. Kroskrity, ed., *Regimes of Language: Ideologies, Polities and Identities*. Santa Fe: School of American Research, 229–257.

Pierce, J. E. (1971). Culture, diffusion and Japlish. *Linguistics*, **9**, 45–58.

Piller, I. and Cho, J. (2013). Neoliberalism as language policy. *Language in Society*, **42**, 23–44.

Platt, J. T. (1975). The Singapore English speech continuum and its basilect 'Singlish' as a 'creoloid'. *Anthropological Linguistics*, **17**, 363–374.

Platt, J. T. and Weber, H. (1980). *English in Singapore and Malaysia*. Petaling, Jaya: Oxford University Press.

Poedjosoedarmo, G. (1995). Lectal variation in the media and the classroom: A preliminary analysis of attitudes. In S. C. Teng and M. L. Ho, eds., *The English Language in Singapore: Implications for Teaching*. Singapore: Singapore Association for Applied Linguistics, 53–67.

Popatial, A. (2010), Double-barrelled listing won't have big impact on ethnic policies: PM Lee. *Channel News Asia*, 15 January 2010. www.channelnewsasia.com/stories/singaporelocalnews/view/1030929/1/.html; accessed 15 January 2010.

Pullum, G. (1999). African American Vernacular English is not Standard English with mistakes. In Rebecca Wheeler, ed., *The Workings of Language: From Prescriptions to Perspectives*. Westport, CT: Praeger Publishers, 39–58.

Quirk, R. (1988). The question of standards in the international use of English. In P. Lowenberg, ed., *Language Spread and Language Policy: Issues, Implications and Case Studies*. Washington, DC: Georgetown University Press, 229–241.

Quirk, R. (1990). Language varieties and standard language. *English Today*, **21**, 3–10.

Rajadurai, J. (2005). Revisiting the concentric circles: Conceptual and sociolinguistic considerations. *Asian EFL Journal*, **7**(4), 111–130.

Rampton, B. (1995). *Crossing*. London: Longman.

Rampton, B. (1998). Language crossing and the redefinition of reality. In P. Auer, ed., *Code-Switching in Conversation*. London: Routledge, 290–317.

Rampton, B. (1999). *Deutsch* in Inner London and the animation of an instructed foreign language. *Journal of Sociolinguistics*, **3**(4), 480–504.

Rampton, B. (2006). *Language in Late Modernity*. Cambridge: Cambridge University Press.

Rappa, A. L. (2000). Surviving the politics of late modernity: The Eurasian fringe community in Singapore. *Southeast Asian Journal of Social Science*, **28**(2), 153–180.

Rappa, A. and Wee, L. (2006). *Language Policy and Modernity in Southeast Asia*. New York: Springer.

Roberts, C. and Sarangi, S. (1999). Hybridity in gatekeeping discourse: Issues of practical relevance for the researcher. In S. Sarangi and C. Roberts, eds., *Talk, Work and Institutional Order: Discourse in Medical, Mediation and Management Settings*. Berlin: Mouton de Gruyter, 473–503.

Romaine, S. (2001). Contact between English and other languages. In John Algeo, ed., *Cambridge History of the English Language*, vol. 6: *English in North America*. Cambridge: Cambridge University Press, 154–183.

Roy, A. (2011). Conclusion: Postcolonial urbanism. In A. Roy and A. Ong. eds., *Worlding Cities: Asian Experiments and the Art of Being Global*. Oxford: Blackwell, 307–335.

Rubdy, R. (2001). Creative destruction: Singapore's Speak Good English Movement. *World Englishes*, **20**.

Rymes, B. (2014). *Communicating beyond Language*. New York: Routledge.

Saravanan, V. (1994). Language and social identity amongst Tamil-English bilinguals in Singapore. In R. Khoo, U. Kreher, and R. Wong, eds., *Languages in Contact in a Multilingual Society: Implications for Language Learning and Teaching*. Clevedon: Multilingual Matters, 79–93.

Sassen, S. (2006). *Territory, Authority, Rights: From Medieval to Global Assemblages*. Princeton: Princeton University Press.

Sbisà, M. (2001). Illocutionary force and degrees of strength in language use. *Journal of Pragmatics*, **33**(12), 1791–1814.

Sebeok, T. A. (1994). *Signs*. Toronto: University of Toronto Press.

Schneider, E. (2007). *Postcolonial Englishes*. Cambridge: Cambridge University Press.

Schneider, E. (2014). New reflections on the evolutionary dynamics of world Englishes. *World Englishes*, **33**(1), 9–32.

Scholte, J. A. (2000). *Globalization: A Critical Introduction*. Basingstoke: Palgrave.

Searle, J. R. (1980). Minds, brains, and programs. *Behavioral and Brain Sciences*, **3**(3), 417–457.

Scollon, R. and Scollon, S. (2007). Nexus analysis. *Journal of Sociolinguistics*, **11**(5), 608–625.

Scollon, R. and Wong Scollon, S. (2004). *Nexus Analysis: Discourse and the Emerging Internet*. London: Routledge.

Shannon, T. A. Jr. (2014). The long diplomacy: How a changing world creates new opportunities for partnership between scholars and practitioners. In A. F. Lowenthal and M. E. Bertucci, eds., *Scholars, Policymakers, and International Affairs: Finding Common Cause*. Baltimore: Johns Hopkins University Press, 187–196.

Siddique, S. (1997). The phenomenology of ethnicity: A Singapore case study. In O. J. Hui, T. C. Kiong and T. E. Ser, eds., *Understanding Singapore Society*. Singapore: Times Academic Press, 107–124.

Siegel, J. (1999). Stigmatized and standardized varieties in the classroom: Interference or separation. *TESOL Quarterly*, **33**(4), 701–728.

Silverstein, M. (1998). The uses and utility of ideology: A commentary. In B. Schieffelin, K. A. Woolard and P. V. Kroskrity, eds., *Language Ideologies: Practice and Theory*. Oxford: Oxford University Press, 123–145.

Silverstein, M. (2003). Indexical order and the dialectics of sociolinguistic life. *Language and Communication*, **23**, 193–229.

Sim, J. J. (2002). Good English campaign reinforces prejudices. *Straits Times*, 14 May.

Slater, D. and Ritzer, G. (2001). Interview with Ulrich Beck. *Journal of Consumer Culture*, **1**(2), 261–277.

Soh, F. (2005). 'You see there got, got. Not there, no got'. *Sunday Times*, 15 May.

Sowell, T. (2004). *Affirmative Action around the World*. New Haven: Yale University Press.

Speak Good English Movement. (2001). *Speak Well, Be Understood*. The Speak Good English Movement Committee. Singapore: Ministry of Information and the Arts.

Speak Good English Movement. (2017). *Grammar Rules*. http://goodenglish.org.sg/~/media/sgem/document/additional%20sgem%20resources/pdf/grammar%20rules%20 20_%20speak%20good%20english%20movement.pdf?la=en; accessed 31 March 2017.

Spivak, G. C. (1988). Can the subaltern speak? In C. Nelson and L. Grossberg, eds., *Marxism and the Interpretation of Culture*. Urbana: University of Illinois Press, 271–313.

Spivak, G. C. (1999). *A Critique of Postcolonial Reason*. Cambridge, MA: Harvard University Press.

Spolsky, B. (2004). *Language Policy*. Cambridge: Cambridge University Press.

Stewart, S. (2013). Tinglish: Thai to English. 28 November, https://prezi.com/vtczmddany9l/tinglish-thai-to-english/; accessed 31 January 2015.

Stroud, C. and Wee, L. (2007). Consuming identities: Language planning and policy in Singaporean late modernity. *Language Policy*, **6**, 253–279.

Stroud, C. and Wee, L. (2010). Language policy and planning in Singaporean late modernity. In L. Lim, A. Pakir and L. Wee, eds., *English in Singapore: Unity and Utility*. Hong Kong: Hong Kong University Press, 181–204.

Stroud, C. and Wee, L. (2011). *Style, Identity and Literacy: English in Singapore*. Clevedon: Multilingual Matters.

Tan, C. (2015). Theatre review: Off Centre revival is profoundly affecting. *Straits Times*, 24 April.

Tan, E. S. (2005). Globalization, nation-building and emigration: The Singapore case. In B. P. Lorente, N. Piper, H. H Shen and B. Yeoh, eds., *Asian Migrations*. Singapore: Singapore University Press, 87–98.

Teschke, B. and Heine, C. (2002). The dialectics of globalization. In M. Rupert and H. Smith, eds., *Historical Materialism and Globalization*. London: Routledge, 165–187.

Toh, P. C. S. (2011). *The Complete Eh, Goondu!* Singapore: Marshall Cavendish.

Uekrongtham, E. (1988). Local drama: Food for thought. *Business Times*, 17 September.

Van Doorn, N. (2014). The neoliberal subject of value: Measuring human capital in information economies. *Cultural Politics*, **10**(3), 354–375.

Vertovec, S. (2006). *The Emergence of Super-Diversity in Britain*. Centre on Migration, Policy and Society, Working Paper No. 25.

Vertovec, S. (2007). Super-diversity and its implications. *Ethnic and Racial Studies*, **30**(6), 1024–1054.

Wade, R. (2001). *Is Globalization Making World Income Distribution More Equal?* London School of Economics DESTIN, Working Paper No. 01-01.

Wee, C. J. W.–L. (2007). Afterword: Language, capitalist development, cultural change. In V. Vaish, S. Gopinathan and Y. –B. Liu, eds., *Language, Capital, Culture: Critical Studies of Language and Education in Singapore*. Rotterdam: Sense Publishers, 249–257.

Wee, L. (2002a). *Lor* in colloquial Singapore English. *Journal of Pragmatics*, **34**(6), 711–725.

Wee, L. (2002b). When English is not a mother tongue: Linguistic ownership and the Eurasian community in Singapore. *Journal of Multilingual and Multicultural Development*, **23**(4), 282–295.

Wee, L. (2003). Linguistic instrumentalism in Singapore. *Journal of Multilingual and Multicultural Development*, **24**(3), 211–224.

Wee, L. (2004). Extreme communicative acts and the boosting of illocutionary force. *Journal of Pragmatics*, **36**, 2161–2178.

Wee, L. (2005). Intra-language discrimination and linguistic human rights. *Applied Linguistics*, **26**, 48–69.

Wee, L. (2007). The hunger strike as a communicative act: Intention without responsibility. *Journal of Linguistic Anthropology*, **17**(1), 61–76.

Wee, L. (2006). The semiotics of language ideologies in Singapore. *Journal of Sociolinguistics*, **10**(3), 344–361.

Wee, L. (2009). English in the Eurasian community. In D. Schreier, P. Trudgill, E. Schneider and J. Williams, eds., *Lesser Known Varieties of English*. Cambridge: Cambridge University Press, 313–326.

Wee, L. (2010). Neutrality in language policy. *Journal of Multilingual & Multicultural Development*, **31**(4), 421–434.

Wee, L. (2010). 'Burdens' and 'handicaps' in Singapore's language policy: On the limits of language management. *Language Policy*, **9**(2), 97–114.

Wee, L. (2011). Metadiscursive convergence in the Singlish debate. *Language & Communication*, **31**, 75–85.

Wee, L. (2013). The evolution of Singlish: Migration and commodification. Paper presented at the 14th Malaysia-Singapore Forum, University of Malaya, 9-10 December 2013. Kuala Lumpur, Malaysia.

Wee, L. (2014). Language politics and global city. *Discourse: Studies in the Cultural Politics of Education*, **35**(5), 649–660.

Wee, L. (2015). The party's over? Singapore politics and the 'new normal'. *Journal of Language and Politics*, **14**(3), 455–478.

Wee, L. and Bokhorst-Heng, W. (2005). Language policy and nationalist ideology: Statal narratives in Singapore. *Multilingua*, **24**, 159–183.

Widdowson, H. G. (1994). The ownership of English. *TESOL Quarterly*, **28**(2), 377–389.

Wise, J. M. (2005). Assemblage. In C. J. Stivale, ed., *Gilles Deleuze: Key Concepts*, Montreal: McGill and Queen's University Press, 77–87.

Wong, J. O. (2004). The particles of Singapore English. *Journal of Pragmatics*, **36**(4), 739–793.

Wong, K. S. (2006). Launch of the Overseas Singaporean Portal. 26 August 2006. www.mha.gov.sg/news_details.aspx?nid=MzIy-WzpmKhqwnZs%3D; accessed 26 October 2012.

Yap, M. T. (2015). Immigration and integration in Singapore: Trends, rationale and policy response. In M. T. Yap, G. Koh and D. Soon, eds., *Migration and Integration in Singapore*. London: Routledge, 25–38.

Yeoh, Brenda. (2007). Singapore: Hungry for foreign workers at all skill levels. *Migration Information Source*. Washington, DC: Migration Policy Institute. www.migrationinformation.org/Profiles/display.cfm?ID=570, accessed 22 September 2007.

Yuen, S. (2016). Who's afraid of 'chao ah beng'? Overseas universities use Singaporean literature to teach. *Straits Times*, 15 February 2016. www.straitstimes.com/singapore/education/whos-afraid-of-chao-ah-beng-overseas-universities-use-singaporean-literature-to; accessed 31 August 2017.

Zukin, S. (2010). *The Naked City: The Death and Life of Authentic Urban Places*. New York: Oxford University Press.

Index